EXPLORE

English for field-specific success

Becky McKnight | Patrick Peachey

Annotated Teacher's Edition

OXFORD

UNIVERSITY PRESS

OXFORD
UNIVERSITY PRESS

Oxford University Press is a department of the University of Oxford.
It furthers the University's objective of excellence in research, scholarship,
and education by publishing worldwide. Oxford is a registered trade mark of
Oxford University Press in the UK and in certain other countries.

Published in Canada by
Oxford University Press
8 Sampson Mews, Suite 204,
Don Mills, Ontario M3C 0H5 Canada

www.oupcanada.com

Catalogage avant publication de Bibliothèque et Archives Canada
Explore 3 : English for field-specific success.
Annotated teacher's edition / Becky McKnight, Patrick Peachey.
ISBN 978-0-19-902872-6 (couverture souple)
1. Anglais (Langue)–Étude et enseignement (Collégial)–
Francophones. I. Peachey, Patrick J., auteur II. Titre.
III. Titre: Explore three.
PE1129.F7M34 2017 Suppl.   428.2'441   C2017-901000-X

Cover images: © iStock.com/ DenGuy; asi© iStock.com/ seeit; © iStock.com/ BraunS;
© iStock.com/ xavierarnau; © iStock.com/ PeopleImages; © iStock.com/ ferrantraite;
© iStock.com/ vgajic; © iStock.com/ South_agency

Cover design: Laurie McGregor
Interior design: Laurie McGregor

Oxford University Press is committed to our environment.
This book is printed on Forest Stewardship Council® certified paper
and comes from responsible sources.

Printed and bound in Canada

1 2 3 4 — 22 21 20 19

Contents

SKILLS UNITS

UNIT 3 | Thinking Outside the Box 43

UNIT 4 | It Just Isn't Right 65

UNIT 5 | United We Stand 87

Projects   109

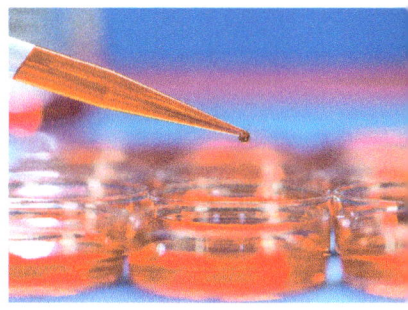

Learning Strategies   115

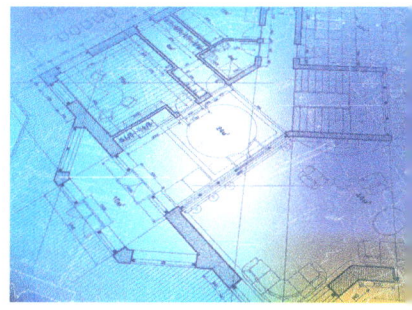

Grammar Guide   151

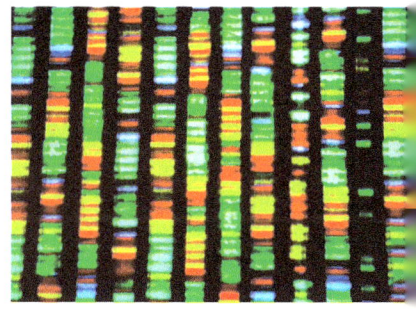

Abbreviations Used in the Text	
• **abbr**	• abbreviation
• **adj**	• adjective
• **adv**	• adverb
• **exp**	• expression
• **n**	• noun
• **n phr**	• noun phrase
• **phr v**	• phrasal verb
• **tr**	• transitive (verb)
• **v**	• verb

Acknowledgements

Thank you very much to David Coombes for giving me the opportunity to work on *Explore*, for his passion, support, and for truly caring for the members of his team. Thank you also to our incredible editor, Nicola Balfour, for her great spirit and wise guidance throughout the project. Thank you to my dear friend and co-author Patrick Peachey, who is such a wonderful person and a great pedagogue. It was an absolute pleasure working with you on this project. Thank you to the reviewers, who offered such thorough and useful advice. Thank you to Sherry Kent and Vanessa Beal for providing models to follow in *Explore 1* and *Explore 2*. Thank you to my colleagues and students at Cégep Saint-Jean, who inspire and teach me daily. Finally, thank you to my amazing family and friends for their love and support (especially Jacques, Jeremy, Jessie, Nicolas, Émilie, Greg, Laura, Spencer, Melissa, Papa John, and Auntie Karen). I would like to dedicate this book to my late and dearly beloved father Fred, mother Madonna, and brother Brad.

Becky McKnight

I would like to thank Nicola Balfour and David Coombes from Oxford for their support, guidance, and encouragement. It was a pleasure working with both of them. I would also like to acknowledge the people I work with every day. They inspire and drive me to do better. Writing is a difficult endeavour and I would not have been involved in this project if it had not been for my co-author and friend, Becky. Finally, I would like to thank my family: my wife Lyne, the love of my life, and my kids Amelie, William, and James.

Patrick Peachey

Oxford University Press Canada would like to express appreciation to the English teachers who generously offered feedback about *Explore* at various stages of the development process. Their feedback was instrumental in helping to shape and refine the book.

Rebecca Baker Collège Montmorency
Vanessa Beal Cégep Édouard-Montpetit
Marie-Hélène Belley Cégep de Jonquière
Félix Maranda Castonguay Cégep Lévis-Lauzon
Jennifer Caylor Cégep de Rimouski
Lisa Deguire Cégep de Jonquiere
Cecilia Delgado Collège Lionel-Groulx
Paola Di Muzio Cégep Limoilou
Marie-Claude Doucet Cégep de Chicoutimi
Suzie Dufresne Cégep Régional de Lanaudière in Joliette
Barry G. Glebe Collège de Maisonneuve
Rebecca Higgins Cégep Édouard-Montpetit
Liana Jalalyn Cégep Régional de Lanaudière
Nancie Kahan Cégep de Saint-Jérôme
Sherry Kent Cégep Saint-Jean-sur-Richelieu
Jerry Kowtalo Cégep de Saint-Jérôme
Christine Lalonde Cégep de Sainte-Foy
Sara Langevin Cégep de Granby
Chiara Laricchuta Collège Ahuntsic
Marie-J. Martineau Cégep Édouard-Montpetit
Laura McGee Collège de Maisonneuve
Catherine Pépin Cégep de Trois-Rivières
Hélène Prévost Cégep de l'Outaouais
Achsa Ramadeen Collège de Valleyfield
Darcy Robb Cégep de Rimouski
Maria Pia Smargiasso Collège Montmorency

Scope and Sequence

	Reading	Writing	Speaking	Listening & Watching
UNIT 1 **Job Satisfaction**	• Read about employee satisfaction and its impact on business performance • Read about unusual job interview questions and how employers use them • **Strategy** Skimming • **Strategy** Scanning	• Take notes to write a report • Describe your personal qualities as skills in the workplace **(Field of Study)** • Analyze paragraph structure • Write a paragraph or email giving professional advice **(Field of Study)**	• Discuss weird jobs and what you learned **(Field of Study)** • Discuss job satisfaction factors and summarize conclusions • Present a PechaKucha to introduce yourself • Research soft and hard skills and discuss the skills you need **(Field of Study)** • Propose ways to introduce humour at school or at work **(Field of Study)** • Conduct mock job interviews • Pronounce -ed endings of simple past tense verbs and past participles	• Listen to audio about positivity, relationships, and job satisfaction in the workplace • Watch a video about the benefits of humour at work • **Strategy** Identify main idea and essential ideas • **Strategy** Effective note-taking
UNIT 2 **Reading Between the Lines**	• Read two articles about antibiotic use and antibiotic-resistant bugs and analyze bias • Read about the impact of misleading headlines on readers' perceptions • **Strategy** Denotative and connotative vocabulary • **Strategy** Identify bias • **Strategy** Annotate a text	• Write sentences comparing news sources • Assess language used in a testimonial and write a persuasive testimonial **(Field of Study)** • List connotative words in a news item and explain their impact on reader **(Field of Study)** • **Strategy** Persuasive language	• Describe media impact and concerns about media • Discuss your news habits • Discuss a comic about bias • Examine the validity of sources • Express your opinion on social media companies' responsibilities • Discuss bias • Present a news report using persuasive language **(Field of Study)** • Discuss bots **(Field of Study)** • Pronounce the -s ending	• Listen to audio about deep fake videos • Watch a video about bots influencing politics • Listen to classmates' testimonials to identify connotative language and other forms of bias • **Strategy** Create a visual summary
UNIT 3 **Thinking Outside the Box**	• Read about innovations in health care, transportation, agriculture, and business • Read about innovations employers are making in workplace design	• Write a descriptive paragraph about a place that affects you positively • Summarize an informative text • **Strategy** Avoid plagiarism by paraphrasing	• Define *innovation* and *creativity* • Describe innovative products **(Field of Study)** • Present situations that require creativity **(Field of Study)** • Describe your ideal work and study environment • Present an innovative workplace **(Field of Study)** • Pronounce the *schwa* (ə) and use correct word stress	• Listen to an interview about creativity and games • Watch a video about the ideal conditions to foster creativity • **Strategy** Predicting
UNIT 4 **It Just Isn't Right**	• Read about corruption and why we should care about it • Read a short text and identify the writer's tone and point of view • Read about how cynicism can blind us to the value of some research • **Strategy** Recognizing tone	• Write a paragraph about ethics and technology **(Field of Study)** • Write a well-researched persuasive essay on the ethics of a new technology • Write a letter to the editor about the ethics of Facebook's experiment on users • **Strategy** Persuasive writing	• Discuss the difference between unethical and corrupt behaviour • Discuss where corruption may exist **(Field of Study)** • Explain your position on sports ethics • Discuss ethical issues and decide on appropriate sentences • Scan and describe a social media company's terms of service • Debate an ethical issue • Pronounce words using appropriate stress patterns	• Listen to an interview on ethics in sport • Watch a video about social media ethics and influence • **Strategy** Create a visual summary (bubble style)
UNIT 5 **United We Stand**	• Read about team building and balancing the needs of individuals • Read about collaboration in construction	• Write a short horror story • Create a writing outline • Write an essay or blog • **Strategy** Using checklists	• Conduct a teamwork survey **(Field of Study)** • Devise rules for effective teamwork • Discuss the importance of teamwork **(Field of Study)** • Describe the value of diversity to effective collaboration **(Field of Study)** • Brainstorm how collaboration can address a societal problem • Present a design challenge solution **(Field of Study)** • Present a survival strategy • Present a news bulletin • Pronounce voiced and voiceless /th/ • **Strategy** Creating and using checklists	• Watch a video about innovation and collaboration • Listen to a broadcast about a zombie apocalypse and the role of collaboration in surviving it

Grammar	Interpreting Data	Vocabulary	Revising and Editing	Wrap Up
• Simple past and present perfect	• Interpret and analyze data and statistics in an infographic about job interview	• Common work-related vocabulary • **Strategy** Use word and context clues to guess meaning of unknown words	• Revise a text to correct use of simple past, present perfect; correct verb tense errors and add transition words; delete unnecessary information in a paragraph	• Interview someone working in your future field and present the results **(Field of Study)** • Oral presentation: create a video resumé or application for an educational program • Write a blog post about long- and short-term goals • Review new words and build personal field-specific vocabulary
• Simple present and present progressive	• Interpret a graph of the media through which people of different ages get news • Expressions to discuss similarities and differences	• Understand denotation and connotation • Words related to media • Use positive and negative words to persuade • Use context clues to acquire new vocabulary	• Revise to correct errors in simple present and present progressive	• Create a graphic organizer **(Field of Study)** • Oral presentation: find and evaluate article(s) for bias • Write a visual summary of an article or a news article **(Field of Study)** • Review new words and build personal field-specific vocabulary
• Active voice and passive voice	• Interpret and analyze data and statistics about the effect of innovation on companies' success	• Use prediction to activate your vocabulary • Use word and context clues to acquire new vocabulary	• Revise to correct errors in the passive voice	• Write about an innovator or innovation **(Field of Study)** • Oral presentation: create and present an innovative workspace **(Field of Study)** • Write a promotional pamphlet **(Field of Study)** • Review new words and build personal field-specific vocabulary
• Past form modals	• Interpret and analyze a graph of youth crime	• Recognize cognates and false cognates • Use word and context clues to acquire new vocabulary	• Revise a paragraph to create a specific tone	• Identify tone in a text, audio, or video **(Field of Study)** • Oral presentation: research a case of corruption and present your findings **(Field of Study)** • Write a persuasive research essay about a debatable issue **(Field of Study)** • Review new words and build personal field-specific vocabulary
• Gerunds	• Interpret and analyze data about the possible sources of a zombie outbreak	• Use word and context clues to acquire new vocabulary	• Revise to correct the use of gerunds and verbs	• Write an informational pamphlet about a collaborative process **(Field of Study)** • Oral presentation: describe a collaborative process or the value of collaboration **(Field of Study)** • Write a journal, short story, or essay **(Field of Study)** • Review new words and build personal field-specific vocabulary

Explore: How to Use the Book

Book Structure

Five theme-based **Skills** units provide contemporary, high-interest, Canadian and international readings, listenings, and watchings chosen to connect with a wide range of students' fields of study and future careers.

Fourteen **Grammar Guide** chapters cover all the key grammar points and give students thousands of practice activities.

Project Files enable students to practice all four skills while developing interesting projects related to their field of study.

A concise **Learning Strategies** section at the back of the book allows students to become more independent and successful at acquiring new language and transferring it to career and academic situations.

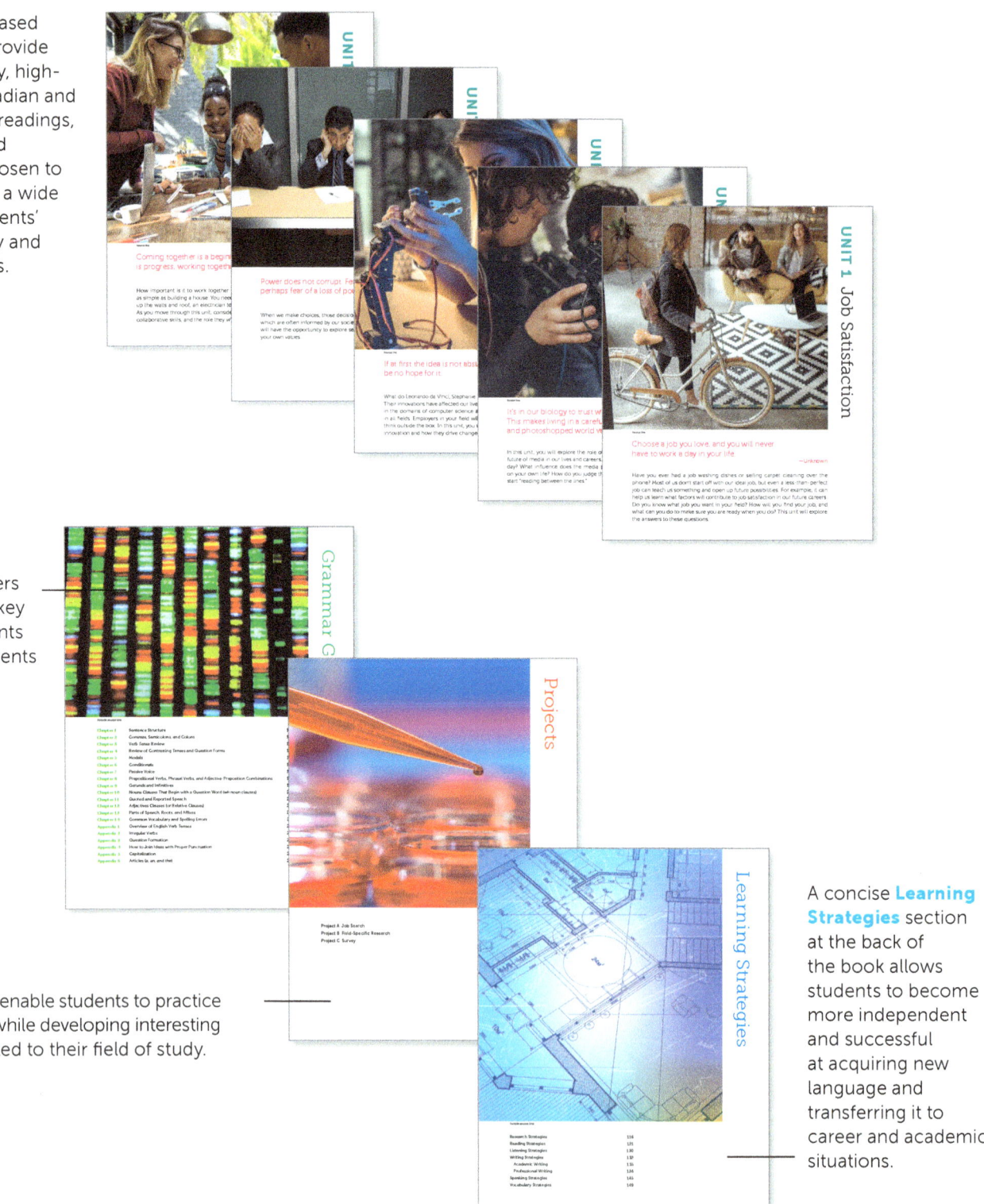

Skills Unit Features

Warm Up

Speaking

In a small group, complete the following activities.

1. Discuss these questions.

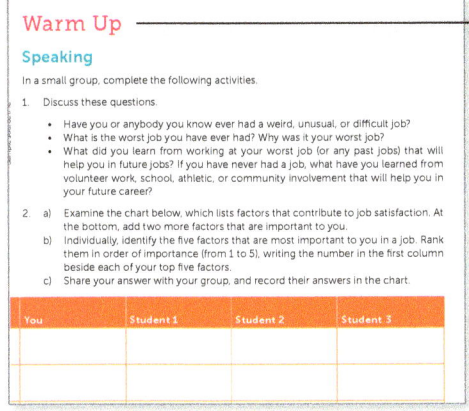

Warm Up activities that practice all four skills connect students to the themes and activate their prior knowledge.

Vocabulary Development

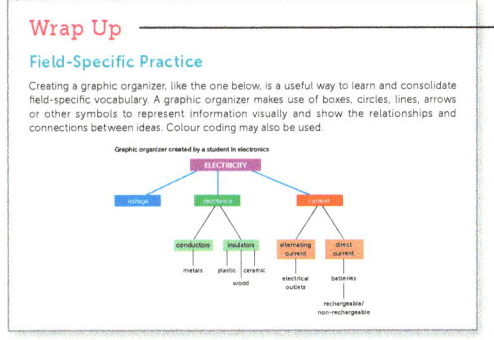

Dynamic vocabulary development activities ensure that students build a rich vocabulary bank related to their individual **fields of study** and **future careers**

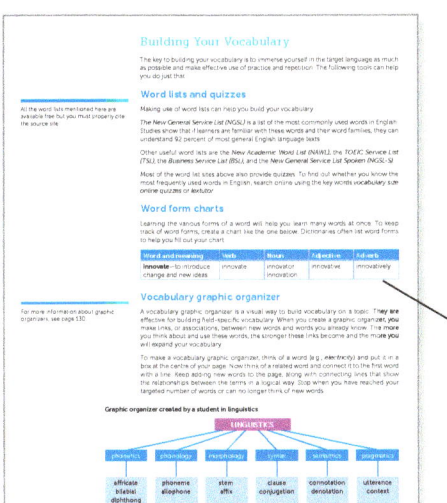

Context clues

Use context to guess the meaning of unknown words. Check to see if any information given within the sentence (or in preceding or following sentences) provides a clue to a word's meaning.

Here are a few ways to find clues within the context of the sentence.

1. Look for **definitions**. Authors sometimes provide definitions within the text to help explain difficult words. The word *or* can sometimes introduce a definition.

   EXAMPLE   Psychosomatic disorders (or illnesses caused by psychological factors) should not be confused with imagined disorders.

2. Look for **synonyms** (words with similar meanings) or **antonyms** (words with opposite meanings) near the unknown word. Writers often give a synonym to explain key terms, or an antonym to define a word by what it is not.

Vocabulary Activities before texts, audios, and videos ensure students are more successful with reading, listening and watching activities.

To help students succeed with their academic studies, *Explore* highlights and practises the **New Academic Word List** (NAWL), 963 words derived from an academic corpus containing about 288 million words.

Reading, Listening, and Watching

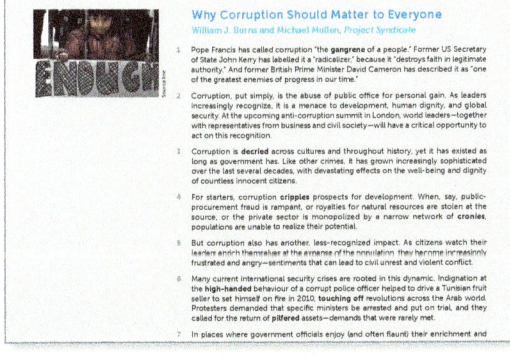

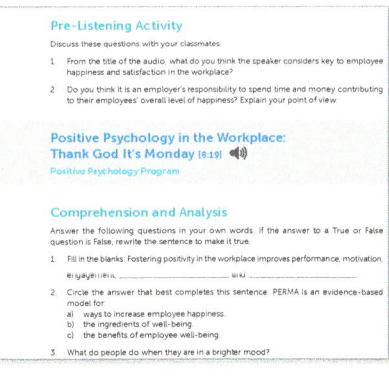

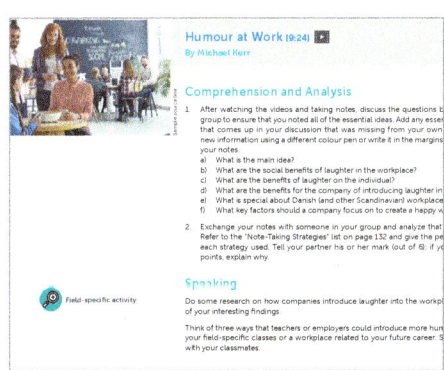

High-interest readings, audios, and videos connected to pre-university and career programs increase students' involvement and motivation.

Speaking, Pronunciation, and Writing

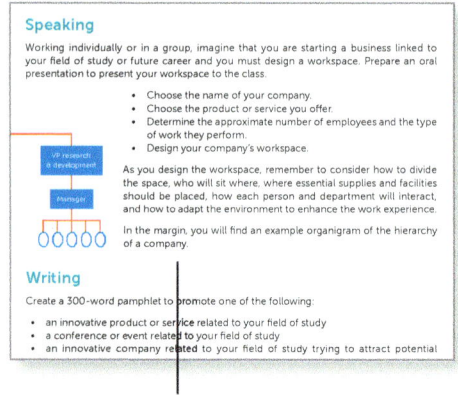

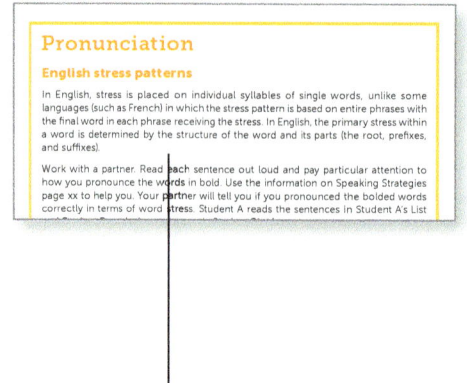

Writing

Choose one of the following activities.

1. Research a company, organization, or institution related to your field of study or future career. You may gather information online or from other sources, such as teachers or professionals in the field, brochures, and so on. Use your findings to write a 450-word blog post. Your objective may be to inform others about your subject or to convince readers of an opinion you have formed based on your research. Be sure to properly cite your sources, within your text where necessary and by including a list of work cited entries at the end.

2. Create a career plan. Describe the short- and long-term goals you will need to achieve to find the job you want. Research the necessary qualifications and skills. What kind

Four to six communicative activities in every skills unit guide students to express themselves on field specific and career related topics.

Pronunciation points in each chapter improve students' speaking skills developing more confident speakers.

Writing activities enable students to master key academic and professional genres and formats.

Field-Specific Practice

 Field-specific activity

Four to six field-specific practice activities in each unit provide students with numerous opportunities to explore and connect to their **fields of study and future careers** making their English language acquisition meaningful and relevant.

Learning Strategies

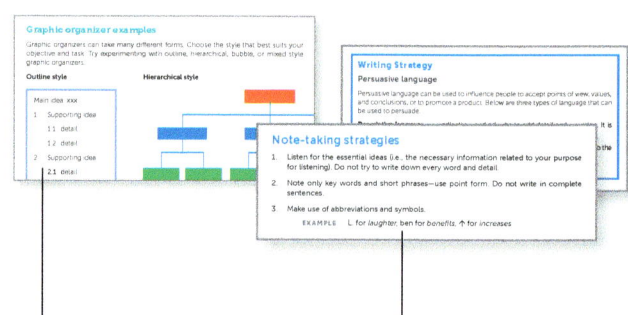

Two or three carefully chosen **Learning Strategies** in each skills unit make learning easier, quicker, and more enjoyable.

Interpreting Data

An **Interpreting Data** activity in every unit with **authentic graphs and diagrams** helps students develop the skills to evaluate and communicate about data and information that is common in all careers and fields of study.

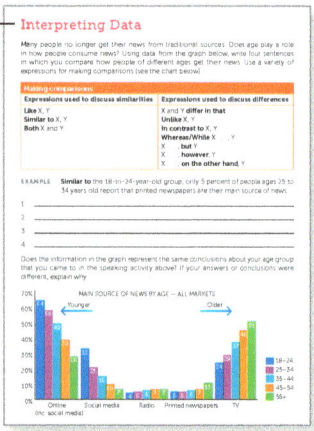

Grammar

Grammar in every skills unit provides a contextualized, student-centred approach that allows students to evaluate their understanding and discover how grammar works in real life.

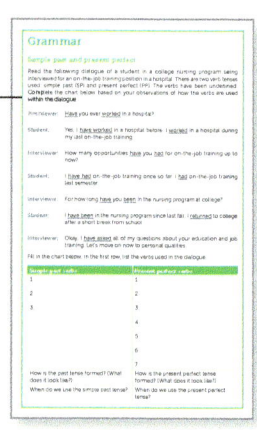

Explore Online

Explore Online is an easy-to-use website that provides students with hundreds of practice activities related to the content in the student book. Students will improve their English through additional practice in vocabulary, listening, watching, reading, pronunciation, revising and editing, and all aspects of English grammar.

Students have access to a full **eBook** version of the text book to study anytime. anywhere.

All **reading texts**, all **audios** and all **videos** are available on the website so students can complete the interactive activities in one place even without their textbook.

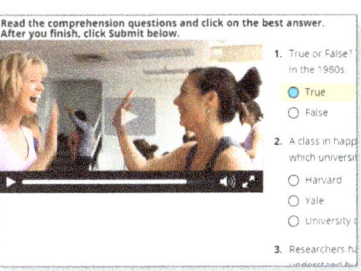

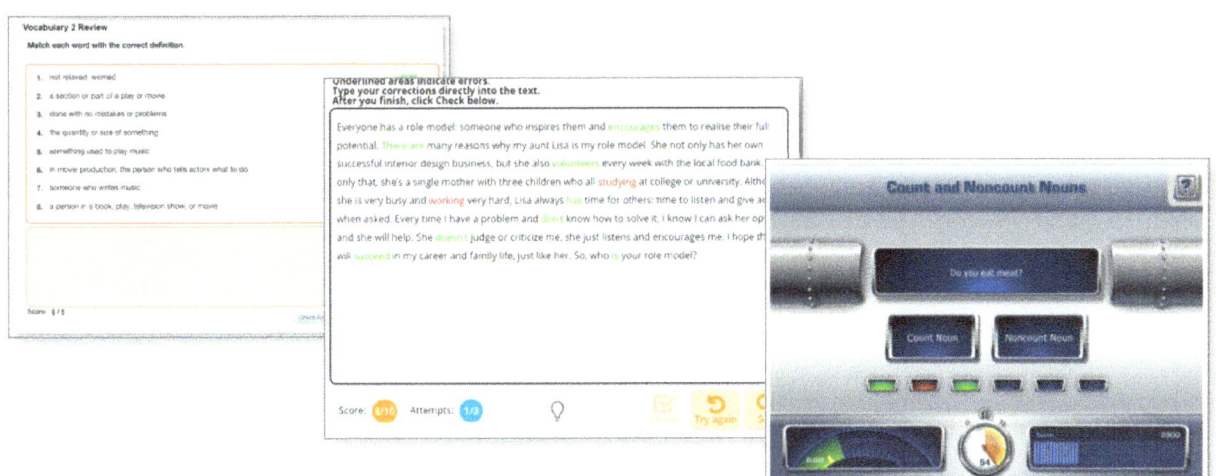

Interactive, self-graded activities, games and tests make learning stimulating and fun!

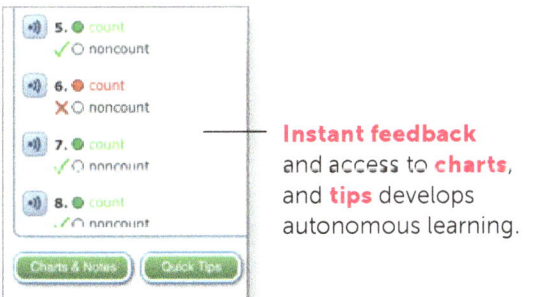

Instant feedback and access to **charts**, and **tips** develops autonomous learning.

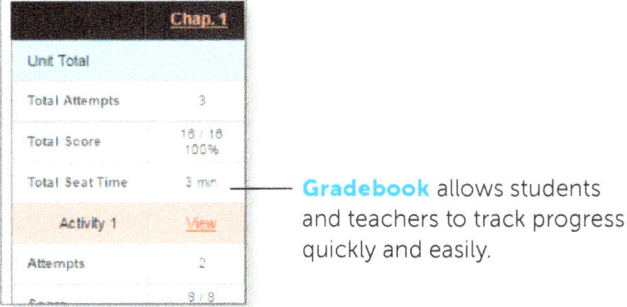

Gradebook allows students and teachers to track progress quickly and easily.

Choose a job you love, and you will never have to work a day in your life.

—Unknown

Have you ever had a job washing dishes or selling carpet cleaning over the phone? Most of us don't start off with our ideal job, but even a less-than-perfect job can teach us something and open up future possibilities. For example, it can help us learn what factors will contribute to job satisfaction in our future careers. Do you know what job you want in your field? How will you find your job, and what can you do to make sure you are ready when you do? This unit will explore the answers to these questions.

Warm Up

Speaking

In a small group, complete the following activities.

Before students discuss the questions, you might want to tell them about famous people who once had less-than-ideal jobs—such as Justin Trudeau, who worked as a bungee-jumping coach, or Stephen King, who pumped gas—or have them research examples of their own.

1. Discuss these questions.

   - Have you or anybody you know ever had a weird, unusual, or difficult job?
   - What is the worst job you have ever had? Why was it your worst job?
   - What did you learn from working at your worst job (or any past jobs) that will help you in future jobs? If you have never had a job, what have you learned from volunteer work, school, athletic, or community involvement that will help you in your future career?

2. a) Examine the chart below, which lists factors that contribute to job satisfaction. At the bottom, add two more factors that are important to you.

   b) Individually, identify the five factors that are most important to you in a job. Rank them in order of importance (from 1 to 5), writing the number in the first column beside each of your top five factors.

   c) Share your answer with your group, and record their answers in the chart.

Factors that contribute to job satisfaction	You	Student 1	Student 2	Student 3
Availability/use of technology in the workplace				
Employer makes you feel appreciated and valued as an employee				
Corporate social responsibility (the company does good for society)				
Employee benefits/perks				
Flexible work schedule				
Interesting work (i.e., responsibilities and tasks)				
Opportunities for training and advancement				
Opportunities to voice your opinion within the company				
Pay/Salary				
Relationships with fellow employees				
Other factors that contribute to job satisfaction: • •				

3. As a group, analyze your responses to question 2. Summarize your group's conclusions about the most important factors that contribute to job satisfaction. Present your findings to the class.

Listening

What brings your classmates job satisfaction may not be the same factors that are important to you. However, according to the audio "Positive Psychology in the Workplace," research suggests that there are certain common factors that contribute most to job satisfaction and happy employees.

> ## Listening Strategy
>
> ### Understanding the main idea
>
> The main idea of a text, audio, or video is the *essential message being delivered*—in other words, the speaker or writer's conclusion (or main message) about the subject under discussion.
>
> To help determine the main idea of an audio or video, do the following:
>
> - check the title
> - read any comprehension questions or introductory information prior to listening
> - listen carefully to the introduction and conclusion
> - listen for key words and repeated concepts
>
> Practise these strategies as you listen to the following audio. You will be asked to identify the main idea in the comprehension questions.

Pre-Listening Activity

Discuss these questions with your classmates.

1. From the title of the audio, what do you think the speaker considers key to employee happiness and satisfaction in the workplace?

2. Do you think it is an employer's responsibility to spend time and money contributing to their employees' overall level of happiness? Explain your point of view.

Positive Psychology in the Workplace: Thank God It's Monday [8:19]

Positive Psychology Program

Comprehension and Analysis

Answer the following questions in your own words. If the answer to a True or False question is False, rewrite the sentence to make it true.

1. Fill in the blanks: Fostering positivity in the workplace improves performance, motivation, engagement, _conflict resolution skills_, and _original thinking_.

2. Circle the answer that best completes this sentence: PERMA is an evidence-based model for:
   a) ways to increase employee happiness
   b) the ingredients of well-being.
   c) the benefits of employee well-being.

3. What do people do when they are in a brighter mood?
   They set higher goals for themselves and spend more time trying to achieve them.

4. According to a study by Virgin, what are two positive effects experienced by employees who have good relationships at work?

a) _increased productivity_

b) _greater ability to deal with stress at work_

5. What is the effect of a PechaKucha presentation?
a) It increases the creativity of employees.
b) It makes employees happier.
c) It encourages employees to work together.

6. Fill in the blanks: The key to increasing employee engagement is to _maximize_ the extent to which people are using and applying their _strengths_.

7. What lesson did Grant's experiment on team productivity demonstrate?
Seeing the impact of our work makes it feel more meaningful.

8. a) The key to happiness is enjoying the feeling of having achieved a goal. ☐ True ☑ False
The key to happiness is enjoying each step along the way to achieving the goal.

b) Your goals should be connected to your strengths. ☑ True ☐ False

c) Receiving a reward has an effect on a person's brain. ☑ True ☐ False

10. What is the main idea of the audio?
By creating a positive work environment and ensuring employees are engaged, employers can contribute to employees' happiness, which will lead to employee job satisfaction and greater productivity.

11. Why do you think even small rewards can have an impact on an employee's work?
Answers will vary.

Credibility Check

When you hear or read information, it is important to apply critical thinking skills and analyze the source. Do you find the information in this audio to be reliable?

Support your answer using criteria from the Evaluating Sources Checklist on page 117.

 Field-specific activity

PechaKucha slides must contain images only (no text), and people can share only things about their lives outside of work. PechaKuchas have caught on internationally. To find out more about them, visit pechakucha.org or check out the many online videos about creating a PechaKucha.

 Field-specific activity

A true PechaKucha consists of 20 images shown for 20 seconds each. You may want to limit the presentation to 10 slides.

Speaking

Imagine you are working in a job related to your field of study or future career. Prepare a PechaKucha presentation (consisting of 20 images for 20 seconds each) that would help your colleagues get to know you. Share your PechaKucha with your classmates. Speak about the images as they advance automatically.

Field-Specific Practice

The audio "Positive Psychology in the Workplace" talked about how being given the chance to use your strengths on the job leads to employee satisfaction. Let's examine your current strengths and the skills you need to develop for your future career.

In the chart on page 5, make a list of eight necessary skills for your field of study or future career. Include a combination of hard skills (educational requirements, specific technical abilities, and knowledge) and soft skills (such as problem solving or adaptability).

Do research to verify the necessary skills in your chosen field.

1. Visit the web pages for university or college programs in your field.

2. Check job postings related to your future career.

3. Search online using key words such as the following (and follow the links):

   - *explore [an occupation] job bank*
   - *occupations guide Government of Canada*
   - *skills needed to be a* _____ (e.g., *mechanical engineer, lab technician, hotel manager*).

S For more information on and examples of hard and soft skills, see Professional Writing Strategies, page 138).

Your field of study or future career: _____ _____	
Hard skills	**Soft skills**
1.	1.
2.	2.
3.	3.
4.	4.

Compare your list with your classmates' lists and discuss the following:

   a) Which skills are common to all of your fields of study or future careers?
   b) Which skills do you not yet possess? How could you develop those skills in the future?

Reading

When you are searching for a job in your chosen career, you will want to research the work culture. What do you know about the predominant work culture in your future profession? Is employee satisfaction generally considered an important value? Should it be? Read the following article to learn what research has revealed about employee satisfaction.

Work culture refers to the values, beliefs, and mentality that a company wants its employees to share. Work culture is reflected in every aspect of a company's operations, such as its workplace policies, hiring decisions, and treatment of its employees and clients.

S For more information about skimming, see Reading Strategies, page 124.

> ### Reading Strategy
> #### Skimming
>
> Skimming gives you some understanding of the main idea and overall content of a text before you read it more deeply.
>
> To skim, read the title, subtitle, and subheadings. Check images or graphs and read the captions. Read the introductory paragraph(s), first sentence of every body paragraph, and concluding paragraph.

Pre-Reading Activity

1. Skim the article on page 7. Then write a sentence explaining what you think the main idea of the article will be.

   _____

   _____

   _____

   _____

2. What questions about the topic do you think will be answered in the text?

   _____

   _____

   _____

   _____

Vocabulary

Word clues refer to information given within a word that offers a clue to the word's meaning. Word clues may include affixes (i.e., prefixes or suffixes), root words, or words within the word.

 S For information about strategies for guessing the meaning of unknown words, see Vocabulary Strategies, page 149.

The following vocabulary words and phrases from the article are useful when we talk about jobs and work environments. Match the vocabulary in the left-hand column with the correct definition on the right. Write the letter of the correct definition in the blank line beside each word or phrase. Use word clues to help you when possible.

EXAMPLE   bottom line → The word *bottom* means "at the last or end point" and the text is discussing a company's income and growth, so *bottom line* means a company's final profit or loss at the end of the year.

Vocabulary		Definition	
f	1. bottom line (n) (para. 2)	a)	a job that generally involves office work and traditionally required wearing a (white) shirt with a collar
e	2. decline (n) (para. 2)	b)	a company's profit after deducting operating costs such as wages, cost of production, etc.
b	3. operating income (n) (para. 2)	c)	to increase quickly to a high amount
h	4. startup (n) (para. 3)	d)	a job that involves physical work and traditionally required wearing a (blue) uniform
c	5. skyrocket (v) (para. 3)	e)	a decrease
a	6. white-collar job (adj + n) (para. 4)	f)	a company's final profit or loss at the end of the year
d	7. blue-collar job (adj + n) (para. 4)	g)	to cause something to happen
g	8. induce (v) (para. 6)	h)	a newly established business

How to Increase Employee Satisfaction for the Long Haul

Eric Siu, Globe and Mail

1   Professor Alex Edmans of The Wharton School of the University of Pennsylvania discovered that businesses with high levels of employee satisfaction perform better than those without. Research from the University of Warwick says happiness makes people 12 percent more productive.

2   And yet a report from Gallup demonstrates that 63 percent of employees today are "not engaged" (24 percent are "actively disengaged") in their jobs. This essentially means that 87 percent of employees have no passion for their work, lack motivation to get the job done, and are unhappy. This has an impact on the **bottom line**, too—according to Tower Perrin, companies with a low level of employee engagement have a 33 percent annual **decline** in **operating income** and an 11 percent annual decline in growth.

3   Considering that three out of four **startups** fail already, the people in charge need to **unearth** ways to **skyrocket** and maintain employee happiness and satisfaction. Your startup's success might depend on it.

unearth (v) find

What makes employees happy?

4   Many factors together contribute to employee satisfaction and happiness. To understand this, The Energy Project teamed up with *Harvard Business Review* to conduct a survey of 12 115 workers. Ninety-four percent of these workers were in **white-collar jobs**. The rest (six percent) were in **blue-collar jobs**.

5   According to the survey, employees are most satisfied and productive when their four core needs are met. These are physical, emotional, mental, and spiritual needs.

6   The good news is that satisfying just one need of the four can improve performance. These steps can kick-start a culture that **induces** employee satisfaction and happiness, which in turn will boost productivity and performance. Just remember everyone's ideas on happiness will vary greatly, so communicating with your current employees and incorporating their wants and needs in the work culture will result in a positively functioning startup.

How should you get new employees to adapt to your work culture?

7   Wondering how to get potential **hires** to adapt to your work culture? You're on the wrong track.

hires (n) new employees, people that you hire

8   Tony Hsieh, Founder and CEO of Zappos, takes work culture so seriously that his company performs two sets of interviews. The hiring manager and his or her team conducts the first set to determine whether the candidate has relevant experience, technical ability, and is a good fit. The HR team conducts the second to ensure that the potential employee would be a good culture fit. Employees have to pass both interviews in order to get hired.

9   Zappos turns down many talented people who just don't fit into their culture. For Zappos, the long-term benefits are more important than the short-term benefits. So instead of looking for methods to get new employees to adapt, look for employees who will directly fit into your culture.

10 You can take it one step further and mandate an employee probationary period like Buffer does. They have a 45-day trial period with an employee called Buffer Bootcamp. During this phase, Buffer assesses the new employee to see if they would fit in with the company. The decision to stay together or part ways depends on how both parties feel at the end of 45 days. Usually 70 percent of new hires stay on.

11 Buffer also takes effective pre-employment steps. They're well-known for their transparency about their culture, salary packages, and everything else offered to make it easy to attract people who fit in.

The secret: Motivating employees to work because it makes them happy

12 On average, people spend 8.7 hours each day working (as compared to 2.6 on leisure and sports). This represents an enormous section of their lives. Businesses need to prioritize bringing fulfillment and happiness to employees. The obvious choice might seem like paying them more, but that does not directly correlate with long-term happiness. Money is a reward that aids as a fuel for a temporary period. Once it's exhausted, employees lose interest.

13 Motivate your employees to work because it makes them happy. Then stand back and watch productivity and overall company performance improve. **[646 words]**

Comprehension and Analysis

Answer the following questions in your own words. If the answer to a True or False question is False, rewrite the sentence to make it true.

1. What is another way to say *for the long haul* (article title)? _____ in the long term _____

2. a) According to the text, what does it mean to say that an employee is *engaged* (para. 2)?

    It means the employee is passionate, motivated, or happy in his or her job.

    b) What word in paragraph 2 means the opposite of *engaged*? _____ disengaged _____

    c) Which word in paragraph 6 is a synonym for *increase*? _____ boost _____

3. In paragraph 2, how does the author come up with the figure of 87 percent?

    The author adds the Gallup results indicating that 63 percent of employees are "not engaged" and 24 percent of employees are "actively disengaged."

4. a) In order to improve employee performance, employers must meet all four core needs: physical, emotional, mental, and spiritual.   ☐ True ☑ False

    Employers can start to improve employee performance by meeting even just one of the four core needs.

skewed (adj) when results are biased or distorted in a way that may make them inaccurate, unfair, misleading

    b) How are the results of the *Harvard Business Review* survey skewed based on the *type of worker*?

    Most workers surveyed (94 percent) worked in white-collar jobs. The sample of blue-collar workers was very small in comparison (6 percent).

5. According to the article, paying employees more is the best way to ensure employee happiness.   ☐ True ☑ False

    According to the article, paying more is only effective in the short term for ensuring employee happiness.

Students may need clarification because the text indicates that money can in fact lead to happiness—but only in the short term.

6. How is the subheading above paragraphs 7 to 11 misleading?

    The subheading suggests workers should be expected to adapt to company culture, but the text indicates that companies should actively look for people who are already a good cultural fit and therefore don't have to adapt.

7. Review the prediction (of the main idea of the article) that you wrote on page 6 after you skimmed the article. Was your prediction correct? If not, write the main idea here.

    Answers will vary.

Speaking

Write five questions you would want answered to help determine if you fit in with a particular company/institution/organization's culture. For example, does your company support any charitable organizations? Compare your questions with those of your classmates.

Watching

Could incorporating humour and laughter into the workplace increase employee satisfaction? Listen to what renowned Canadian business and motivational speaker, and author of *The Humor Advantage*, Michael Kerr, has to say.

Pre-Watching Activity

In a small group, discuss the following questions.

1. Is laughter in the workplace a good or bad thing? Support your opinion with reasons, facts, examples, or anecdotes.

2. Do you like to watch or listen to comedy programs or hang out with funny people? Think about how you feel when you laugh. What does laughter do for you?

3. Do you think fake laughter has the same benefits as real laughter? Explain.

> ### Watching Strategy
>
> **Note-taking**
>
> The goal of note-taking is to concisely record essential ideas. Note-taking can help you process and remember what you hear, and it provides a reliable reference to consult later.
>
> When taking notes, consider your purpose: What will you need to do with the information? What specific information do you need to listen for? Do you need to write down just main ideas or is it necessary to include specific details?

As you watch the following videos, imagine the company you work for is considering introducing more laughter into its work culture. You've been asked to watch Michael Kerr's videos and take notes of the essential ideas to present at your next company meeting to help them come to a decision about whether or not to add more laughter to your workplace.

Considering your purpose for watching, write down four questions you want answered in the videos in order to report effectively at your next company meeting.

Why do we need laughter in the workplace? What are the benefits?

How can companies incorporate laughter into the workplace?

What advice is given about how to implement changes?

Are there any negative aspects to laughter in the workplace? What problems might

companies face in trying to incorporate laughter?

What is some advice regarding how to go about the process of implementing more

laughter in the workplace?

Now watch the video and take notes of the essential ideas. Keep the purpose for listening in mind; the purpose determines what ideas are essential. Use good note-taking strategies.

Discuss the students' preparatory questions as a class before they watch the video to determine what information will be essential for them to jot down in order to give a successful presentation at the upcoming company meeting.

This is a good opportunity to discuss when it is necessary to include details and specific examples in your notes. For this situation, noting specific details in terms of benefits (to health, company profits, etc.) and examples (how other companies introduce laughter) would be advisable.

Sample questions are provided. Students may suggest other useful questions.

It is pedagogically useful to tell students to use good note-taking strategies without discussing strategies beforehand. Just tell them to do their best. Then go over the list of good note-taking strategies with them after the listening and have students evaluate another student's notes to determine if the student used those strategies.

Humour at Work [9:24]

By Michael Kerr

It is highly recommended that you go through the note-taking strategies list (Listening Strategies, page 130) one by one with your students as they evaluate their partner's notes.

Comprehension and Analysis

1. After watching the videos and taking notes, discuss the questions below in a small group to ensure that you noted all of the essential ideas. Add any essential information that comes up in your discussion that was missing from your own notes. Add the new information using a different colour pen or write it in the margins or at the end of your notes.
   a) What is the main idea?
   b) What are the social benefits of laughter in the workplace?
   c) What are the benefits of laughter on the individual?
   d) What are the benefits for the company of introducing laughter in the workplace?
   e) What is special about Danish (and other Scandinavian) workplaces?
   f) What key factors should a company focus on to create a happy workplace?

2. Exchange your notes with someone in your group and analyze that person's notes. Refer to the "Note-Taking Strategies" list on page 130 and give the person a point for each strategy used. Tell your partner his or her mark (out of 6); if you withheld any points, explain why.

Speaking

Do some research on how companies introduce laughter into the workplace. Take notes of your interesting findings.

Think of three ways that teachers or employers could introduce more humour into one of your field-specific classes or a workplace related to your future career. Share your ideas with your classmates.

Reading

Many employers now include some unusual questions in the job interview process. As part of your preparation for future job interviews, you should learn how to approach common interview questions as well as the more unexpected ones.

Pre-Reading Activity

1. In a small group, write down what you think are *common* job interview questions regularly asked in all professions.

   a) _____

   b) _____

   c) _____

   d) _____

   e) _____

2. How about more unusual or unexpected questions? Have you ever been surprised or stumped by a question in a job interview? If so, describe the question and how you answered it at the time. Ask if anyone has suggestions about how you could have responded more effectively.

Field-specific activity

You might suggest that your students watch the online video "Laughter: Serious Business" by Eric Tsytsylin or Michael Kerr's "Interview with Happiness in the Workplace Author (Part 2)" for some fun and interesting ideas on how companies introduce laughter into the workplace.

Credibility Check

When you hear or read information, it is important to apply critical thinking skills and analyze the source. Do you find the information in these videos to be reliable?

Support your answer using criteria from the Evaluating Sources Checklist on page 117.

You may want to discuss students' answers to this question as a class and then have students check to see how many of their questions are on the list of common job interview questions found on page 142 of the Professional Writing Strategies section.

Read Part 1 on your own. For Part 2, you will work with a partner.

Top 10 Weird Job Interview Questions (Part 1)

Aimee Picchi, CBS Money Watch

1 When it comes to hiring, more employers are going beyond standard questions such as asking candidates to list their biggest strengths and weaknesses.

2 Job applicants need to be prepared to answer a range of seemingly **oddball** questions, because employers are increasingly throwing these **zingers** into their interviewing repertoire, according to employment site Glassdoor.

3 Think of it as the Google-ization of the interview process: the Internet giant has asked tough, open-ended interview questions for more than a decade as a way to sort the analytical thinkers from the **chaff**. And now the rest of corporate America is catching on, according to Glassdoor's analysis of 250 000 interview questions that its members have posted to its site.

4 "We're seeing tougher and more unexpected questions asked for a variety of positions and variety of industries," said Scott Dobroski, associate director of corporate communications at Glassdoor. "Employers are looking to test a candidate's critical thinking skills, as well as how they problem-solve on the spot and how they handle an unexpected challenge."

5 So how can interviewees avoid getting **flummoxed** by an unexpected question? First, be aware of the types of questions that are now asked by companies, whether it's analytical or trying to find out what type of worker you are. Secondly, ask friends or family to pose similar questions, and get used to answering them out loud and on the spot, Dobroski said.

6 There are also two *faux pas* that potential hires should avoid. Never answer one of these odd questions with a one-word response, Dobroski said. Interviewers want to hear that applicants can create a thoughtful response and rise to the challenge.

7 Lastly, avoid laughing or **smirking** at the question, even if it seems off-base. "Employers take these questions very seriously, and if you **mock** them it won't bode well for you," he added.   **[310 words]**

oddball (adj) strange or unusual

zinger (n) a surprising or amusing remark

chaff (n) something not worthy, of less value

flummoxed (adj) confused

smirk (v) to smile, often condescendingly

mock (v) to laugh at or make fun of

Comprehension and Analysis

Answer the following questions in your own words. If the answer to a True or False question is False, rewrite the sentence to make it true.

1. According to the text, what is one common interview question?
   List your greatest strengths and/or weaknesses.

2. Why is the trend of asking weird job interview questions referred to as the "*Google-ization* of the interview process"?
   Google was the company that started the trend of asking unusual questions and now other companies are doing it as well.

3. According to the text, generally only computer-related companies ask unusual interview questions.   ☐ True ☑ False
   Unusual interview questions are now being asked "for a variety of positions and a variety of industries."

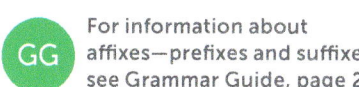 For information about affixes—prefixes and suffixes—see Grammar Guide, page 213.

4. One reason employers ask oddball questions is to see how well a person tackles problems that arise suddenly. ☑ True ☐ False

_____

5. What advice is given to help people avoid being stumped by oddball interview questions?

   a) Be aware of the types of questions that are asked at job interviews.

   b) Practise answering oddball interview questions with friends or family.

6. What advice is given about how to respond to such questions?

   Never answer with a one-word response or laugh at a question.

_____

Students are meant to read to extract information from the Part 2A and 2B articles: to read, analyze, and determine which information from the text is necessary to perform a specific task (described in the speaking activity that follows).

Read about and practise asking and answering some of the wacky interview questions asked at some well-known companies!

Before you read Part 2 of the text, get into a group of four students. Two students from your group will read Part 2A, and two students will read Part 2B. When you and your partner both finish reading your text, go to the speaking activity on page 14. Your group of four will get back together during the speaking activity.

Top 10 Weird Job Interview Questions (Part 2A)

8 **"What would you do if you were the one survivor in a plane crash?"** —This question was asked of an Airbnb trust and safety investigator job candidate.

As with all the oddball questions, interviewees should relate their answers back to the workplace, Dobroski noted. In this case, a potential response could include how to **ensure** the survivor's safety, as well as checking the rest of the plane to make sure there were no other survivors. Asking about nearby resources, such as radio or cellphone towers, could also help show the interviewer that the applicant can think ahead and plan for emergencies.

9 **"What's your favourite '90s jam?"** —A Squarespace customer care job candidate.

ensure (v) to make sure or certain

jam (n) a song

goofy (adj) silly

While this might seem **goofy**, Dobroski notes that this open-ended question is a way for a candidate to show off their positive qualities. "I could answer, 'All Star' by Smash Mouth. This reminds me to keep reaching for the stars,'" Dobroski said. "These can be very short responses, as long as you relate it back to the workplace."

10 **"If you woke up and had 2000 unread emails and could only answer 300 of them, how would you choose which ones to answer?"** —Dropbox rotation program job candidate.

This is the type of situation that almost everyone deals with today, but it also allows the candidate to show how he or she would prioritize in a potentially stressful situation, Dobroski noted. Candidates could note that they'd search for names of people and subject line terms that would need attention first, for example.

11 **"Who would win in a fight between Spiderman and Batman?"** —Stanford University medical simulationist job candidate.

circumstantial (adj) relating to a particular situation or circumstance

This is a **circumstantial** type of question where a candidate could ask the interviewer for more information, such as whether the fight is in a cave (giving Batman an edge) or the top of a building (Spiderman). "This shows how you assess an unexpected challenge," Dobroski noted. Giving a one-word answer such as "Spiderman" isn't what employers want to hear (no matter how much you love Spidey).

12 **"If you had a machine that produced $100 bills for life, what would you be willing to pay for it today?"** —Aksia research analyst job candidate.

glut (n) too much of something, such that supply exceeds demand

targeted (v) attacked

Candidates could ask the interviewer for more information, such as whether there is only one of these machines available or if there's a **glut**. Asking about whether there is risk involved—such as whether the owner could be **targeted** by criminals—could also help show analytic skills, Dobroski noted. **[418 words]**

Top 10 Weird Job Interview Questions (Part 2B)

13 **"What did you have for breakfast?"** —Banana Republic sales associate job candidate.

This sounds like small talk, but it allows the interviewer to **gauge** whether the candidate is an upbeat person and can relate to other people. Sales associates are asked questions all day long by customers, and keeping upbeat energy is important.

gauge (v) measure or judge

14 **"Describe the color yellow to somebody who's blind."** —Spirit Airlines flight attendant job candidate.

This question tests a candidate's sensitivity and how they gather information. An applicant could ask whether the person is partially blind and when they became blind, helping to formulate an answer and deal with someone's disability. "There are times when they have to work with passengers with special needs," Dobroski noted.

15 **"If you were asked to unload a 747 full of jellybeans, what would you do?"** —Bose IT support manager job candidate.

Unloading a plane full of jellybeans is no small task, so this allows a candidate to show off their project management skills. An interviewee could ask what the budget is, when the **deadline** is for unloading the plane, and whether they have machinery or **staff** to work with. That will help demonstrate the candidate's ability to think through all the possible dimensions of the challenge.

deadline (n) the date by which something must be finished

staff (n) employees, workers

16 **"How many people flew out of Chicago last year?"** —Redbox software engineer II job candidate.

This question for an entry-level engineering job is, not surprisingly, **geared** toward assessing a candidate's analytic skills. The interviewee could walk through their thinking, such as how many flights go in and out of Chicago each day, how traffic surges at the holidays, and come up with an answer. The interviewer isn't interested in the correct answer, Dobroski noted. Rather, it's all about how a candidate **handles** such problems.

geared to/toward (adj) designed for/suitable for

handle (v) deal with, manage

17 **"What's your favorite Disney princess?"** —Coldstone Creamery crew member job candidate.

This question is all about getting a candidate to show off their personality. Responses should link back to the business, Dobroski noted. "You might say, 'I like Cinderella. She epitomizes someone who works hard, is well liked and has overcome some challenges. That's how I approach work,'" he said. **[346 words]**

Speaking

With a partner who read the same text as you (either 2A or 2B), follow the steps below to complete this speaking activity.

1. Imagine that you and your partner work at the same company and are on the hiring committee. You must conduct job interviews for a position in your company. With your partner, choose three of the five oddball interview questions from the text you read. Write the questions in the box below. You will ask the candidates those questions at the job interviews.

2. Next, imagine that the two other students from your original group of four have applied for a job at your company. You and your partner will, individually, interview one of the other students from your group. Ask your candidate the three oddball interview questions that you wrote in the box below and take notes of that student's answers. Your partner will do the same with the fourth member of the group.

3. After your group has completed its interviews, rejoin your partner and decide which of the two candidates had the best answer to each of the three job interview questions. Use the explanation that follows each oddball question in the text—describing the purpose of that specific question—to make your decisions.

4. Select the student with the best overall answers to your questions. Announce the winning candidate and explain why his or her answers were the best. Provide details about what the answers told you about the person and why that person was the best candidate for the job. The other pair in your group will do the same.

Oddball interview questions	Candidate's answers Name: _____
1.	
2.	
3.	

Results Write the name of the student who had the best answer to each question.

Question 1: _____

_____

Question 2: _____

_____

Question 3: _____

_____

Name of winning candidate: _____

Grammar

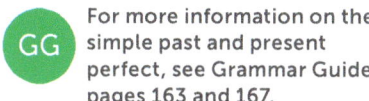
GG For more information on the simple past and present perfect, see Grammar Guide, pages 163 and 167.

Simple past and present perfect

Read the following dialogue of a student in a college nursing program being interviewed for an on-the-job training position in a hospital. There are two verb tenses used: simple past (SP) and present perfect (PP). The verbs have been underlined. Complete the chart below based on your observations of how the verbs are used within the dialogue.

Interviewer: Have you ever worked in a hospital? [PP]

Student: Yes, I have worked [PP] in a hospital before. I worked [SP] in a hospital during my last on-the-job training.

Interviewer: How many opportunities have you had [PP] for on-the-job training up to now?

Student: I have had [PP] on-the-job training once so far. I had [SP] on-the-job training last semester.

Interviewer: For how long have you been [PP] in the nursing program at college?

Student: I have been [PP] in the nursing program since last fall. I returned [SP] to college after a short break from school.

Interviewer: Okay, I have asked [PP] all of my questions about your education and job training. Let's move on now to personal qualities.

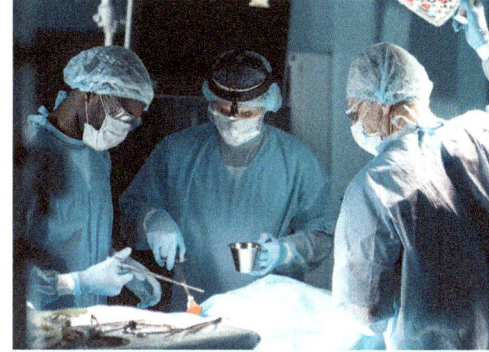

Fill in the chart below. In the first row, list the verbs used in the dialogue.

Simple past verbs	Present perfect verbs
1. worked	1. Have you ever worked
2. had	2. have worked
3. returned	3. have you had
	4. have had
	5. have you been
	6. have been
	7. have asked
How is the past tense formed? (What does it look like?)	How is the present perfect tense formed? (What does it look like?)
When do we use the simple past tense?	When do we use the present perfect tense?

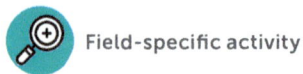

Field-specific activity

Field-Specific Practice

Use positive descriptive words (adjectives and action verbs) in your cover letter and resumé, and in your job interview, to highlight your professional qualities, skills, and accomplishments.

1. Choose three adjectives to describe yourself, focusing on those qualities that are particularly valued in your field of study or future career. Describe how those qualities translate into skills and positive behaviours in the workplace. See the example provided in the chart.

2. Use action verbs to give examples of how you demonstrated each skill in the past. Refer to a professional or academic situation if possible. See the example provided in the chart.

S For a list of suggested adjectives and action verbs, see Professional Writing Strategies, page 139.

You could have students do this as a speaking activity or include it as part of the job search project (Project A) described on page 110.

Adjective to describe a skill or quality	Example of how you demonstrated that skill
I am cooperative, which means that I work well with others.	In my final year of college, I collaborated with three classmates on the final project. I strengthened the team's spirit and motivation, which contributed to our A grade.
1.	
2.	
3.	

Pronunciation

-ed endings of simple past tense verbs and past participles

The -ed ending at the end of verbs can be pronounced three different ways.

/d/	/t/	/id/
For verbs that end with /b/, /g/, /j/, /l/, /m/, /n/, /r/, /v/, /w/, /y/, /z/, and all vowel sounds, the -ed is pronounced /d/.	For verbs that end with /f/, /k/, /p/, /s/, /ch/, /sh/, and /x/, the -ed is pronounced /t/.	For verbs that end with the sounds /t/ or /d/, the -ed is pronounced /id/.
EXAMPLES controlled, learned, played	**EXAMPLES** worked, finished, passed	**EXAMPLES** started, added, wanted

Why does the pronunciation of the -ed change depending on the sound that precedes it?

Hint: Put your fingers on your throat and pronounce each example word above before the -ed was added to it.

1. Read the following paragraph out loud. After each underlined verb, circle the correct pronunciation (/t/, /d/, or /id/) of the -ed ending.

> When I travelled (d t id) to the Dominican Republic on my last vacation, I met the owner of a successful steel processing company who treated (d t id) me to an interesting story of a job interview he had recently conducted (d t id). During the interview, he mentioned (d t id) to the job candidate that he had to leave for a short time and he handed (d t id) her a piece of paper and pen and asked (d t id) her to write something on the paper during his absence. He stated (d t id) that she could write anything she wanted (d t id), without further instruction. Then off he went. When he returned (d t id), he took the piece of paper from her and without even looking at it, he crumpled (d t id) it up and threw it into the garbage. He explained (d t id) to me that it hadn't mattered (d t id) to him what she had written. What he wanted (d t id) to see was how she reacted (d t id) to the situation. He finished (d t id) his story by saying how pleased (d t id) he was with his new-found interviewing technique and that he planned (d t id) to use it again in the future.

2. Listen to the online recording of the paragraph being read out loud and check your answers.

Students may want to record themselves using their phones to compare their pronunciation.

A voiced sound is one that makes the vocal cords vibrate when the sound is made. A voiceless sound does not make the vocal cords vibrate. To see if a sound is voiced or voiceless, put your fingers on your throat and make the sound. If the sound is voiced, you will feel the vibration.

The interview technique described here is real and is used by the employer described in the paragraph.

Students may go to Explore Online to hear a recording of all *Explore 3* Pronunciation features.

Interpreting Data

Job interviews can be very stressful, as you never know exactly what to expect. However, the better prepared you are and the more you learn from your own and others' experiences, the less stressful job interviews will be.

Reading Strategy

Scanning

Scanning means to look quickly over written material to find a specific piece of information such as a word, name, or number.

What You Wish You'd Known Before Your *JOB INTERVIEW*

In a survey of 2000 bosses, 33% claimed that they know within the first **90 seconds** of an interview whether they will hire someone.

The average length of an interview is approximately **40 minutes**.

Common nonverbal mistakes made at a job interview

From a survey of 2000 bosses.

21% Playing with hair or touching face

47% Having little or no knowledge of the company

67% Failure to make eye contact

38% Lack of smile

33% Bad posture

21% Crossing arms over the chest

9% Using too many hand gestures

26% Handshake that is too weak

33% Fidgeting too much

Things that have an impact on first impression

Statistics show that when meeting new people the impact is:

7% from what they actually say

38% the quality of their voice, grammar, and overall confidence

55% the way they dress, act, and walk through the door

Clothes

Is how you dress important?

65% of bosses said clothes could be a deciding factor between two similar candidates.

So, how should you look during an interview?

70% of employers claim they don't want applicants to be fashionable or trendy. You may also want to stay away from bright colors since they are typically a turnoff.

Most common interview tips

1. Learn about the organization.
2. Have a specific job in mind.
3. Review your qualifications for the job.
4. Be ready to briefly describe your experience.

Questions most likely to be asked

1. Tell me about your experience at _____.
2. Why do you want to work for us?
3. What do you know about our company?
4. Why did you leave your last job?

Comprehension and Analysis

Read each comprehension question and scan the infographic to find the answer as quickly as you can. If the answer to a True or False question is False, rewrite the sentence to make it true.

1. When meeting someone for the first time, we make the most impact with what we say. ☐ True ☑ False

   The greatest impact is made by the way we dress, act, and walk through the door. (55 percent)

2. According to just over 30 percent of bosses, how long does it take them to decide if they will hire somebody?

   90 seconds

3. What is the most common nonverbal mistake candidates make at a job interview?

   The most common nonverbal mistake is failure to make eye contact. (67 percent)

4. Employers want job applicants to dress fashionably. ☐ True ☑ False

   The majority (70 percent) said they do not want candidates to be trendy or fashionable.

5. On average, how long is a typical job interview?

   40 minutes

6. When meeting new people, 70 percent of the impact people make is based on what they say. ☐ True ☑ False

   Only 7 percent of the impact is based on what someone says.

7. The majority of employers are not influenced by what you wear. ☐ True ☑ False

   How you dress could be a deciding factor for 65 percent of bosses.

8. Which most common job interview question matches with common interviewing tip no. 1?

   Question no. 3: What do you know about our company?

Before or after students have completed the exercise, you could go over each question and discuss what key words, numbers, or symbols students would (or did) use while scanning to find the answer to the question.

You might want to talk about cultural differences when discussing question 3. For example, in Japan, making direct eye contact would actually be a bad thing to do at a job interview.

Writing

To review paragraph structure and see a list of transition words, refer to Writing Strategies, page 134.

1. Analyze this paragraph, which summarizes a video, by completing steps a) through e) below.

> In her video "How to Ace an Interview," Linda Spencer (a Harvard University career counsellor) gives the following advice about how to succeed in a job interview. First, you must do research about yourself, the position, the employer, and the industry. You need to be clear about your relevant qualifications, what you can bring to the company, exactly what the position entails, the employer's history, its products and services, and the competition. Second, you need to prepare short, relevant stories about yourself that highlight your abilities and accomplishments. Be ready to insert these in the interview at appropriate moments. Next, you need to practise your answers to common interview questions, alone or with a friend or professional career counsellor. Furthermore, on the day of the interview, you must be punctual. Spencer suggests arriving in the vicinity 30 minutes ahead of time and announcing yourself at the reception 10 to 15 minutes early. Finally, you need to make a good first impression. To do this, you need to make good eye contact, have a firm handshake, and appear positive, confident, and upbeat with a good energy level. Spencer concludes that following these five tips will help you ace your job interviews.

a) Circle the **topic sentence**, which introduces the **main idea** of the paragraph.
b) Underline (with a straight line) the **main supporting points**.
c) Underline (with a wavy line) any further **details** given for each supporting point.
d) Highlight the **transition word(s)** that introduce new supporting points.
e) Circle the **concluding sentence**, which rephrases the main idea.

2. Write a paragraph (150–200 words) in which you give professional advice of some kind related to your field of study or future career. For example, if you are a psychology student, you could write about what to do if somebody is having a panic attack or if you are a technology student, you might explain how to choose the best computer for your needs. When you have finished, exchange your paragraph with a partner and analyze each other's use of good paragraph structure the same way you did above with the paragraph on how to ace an interview.

_____

_____

_____

_____

_____

_____

_____

_____

_____

_____

_____

In an academic text, you must indent the first line of every paragraph by half an inch (1.27 cm). Use the tab key rather than the space bar.

It might be useful to go over the definitions of main idea, supporting ideas, and details here, as explained in the Reading Strategies section on page 121.

 Field-specific activity

You may also offer the choice of giving advice related to a general academic situation (e.g., how to decrease your stress before an oral presentation).

have happened/happened

arrived
(irrelevant)

complained
(irrelevant)

interview. Then,/After that, there was. . .
(Add a transition word.)
gave
drank
it. Also,/In addition, he often invaded
(Add a transition word.)

answer

Field-specific activity

Revising and Editing

1. Correct the errors in the use of the simple past or present perfect tense in the following paragraph. There are six verb errors.

2. Add any missing transition words and delete any unnecessary information to improve paragraph structure.

> In the video entitled "Interview Mistakes Right and Wrong," Stephanie Cruz, a director of a career services and recruitment agency, re-enacts blunders that <u>have happen</u> in real-life job interviews so that her viewers will not make the same mistakes. The first candidate was talking on her cellphone when the interviewer <u>is arrived</u> and the interviewer had to wait while she ended the call. ~~The candidate was talking to her boyfriend~~. The second interviewee showed a lack of preparation by responding "What would you like to know?" when asked "Tell us about yourself." Another mistake was made by a potential employee who <u>have complained</u> about his previous employer when asked about his last job. ~~His previous boss was not much older than he was~~. Next was a young woman who answered her cellphone during the <u>interview. There</u> was a man who <u>gived</u> too much personal information when asked about his shortcomings. He answered that he <u>drunk</u> too much on the weekends. Moreover, when he stated a weakness related to the job, he did not follow it up by explaining how he was working to overcome <u>it. He</u> often invaded the personal space of the interviewer by reaching over and touching her arm. The final interviewee could not <u>answered</u> when asked why he wanted to work there. He knew nothing about the company, its mission, or culture. Cruz concludes by stating that the viewer now knows which errors to avoid in order to triumph at that next job interview.

Wrap Up

Field-Specific Practice

Interview a person who works in your field of study or in a job related to your chosen profession. Prepare at least 10 interview questions. Your goal is to gain information that will be useful for you in your job search and increase your knowledge about your future career. You may ask for job interview advice, information about company culture, the most satisfying and dissatisfying aspects of the job, how to succeed in your chosen career, or any other information relevant and useful to you. Record the interview or take good notes.

Give an oral presentation in which you present the interesting findings from your interview. Be sure to state the name of the person you interviewed, where that person works, and his or her job title or position. Your teacher will specify the required length of your oral presentation..

Speaking

 Field-specific activity

Choose one of the following options and create a video resumé (2 minutes in length). You should watch some examples online before you prepare your own.

You might want to have students create a video resumé for an actual job ad that they find.

Option 1. Prepare a short job application video for a position related to your field of study or future career. State your name and identify the job you are applying for. Convince your potential employer that you are the person for the job! Try to be unique and creative and say something that will catch the employer's attention.

Option 2. Prepare a short application video for a specific university or educational program. State your name and the institution and program for which you are applying. Convince the admissions officer that you are right for that program and a good fit for their post-secondary institution. Do some research on the institution and program before you begin.

Writing

 Field-specific activity

Choose one of the following activities.

1. Research a company, organization, or institution related to your field of study or future career. You may gather information online or from other sources, such as teachers or professionals in the field, brochures, and so on. Use your findings to write a 450-word blog post. Your objective may be to inform others about your subject or to convince readers of an opinion you have formed based on your research. Be sure to properly cite your sources, within your text where necessary and by including a list of work cited entries at the end.

S For information on writing a blog, see Writing Strategies, page 144.

S For information on citing sources, see Research Strategies, page 118.

S For information on writing an email, see Writing Strategies, page 136.

2. Create a career plan. Describe the short- and long-term goals you will need to achieve to find the job you want. Research the necessary qualifications and skills. What kind of experience will you need and how will you get it? Use your findings to write a 450-word personal journal entry called "My Career Plan."

You may want to change the genre of the text (e.g., have students write an informational pamphlet or create a poster for option 1). Or have students create a poster and/or present their ideas at a booth. Another option: students write an email or another type of text giving advice.

3. Imagine that you are the employee representative at a company or institution related to your field of study or future career and that the employees are extremely dissatisfied. Write a 400-word email to the appropriate person (e.g., CEO) explaining why the employees are dissatisfied and make recommendations about how to increase employee satisfaction.

 Field-specific activity

 Go to Explore Online to download a template for creating a personal vocabulary list.

Vocabulary

Fill in the chart below with useful words that you learned in this unit. Transfer these words to your own personalized digital vocabulary list that you can organize and add to.

Field-specific vocabulary			
Word	Part of speech	Definition	Example sentence

Theme-specific vocabulary			
Word	Part of speech	Definition	Example sentence

It's in our biology to trust what we see with our eyes. This makes living in a carefully edited, overproduced, and photoshopped world very dangerous.

—Brené Brown

In this unit, you will explore the role of news media, bias in the media, and the future of media in our lives and careers. How much media do you consume each day? What influence does the media play in society? What effect does it have on your own life? How do you judge the validity of media sources? Get ready to start "reading between the lines."

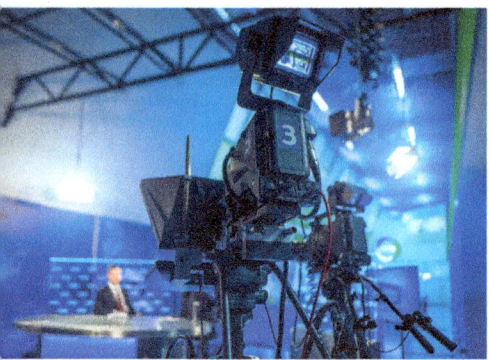

Warm Up

Speaking

1. In a small group, discuss the following questions.

    *   How will keeping up with current news help you in your studies? In your professional life? In social contexts?
    *   What effect has the Internet had on news media?
    *   What are some concerns or complaints that people have about the news media?
    *   How often do you check the news? How often do you check it in English?
    *   What medium do you use most to get your news?
    *   What are some of your favourite English news sources?

2. Summarize your group's answers and share your findings with the class.

Interpreting Data

Many people no longer get their news from traditional sources. Does age play a role in how people consume news? Using data from the graph below, write four sentences in which you compare how people of different ages get their news. Use a variety of expressions for making comparisons (see the chart below).

Making comparisons	
Expressions used to discuss similarities	**Expressions used to discuss differences**
Like X, Y . . . **Similar to** X, Y . . . **Both** X and Y . . .	X and Y **differ in that** . . . **Unlike** X, Y . . . **In contrast to** X, Y . . . **Whereas/While** X . . . , Y . . . X . . . , **but** Y . . . X . . . ; **however**, Y . . . X . . . ; **on the other hand**, Y . . .

EXAMPLE   **Similar to** the 18-to-24-year-old group, only 5 percent of people ages 25 to 34 years old report that printed newspapers are their main source of news.

1. _____

2. _____

3. _____

4. _____

Does the information in the graph represent the same conclusions about your age group that you came to in the speaking activity above? If your answers or conclusions were different, explain why.

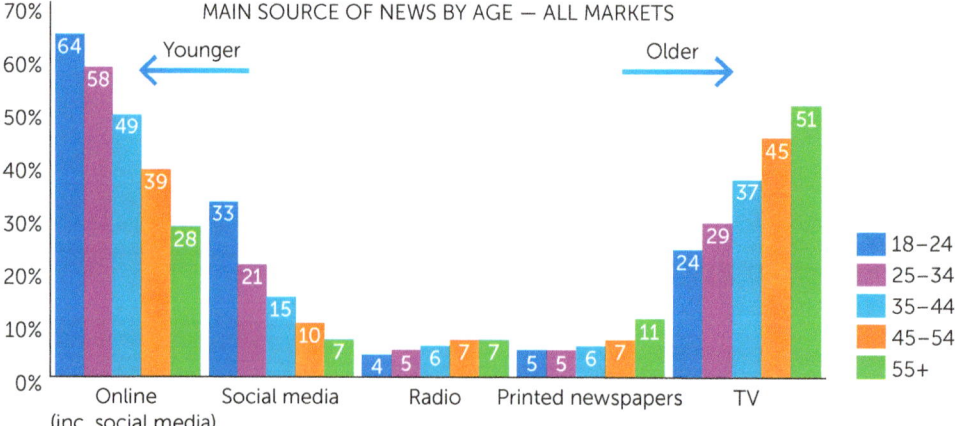

MAIN SOURCE OF NEWS BY AGE — ALL MARKETS

Reading

> ## Reading Strategy
>
> ### Recognize and use denotative and connotative vocabulary
>
> Being aware of a writer's use of denotative and connotative vocabulary will help you read critically and understand the writer's purpose. *Denotation* refers to a word's objective or literal meaning—the meaning in a dictionary. *Connotation* refers to associations and sentiments attached to words that add meaning. Words can have positive, negative, or neutral connotations, depending on the context.
>
> ### Identify bias
>
> The ethics of journalism require that journalists be accurate, fair, independent, and unbiased when reporting news. Despite this, bias in the media still occurs. To assess whether a text shows bias, ask yourself: What evidence is provided? Does the text favour one perspective more than another? Does the writer or publisher have a vested interest in the matter?

When you have a word in mind but want a more precise word to express your meaning, look up the word in a thesaurus or check the list of synonyms given in the dictionary. Always try to find examples of words used in context.

 For more information and examples of denotative and connotative vocabulary, see Reading Strategies, page 123.

bias (n) a prejudice or inclination to support or oppose a particular person, group, or point of view

vested interest (exp) having a stake or involvement in the matter, for financial or other personal gain

Pre-Reading Activity

1. Read this paragraph from "Canadian News and Media" by J.J. McCulloch. Find words in the paragraph that have negative connotations but similar meanings to the more neutral words in the chart. Notice how the vocabulary choice contributes to the negative tone.

> Today, more than 80 percent of Canadian media is owned by a <u>cartel</u> of five corporations: Bell Media, Rogers Media, Postmedia, Corus, and Torstar, each of which owns dozens of different publications and networks under various subsidiaries and affiliates. It's hard to keep track of who owns what on any given day because the "big five" are almost constantly engaged in various <u>schemes</u> to merge, buy out, or take over each other and their properties. The degree to which this cartel <u>conspires</u> to do various <u>nasty</u> things, such as raise cable rates, <u>drive</u> independent media outlets <u>out</u> of business, <u>foist</u> a certain political agenda, or collaborate with the government are all much-discussed in contemporary Canada, and tend to be <u>hot-button</u> issues for the left and right alike.

Research, such as a large-scale study done by Sumo (a content marketing analytics company), suggests that the average visitor to their site reads only about 25 percent of an article. (https://sumo.com/stories/how-many-visitors-read-article)

Go to Explore Online for the complete article by J.J. McCulloch, including comprehension and analysis questions.

Synonym (with more neutral meaning)	Author's word choice	Synonym (with more neutral meaning)	Author's word choice	Synonym (with more neutral meaning)	Author's word choice
1. group or band	cartel	4. cause . . . to leave	drive out	7. disagreeable or objectionable	nasty
2. plans	schemes	5. promote	foist		
3. works together	conspires	6. debatable/emotional	hot-button		

2. Complete the chart by writing down elements that could create bias in a news article—and how those elements create bias. Note any examples you have seen.

Elements	How it could create bias
a) the headline and/or subtitles	**It can reflect one point of view.**
b) photos and/or photo captions	can show subject in a flattering or unflattering way
c) choice of information included or excluded	may only include information from one perspective
d) choice of references/experts mentioned	may include opinions from biased individuals or laypersons vs. experts
e) the placement of information within the article	view expressed at start of article more likely to be read than view that follows (people often read only first few paras)
f) the interpretation of statistics	the same stats can be presented in different ways (e.g., glass half empty vs. half full)
g) the choice of words/vocabulary	use of connotative language (e.g., describing person as childish vs. youthful)
h) placement of report within the news source	front page vs. hidden in the back pages
i) funding or sponsors mentioned	research or a poll that has been funded by a biased source

Compare your answers with those listed in Recognizing Media Bias, page 123.

Read the following two articles that report on the same issue: the problem of antimicrobial resistance. Answer the comprehension and analysis questions to analyze the content of each article and consider how some of the elements from the chart on page 25 create bias.

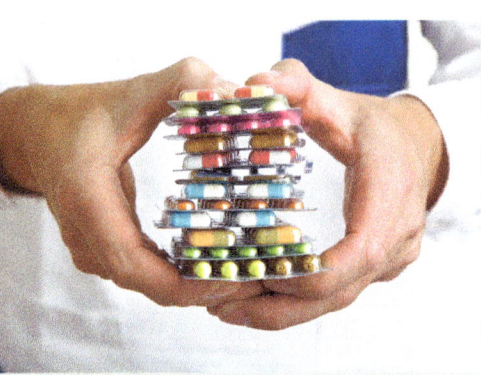

Shortages of vital drugs mean patients are left untreated.

Article 1: Global Shortage of Lifesaving Drugs Fuels Rise in Superbugs

by Anne Gulland, *The Telegraph*

1 A crisis in the global antibiotics market is fuelling the rise in antimicrobial resistance, as shortages of the vital drugs are leading to patients being given poor quality alternatives or even left untreated.

2 A new report warns that antibiotic supply chains are on the "brink of collapse," with many countries experiencing shortages of key drugs such as penicillin. Doctors are either forced to treat patients with inferior second choice treatments, switch to a lower dose, or delay treatment—all of which can fuel the rise in antibiotic resistance.

3 The report, by the Access to Medicine Foundation, highlights the global scale of antibiotics shortages and supply problems. For example, between 2002 and 2013, 148 national antibiotic shortages occurred in the United States alone. In 2010, 15 countries, including the UK, reported national shortages of injectable streptomycin, which is used to treat tuberculosis.

4 And an ongoing shortage of penicillin—described by the report's author as a "fundamental bread and butter" treatment—is affecting at least 39 countries, including Brazil, Germany, the Netherlands, India, and the US.

5 In Brazil, this shortage coincided with an outbreak of syphilis, which led to the number of babies born with the disease doubling between 2012 and 2015.

6 The report highlights the fragile nature of the antibiotic market with only a small number of factories manufacturing the active ingredient in many drugs. For example, an explosion at a Chinese factory in 2016 triggered an ongoing global shortage of the key broad spectrum antibiotic piperacillin-tazobactam.

7 The report says that the pharmaceutical industry has little incentive to take action—research and development is risky and expensive and antibiotics offer poor margins.

8 Jayasree Iyer, executive director of the foundation and report author, said the world was becoming more reliant on just a handful of manufacturers of antibiotics. "Pharmaceutical companies—whether they manufacture the active ingredients or the finished antibiotic—are leaving the antibiotic market in droves," she said.

9 She said that when a first-line treatment is out of stock, doctors might use an alternative, which could be of lower quality. They may ration the drug or even delay treatment.

10 "An alternative drug may be more expensive or doctors might use a different treatment regimen that requires a hospital stay. It creates a cost to society and to an individual's health," she said.

11 While the issue of antimicrobial resistance has been high on the international agenda—spearheaded by England's chief medical officer Professor Dame Sally Davies—the link with the global supply chain has not been so well recognized, said Dr. Iyer.

12 But she added that it was not up to the pharmaceutical industry alone to solve the problem.

13 "Pharma companies need to be incentivized to keep producing antibiotics. There is definitely no easy fix. But without a global push to address the systemic causes we risk being unable to treat common infections, such as from contaminated food or simple wounds," she said. **[482 words]**

Article 2: Antibiotic-Resistant Superbugs in Spotlight at High-Level UN Meeting

CBC News

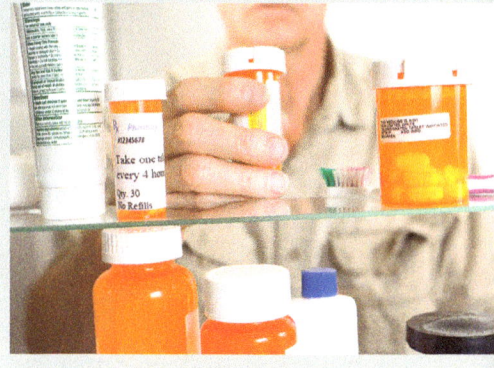

Overuse of medications contributed to the rise of antibiotic-resistant organisms but modern medicine depends on effective antibiotics.

1   The United Nations General Assembly will hold a historic, high-level meeting on Wednesday to discuss a plan to fight antibiotic-resistant superbugs.

2   We fall sick when bacteria infect us and we take antibiotics to fight off those infections, but bacteria can evolve to withstand antibiotic drugs.

3   And the medical world is losing the ability to keep ahead of microbial resistance. Antimicrobial resistance in bacteria, viruses and fungi already kills 700 000 people worldwide each year, according to a report to the British government.

4   On Wednesday at the UN General Assembly, world leaders will talk about ways to fight antimicrobial resistance. It's rare for a health topic to reach this level at the UN. The Ebola and HIV epidemics and non-communicable or chronic diseases such as heart attacks and stroke, cancer, diabetes, and asthma were the other instances.

5   "By the year 2050, it's been estimated that more people will die from these kinds of infections than die from cancer today," said Keiji Fukuda, special representative for antimicrobial resistance in the office of the World Health Organization's director general.

6   When bacteria resist all available antibiotics, routine surgeries such as C-sections and transplants or chemotherapy will become more dangerous without an effective way to keep infections at bay, said Ramanan Laxminarayan, director and senior fellow at the Center for Disease Dynamics, Economics and Policy in Washington.

7   Outbreaks such as Ebola or Zika generate headlines, but antimicrobial infections haven't grabbed the attention of government and state leaders the same way, said Dr. Andrew Morris, director of antimicrobial stewardship at Sinai Health System and Toronto's University Health Network.

8   Fukuda hopes the UN meeting about antimicrobial resistance will galvanize the attention of leaders around the world and lead them to find the money and political will to act on a problem that demands coordination from the health, agricultural, and economic development sectors.

9   Individuals also need to use antibiotics in a responsible way, which will require the kind of culture shift that second-hand smoking faced, he said.

10 "Countries are now on notice," said Laxminarayan. "If they fail to act, the consequences are basically the dismantling of modern medicine as we know it. It all depends on effective antibiotics."

11 The UN spotlight lends support to individuals, professional societies, and patients because it offers "a document to put in front of governments and say, 'You promised to do this and people are dying because you have not acted.'"

12 At the meeting, delegates will talk about solutions such as reducing the use of antibiotics in animal agriculture, discovering new ways to kill bacteria, and finding ways to make new drugs economically viable and available to everyone who needs them.

13 On Tuesday, 13 drug makers pledged to clean up pollution from factories making antibiotics and take steps to curb overuse of the medicines as part of the effort.

14 Their efforts to prevent overuse of antibiotics will involve a review of promotional activities and the implementation, by 2020, of concrete measures such as the removal of incentives to sell the drugs in larger volumes.   **[501 words]**

Comprehension and Analysis

Article 1 (page 26)

Answer the following questions in your own words.

1. Read the first three paragraphs of Article 1. What is the main message?
    Pharmaceutical companies need to keep producing antibiotics, and they need to produce more of them. The shortage of antibiotics is causing the ineffectiveness of antibiotics.

2. Now read the rest of the article. Does it give any information that indicates there may be opposing views to the main message you noted in the previous question?
    No

3. What evidence does the article mention to support its message? Does the text include information from different sources?
    All the information is based on one source: a report published by the Access to Medicine Foundation.

4. Examine the headline, accompanying photo, and photo caption. What impressions do they give the reader?
    They support the view that companies need to produce more antibiotics. The photo shows a variety of neatly organized, colourful (appealing) pills held in two hands (perhaps implying a small supply) by a person in a white coat (perhaps a doctor, a person generally trusted and respected).

Article 2 (page 27)

1. Read the first three paragraphs of Article 2. What is the main message?
    We must stop antibiotic resistance by using fewer antibiotics. If not, it will mean dire consequences. Already thousands of people worldwide are dying from antibiotic resistance.

2. Now read the rest of the article. Does it give any information that indicates that there may be opposing views to the main message you noted in the previous question?
    No (although it does mention some other possible solutions to combating antibiotic resistance).

3. What evidence does the article mention to support its message? Does the text include information from different sources?
    It is based on three sources: Keiji Fukuda at the World Health Organization, Ramanan Laxminarayan at the Center for Disease Dynamics, Economics and Policy in Washington, and Dr. Andrew Morris of Sinai Health System and Toronto's University Health Network.

4. Examine the headline, accompanying photo, and photo caption. What impressions do they give the reader?
    They support the view that the world needs to use fewer antibiotics. The photo shows a hand reaching into a medicine cabinet crammed with prescription drugs.

Both articles

1. The Access to Medicine Foundation (the source of the information in Article 1) is a non-profit organization that works with pharmaceutical companies to improve access to medicine in poor countries. According to the Foundation's website, its research helps companies to enter new markets in an ethical, responsible way. In terms of the issue of fighting antimicrobial resistance, would you say they have an unbiased or impartial viewpoint? Explain.

   Answers will vary. The goal is to get students thinking about where information comes from and whether the informer may have a vested interest or biased opinion.

2. If you knew nothing about the issue of antimicrobial resistance and read only Article 1, what impression would you be left with? What if you read only Article 2?

   Article 1 leaves the reader with the impression that the world needs to produce more antibiotics and Article 2 leaves the impression that we need to produce fewer antibiotics.

3. What lesson(s) did you learn from completing the questions on the articles above?

   The selection of whom to interview and what information to include in an article can be biased. Reading only one article on a subject from one source can leave you with an incomplete and possibly biased understanding of the subject matter. You should get your news from various sources.

Speaking

Media outlets often commission and publish their own public opinion polls, which may then be republished by other media outlets. The comic below examines the use of polls in the media and how the media can introduce bias when including or reporting on a such a poll.

In a small group, discuss the following questions.

1. Why would a media outlet want to commission and publish its own poll?

2. Do you see any problems with a media outlet commissioning and publishing its own poll? Support your opinion.

3. What messages do you take away from the comic below? What points are being made by comments 1 through 4?

4. Find a public opinion poll published by a media outlet and present it to your classmates. Address the following questions in your presentation:

- Who created the poll and why?
- Who were the people surveyed? How many people were polled?
- What were the conclusions of the poll?
- Do you see any evidence of possible bias in the poll, its conclusions, or in the way it is presented? Support your answer.

 Field-specific activity

Writing

> ## Writing Strategy
>
> ### Persuasive language
>
> Persuasive language can be used to influence people to accept points of view, values, and conclusions, or to promote a product. Below are three types of language that can be used to persuade.
>
> **Descriptive language** uses adjectives and adverbs to add detail and precision. It is used to create a vivid image in the mind of the reader.
>
> **Emotive language** is language that has an emotional impact. It is used to appeal to the emotions of the audience.
>
> **Hyperbole** is exaggeration. It is used to emphasize or make a point.

In business, *testimonials* are endorsements by celebrities or customers promoting the quality or value of a particular product or service. When writing a testimonial, you should

- explain the problem (the need for the product or service)
- discuss your situation
- describe the product or service and why/how it solved your problem
- make it personal

Below is an example of a testimonial. As you read, underline all the examples of persuasive language and identify each type: write D above descriptive language, E above emotive language, and H above hyperbole.

Choosing a university that was right for me was the most difficult and unpleasant experience of my life. That is, until I visited Capulet University.

With its expansive green spaces and its strategic location near downtown, it is definitely the only university for me. I love sitting outside under one of the many magnificent trees to eat my lunch, study, and recharge my batteries before classes. The trees make me feel as if I am home.

Not only is the campus beautiful, the teachers are the best in the world. The professors truly care about the success of their students. They are always asking students if they understand and if everything is okay. It is like being part of a big family.

If you are looking for an enriching and rewarding university experience, Capulet is for you!

Write a testimonial for a product or service. Your testimonial must have some connection to your field of study or future career and should be 100 to 150 words in length. Include some descriptive language, emotive language, and hyperbole.

Speaking

You can give students some examples of possible topics such as cannabis use (social science or health field), the elimination of cars from major cities like Montreal (urban planning), or green energy (environmental studies).

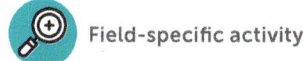

Field-specific activity

Prepare a news report (2–3 minutes) on a subject related to your field of study or future career. Your news report should be biased in some way. Include persuasive and connotative language and some of the elements listed in the chart on page 25 to help create the bias. (Your teacher may ask you to submit a list of the ways that your report is biased.) Include some research data on your topic in the report.

Present your news report to the class.

When listening to your classmates' reports, identify the ways in which each report is biased and the elements that contributed to the bias.

Field-Specific Practice

Find a media article on a news item related to your field of study or future career. Read the article and circle any words that have a negative or positive connotation. Make a list of the positive or negative words. Does the use of these words have any effect on the reader? Discuss with a partner and justify your conclusions.

Listening

We can train ourselves to look for bias in the media we consume, but what if that media is showing us images and videos that look real but are in fact fake? Listen to the CBC report "The Fight Against 'Deep Fake' Videos" to learn about this growing threat.

Pre-Listening Activity

As a class, discuss the following questions.

1. Have you ever thought something you saw in the media was real or true only to find out later it was fake or false? If you haven't experienced this, do you know of anyone who has? Describe what happened.

2. How do you decide if something you see or read in the media is real or true? Make a list of factors that you consider.

3. Are there media sources that you trust that perhaps you should question? Explain.

The Fight Against "Deep Fake" Videos [12:12] 🔊

CBC The Current

Comprehension and Analysis

Answer the following questions as you listen to the audio. If the answer to a True or False question is False, rewrite the sentence to make it true.

1. Michael McFaul says he is most worried about the harm that deep fakes could do to someone's reputation.　☐ True　☑ False

   He is most worried that deep fakes will blur the lines between fact and fiction.

2. According to researcher Hany Farid, what is new about the deep fakes of today? Circle all elements mentioned.
   a) how they are being made
   b) the purpose for making them
   c) the organizations that try to detect them
   d) how easy it is to make them

3. What is a deep fake?

A deep fake is an image or video that is not real, created using advanced technology that takes input from a user to create something new.

4. What were some of the challenges with creating fake content before deep fake technology came along?

It was time-consuming and difficult to make and it required a lot of skill to make good fakes.

5. Farid explicitly says we should worry about the high quality of deep fakes he is seeing today. ☐ True ☑ False

Farid says we should worry about the pace at which the technology is accelerating.

6. Give one example of how deep fakes are already causing problems in the world.

They are disrupting democratic elections and creating violent uprisings in Myanmar, Sri Lanka, and India.

7. What problem does DARPA face when it comes to sharing its detection techniques publicly?

Sharing information publicly allows the computer algorithms to learn DARPA's techniques and therefore circumvent them.

8. Describe two ways that social media contribute to the growth and increasing influence of deep fakes. Support your answer with information from the audio.

a) Social media companies promote deep fakes because they engage users, and increase the speed and scale at which fakes are distributed.

b) The use of social media increases the amount of online data available to create a deep fake.

9. What is the main idea of the audio?

Answers will vary. Possible answer: Deep fakes make it more difficult to tell what is real and what's not and they will continue to cause problems as the technology improves.

Speaking

What is your opinion about whether social media companies should be held responsible for the fake news or deep fakes distributed on their platforms?

Think of two reasons why they should be responsible and two reasons why they should not be. Discuss your reasons with your classmates. Do you come to the same or different conclusions?

Reading

What is the purpose of a news headline? What effect does a news headline have on you? Read the following article to find out just how deep the influence of a headline goes.

Pre-Reading Activity

In a small group, read the headlines below from three different media sources about the same news story and discuss the questions that follow.

HEADLINES   Heading for Extinction?

Earth on Brink of "ANNIHILATION": Humans have just 30 years to SAVE Earth from Extinction

Window for Saving Earth from Ecological Annihilation Closing

- Which of the three headlines attracts you the most and makes you want to read the accompanying article? Explain why.
- Based on the headlines, what perspective do you think each article will take on the story?
- Do you think any of the headlines could affect how you read the article? If so, how?

Vocabulary

Read the sentences in the reading on page 34 that contain the vocabulary words in the chart below. The paragraphs containing the words are identified and the words are bolded in the reading. Use context clues to determine the correct definition and match the terms in the left-hand column with the definition on the right by writing the letter of the definition in the blank line beside each term.

Vocabulary	Definition
__c__ tabloid (n) (para. 3)	a) to put forward or assume as a fact or principle; postulate
__h__ hard news (n) (para. 3)	b) a person who is not specifically trained or educated in a particular subject; a non-expert
__d__ news junkie (n) (para. 3)	c) a newspaper concentrating on sensational and lurid news
__a__ posit (v) (para. 3)	d) a person who is passionate about keeping up with the news and who reads multiple newspapers daily
__g__ slant (n) (para. 5)	e) elevated in style, tone, or sentiment (in writing or speech)
__b__ layperson (n) (para. 6)	f) an action that causes harm
__e__ lofty (adj) (para. 7)	g) bias; the point of view from which something is presented or seen
__f__ disservice (n) (para. 7)	h) serious news of widespread importance, concerning politics, foreign affairs, or the like

How many of the vocabulary words in the chart can you use in one sentence? Write a sentence using as many of the words as possible. Then compare it with classmates' sentences.

_____

_____

_____

_____

_____

Reading Strategy

Text annotation

When you annotate a text, you mark it up (highlight, underline, circle words, or colour code information) and add marginal notes to identify subtopics and/or the essential ideas and note how they are organized and connected. Annotation can help increase your understanding and retention of the ideas in a text.

Context clues refer to information given within the sentence itself (or in preceding or following sentences) that gives clues to a word's meaning.

For more information about how to guess the meaning of unknown words, see Vocabulary Strategies, page 149.

When reviewing the answers, you can discuss with students which context clues they used to guess the meaning of each term.

You can make this a game to see which student can fit the most words into one sentence.

Read the section on text annotation (Reading Strategies, page 124) and then practise by annotating the text "Misleading Headlines Can Influence Readers More Than Actual Content."

Misleading Headlines Can Influence Readers More Than Actual Content

by T. J. Anderson, Content Customs

1. You've probably run into it dozens of times: you click on an interesting article headline only to be taken to content that doesn't exactly fulfill the headline's promise. Sites that have been labelled as *click-bait farms*, such as BuzzFeed and Upworthy, are often accused of this. However, even long-standing and reputable publishers have started using misleading headlines to attract traffic.

2. Now, a new study shows that these headlines can have more of an effect on a reader's interpretation of an article than the text in the article itself—even if the whole article is read.

Examples of misleading headlines

3. Everybody's familiar with **tabloid**-style headlines that are clearly exaggerations or fabrications. Misleading headlines in supermarket tabloids and gossip magazines are to be expected. But what happens when the line between tabloid and **hard news** starts to blur? For example, anybody who isn't a **news junkie** would likely consider a source called *The Washington Times* to be a reputable publication. However, consider an article titled "Take it to the bank: Sen. Elizabeth Warren wants to raise minimum wage to $22 per hour." That headline might grab you, but a quick read of the article will reveal that Warren never *truly* **posited** the minimum wage should be raised to $22.

4. A little research reveals that *The Washington Times* has long had a conservative bias. Stuff like this can be found everywhere—there's no shortage of biased news sources for both liberals and conservatives. But what happens when one of the most well-known, supposedly unbiased news outlets is just as misleading? Consider a CNN article from earlier this year titled "Ebola in the air? A nightmare that could happen." Again, this headline is definitely going to get some clicks (*ebola* was the top search term this year), but the experts interviewed for the story claimed that the chances of ebola mutating to spread through the air are actually very small. The headline could just as easily have been "Ebola in the AIR? Experts say it's unlikely."

Study shows headlines skew readers' thoughts about content

5. The Australian study, published in the *Journal of Experimental Psychology: Applied*, gave participants four articles to read—two factual pieces and two opinion pieces, all of which were 400 words or less. The articles presented different **slants** in their headlines. For example, one of the factual pieces concerned burglary rates, which had decreased by 10 percent in the past decade but showed a 0.2 percent rise in the last year. Readers read two articles on this topic, one titled "Number of burglaries going up" and one called "Downward trend in burglary rate." When the study participants faced a surprise quiz after reading the articles, they were better at recalling information that was **congruous** with the headline. In other words, readers could remember more details about the declining trend in the article titled "Downward trend . . . " while also having better retention of the 0.2 percent increase in the article titled "Number of burglaries going up." The headlines told readers what to focus on, and those are exactly the details they retained. On the other hand, most readers were able to infer that the burglary rate would decrease next year regardless of article headlines.

6. In the opinion pieces, however, both inference and retention were skewed due to misleading headlines. Readers were presented with a piece about genetically modified food. The article contained contrasting information from an expert and a

congruous (adj) in agreement

Genetically modified foods are crops that have had their DNA altered to produce a desired characteristic.

layperson, the food expert stating that genetically modified (GM) foods are safe and the layperson expressing concerns. Some participants read the article under the title "GM foods are safe," while others saw the headline "GM foods may pose long-term health risks." Despite reading the same exact article, participants were found to side with whatever slant the title took. Readers of "GM Foods may pose . . . " were also more willing to pay extra money for organic food in the future.

What does this mean for writers?

7 The main problem here is that publishers are posting articles with **lofty** headlines that generate clicks but end up actually leaving readers with skewed versions of the truth. This happens even if the whole article is read. Thus, the study suggests that content creators are doing a serious **disservice** to their readers by using headlines such as these. The question is this: if publishers and article writers know that readers retain information from the headline more than anything else in the article, don't they have a responsibility to avoid headlines that bend the truth? Can readers be blamed for not examining content more closely and getting to the true **crux** of a story? **[763 words]**

crux (n) most important point

Comprehension and Analysis

Answer the following questions in your own words. If the answer to a True or False question is False, rewrite the sentence to make it true.

1. With a partner, compare your annotated texts and explain to each other what you annotated and why. Then answer the following questions.

   a) What similarities and differences are there in how you each annotated the text?

   _____

   _____

   _____

   b) Would you do anything differently the next time you annotate a text? Explain.

   _____

   _____

   _____

When students have finished annotating the text individually and analyzing it with a partner, you can go through the text as a class (while projecting it on a whiteboard) and discuss how students annotated each section, simultaneously annotating the text on the board based on your class discussion.

2. How does the author try to grab the reader's attention in the beginning of the text?
   a) makes the subject relevant to the lives of students
   b) starts with a surprising or disturbing claim
   c) starts with a relevant example
   d) all of the above

3. Why do sites use misleading headlines?

   Misleading headlines get people's attention—they attract traffic and viewers and presumably increase revenue.

4. "Take it to the bank: Sen. Elizabeth Warren wants to raise minimum wage to $22 per hour." According to the author, what is misleading about this headline?
   a) The senator never said this.
   b) *The Washington Times* never printed this.
   c) Only news junkies would understand the headline.
   d) None of the above.

5. "Ebola in the air? A nightmare that could happen." Why does the author think this headline would "get some clicks"?

   because *Ebola* was the top search term this year

   _____

6. The Australian study indicates that headlines "told readers what to focus on." If this is correct, how can newspapers use headlines to their advantage?

Readers remembered more details when the headline matched the information in the text. Newspapers could exert more influence over readers by matching headlines with content.

7. In paragraph 6, the author writes about an article on genetically modified foods. Are readers more likely to believe the expert or the layperson? Explain.

Neither. It all depends on the headline. Despite reading the same exact article, participants were found to side with whatever slant the title took.

8. In the conclusion, the author asks: "If publishers and article writers know that readers retain information from the headline more than anything else in the article, don't they have a responsibility to avoid headlines that bend the truth?" What is the media's responsibility? Explain your answer in 4 to 5 sentences.

Answers will vary.

Watching

After the 2016 US election, it was discovered that 50 000 Twitter accounts that actively tweeted information and opinions about the election were actually run by Russian bots. This interference may have had an impact on the election result. You are going to watch a video that discusses the potential of bots being used to influence Canadian politics.

Pre-Watching Activity

With a partner, discuss the following questions.

1. What do you know about bots?

2. What are some potential issues with computer programs pretending to be human on social media?

3. Who do you think might benefit from using bots?

Watching Strategy

Create a visual summary to illustrate essential ideas

A visual summary is a type of graphic organizer in which you represent the essential ideas of an audio, video, or text in a visual way. Creating a visual summary can help you understand and retain information better. There are different styles of visual summaries.

For more information about visual summaries and examples of different styles, see Reading Strategies, page 128.

Are Twitter Bots Invading Canadian Politics? [8:13] ▶

CBC The Weekly Briefing

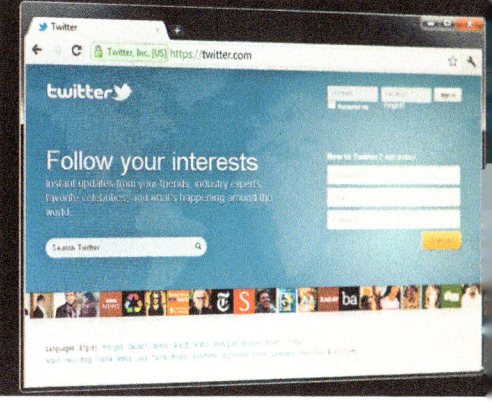

Comprehension and Analysis

Complete the visual summary below with the missing information from the report. This visual summary uses outline style.

Video Summary "Are Twitter Bots Invading Canadian Politics?"

Main idea: _____

_____

A bot is: _an online account created by a person to look real but that is run by_

artificial intelligence; a fake account that spreads stories _____

Study by Fenwick McKelvey and Elizabeth Dubois:

They analyzed ___3000___ (#) Twitter accounts; found ___20___ (#) that were suspicious

Three reasons why the accounts seemed suspicious:

a) _many were created within minutes of one another_ _____

b) _the number of times they tweeted was inhuman_ _____

c) _they had fake avatars_ _____

Their conclusion:

They suspect these accounts are involved in media manipulation—the spread of false

or misleading information. _____

Interview with Jesse Hirsh:

Two ways bots undermine the integrity of the electoral process:

a) _Bots could affect the outcome of the election by influencing people._ ____

b) _Bots marginalize what real people are saying—we question which voices are real._

Three possible effects of using bots in politics:

a) _A politician can have thousand of robots as supporters._ _____

b) _Bots can turn voters against a certain candidate._ _____

c) _Using bots can change the narrative before the election._ _____

His solution to the problem of bots:

We need rules and transparency for when bots are being used. _____

Case of Chris Wiley:

What he admitted to doing: _He harvested 50 million Facebook users' accounts_

during the American election and used them as a weaponized tool. _____

---

avatar (n) an icon or figure representing a person

astroturfing (n) activity (often political) that appears to have been started by the public but has actually been started secretly by a large organization

slippery slope (n phr) an idea or action that will lead to a larger, negative trend

whistleblower (n) a person from within an organization who exposes that organization's illegal or immoral activity

account harvesting (n phr) collecting all the account names in a system

tip of the iceberg (exp) the first, small part of a much larger problem

You may want to expand this question to include all forms of artificial intelligence.

 Field-specific activity

It would be good to have students from different fields of study represented in each group.

Speaking

Bots are software programs that perform repetitive and automated tasks, but they can be used to spread false or misleading information. In a small group, discuss the following questions.

1. Are bots currently used in your field of study? If so, describe how they are used.

2. How might bots be used in your field of study in the future (in positive or negative ways)? Complete the chart below with the members of your group.

Field of study	Positive use of bots in that field	Negative use of bots in that field

Grammar

Simple present and present progressive

GG For more information about the simple present and present progressive, see Grammar Guide, pages 163 and 165.

Read the following paragraph. Put the underlined verbs in the chart according to the verb tense used and answer the questions regarding their use and form.

People always <u>ask</u> me why I quit social media. I <u>am writing</u> this blog post today to explain. Social media <u>comes</u> with many positives—it <u>fosters</u> connection, <u>combats</u> loneliness, and <u>entertains</u>—but I <u>am no longer ignoring</u> the negatives. Algorithms <u>track</u> your every move. Huge companies <u>own</u> your personal information. Worse, social media companies' success <u>depends</u> on their ability to manipulate your behaviour. Trust me, right now, in your everyday life, you <u>are being</u> manipulated. Until social media companies <u>change</u> their business model, I <u>am staying</u> away. I heard on the news that leaders in the technology sector <u>are meeting soon</u> to discuss their social responsibility. Even those in the industry <u>are realizing</u> that things <u>need</u> to change.

	Simple present	Present progressive
Verbs from the paragraph	ask, quit, comes, fosters, combats, entertains, track, own, depends, change, need	am writing, am no longer ignoring, are being, am staying, are meeting, are realizing
Why is this tense used? What does it indicate?	1. to indicate a fact 2. to indicate a generalization	1. to indicate an action in progress 2. to indicate a planned future event
How is the tense formed?	subject + verb (base form, except add -s or -es with third-person singular subjects)	subject + be (conjugated in the present tense) + verb + -ing (present participle)
Verbs that cannot be used in this tense	X	stative verbs (e.g,. believe, know, seem)

Pronunciation

The -s ending

In English, the -s is almost always pronounced at the end of words, including the third-person singular -s used with simple present tense verbs and plural count nouns. The -s can be pronounced three different ways, depending on the sound at the end of the word before the -s is added.

/z/	/s/	/iz/
For words that end with the sounds /b/, /d/, /g/, /l/, /m/, /n/, /r/, /v/, /w/, /y/ or a vowel sound, the -s is pronounced /z/.	For words that end with the sounds /f/, /k/, /p/, /t/, the -s is pronounced /s/.	For words that end with the sounds /ch/, /sh/, /j/, /s/, /x/, /z/, the -s is pronounced /iz/.
EXAMPLES volunteers, subscriptions	**EXAMPLES** tests, desks	**EXAMPLES** teaches, wages

Why does the pronunciation of the s change depending on the sound that precedes it?

Hint: Put your fingers on your throat and pronounce each example word above before the -s was added to it.

Read the text below to a partner. Your partner will listen and tell you if you forget to pronounce the -s or if you pronounce it incorrectly. (Student A should check the answer key while listening to Student B, then Student B should check the answer key while listening to Student A. The answer key is available on Explore Online.)

Student A Every month, thousands of jobs are created and others are lost. Sometimes governments can play an important role in the creation of jobs. For example, if the federal government lowers interest rates, companies will be more willing to invest in their own businesses and hire more employees. This leads to an increase in employment. On the other hand, if a government raises minimum wages, employers will be more likely to cut positions or hire fewer employees. The government has to make these types of decisions that affect people's lives.

Student B Deciding what to do after high school is difficult for students nowadays. There are many choices. A student who chooses to go to university has to study for three years to get a bachelor's degree. In Canada, an undergraduate degree costs an average of six thousand five hundred dollars, depending on the program (Attfield and Havlak). On the other hand, a student may decide to complete a technical program at a college. This type of degree takes two or three years and tuition fees are about two thousand five hundred dollars per year ("Paying for College"). Making such decisions sometimes presents challenges. There are many factors to consider, but this is a very exciting time for students.

You may also listen to the recording online to check your pronunciation and practise saying the final -s correctly.

Students can record themselves as they read the paragraph(s) and then listen to and correct their own errors.

Point out that this paragraph describes the educational system in English-speaking provinces but not in Quebec.

Info sources:

Attfield, Paul, and Caitlin Havlak. "Canadian University Report—Paying for It." *Globe and Mail* 6 Sept. 2017, https://www.theglobeandmail.com/news/national/education/canadian-university-report/what-it-costs-to-go-to-university-in-every-province/article32375427/.

"Paying for College—Tuition and Financial Assistance." *Ontario Colleges*, http://www.ontariocolleges.ca/colleges/paying-for-college. Accessed 21 Jan. 2019.

Revising and Editing

Correct the errors in the use or form of the simple present and present progressive tenses in the following paragraph. There are 10 verb errors. The first error has been corrected for you.

believes   exist
says

refers

make

making
has

cut   wants

contribute

David Sedell, a photojournalist who has worked for many major news media networks, is believing that complete objectivity cannot exists when reporting events in the media. Sedell is saying that although reporters must strive to produce balanced and unbiased news reports, approaching an event without any opinion or emotion is impossible. There are multiple choices that are made in the process of creating a news report and the moment a decision is taken, it immediately becomes subjective in some way. Sedell is referring to these decisions as the five filters that affect objectivity. The first filter is the assignment, the choice of which events to cover in a news report. The people who makes that decision always consider what is important for their viewers, but still they do so based on their knowledge, experiences, and feelings, which are subjective. The second filter is the reporter, who relays and edits the words of others, which involves personal interpretation and make choices about what information to include or cut. Next is the photojournalist, the person behind the camera, a human who is having opinions and experience (or not) that will influence his or her decisions about which shots to take or how to shoot a scene. After that, at the editing stage, the editor can cuts whatever he is wanting from a news clip, which can end up giving the viewer a restricted view. Finally, there is the lineup—the order in which items will be presented and the time they will be aired. All of these filters are contributing to the fact that a news report can never be completely objective.

 Field-specific activity

Wrap Up

Field-Specific Practice

Creating a graphic organizer, like the one below, is a useful way to learn and consolidate field-specific vocabulary. A graphic organizer makes use of boxes, circles, lines, arrows or other symbols to represent information visually and show the relationships and connections between ideas. Colour coding may also be used.

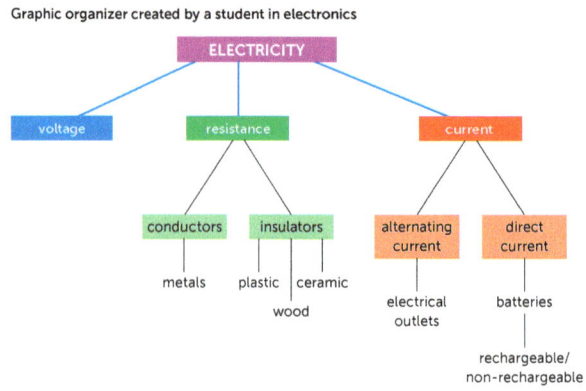

Graphic organizer created by a student in electronics

Create a graphic organizer that includes 15 to 20 vocabulary words related to your field of study or future career. Choose a field-specific word (e.g., electricity), and then think of related terms and continue to connect the words in a logical way that connects the words semantically. Be ready to explain your diagram in words.

You can ask students to find a field-specific news item for both activities. Students could do their presentation in small groups or in front of the class. You may want to have students prepare a visual summary of their news item to refer to during their presentation. Additionally, you may have them prepare two thought-provoking questions about their news topic to ask their classmates.

This could also be adapted into a writing activity.

 Field-specific activity

Speaking

Choose one of the following activities and prepare a short oral presentation (3–4 minutes).

1. Find an article linked to your field of study or future career and evaluate it for bias. Refer to the factors that can create bias on page 25. Be sure to use examples from your article to support your argument.

2. Find two news articles on the same topic from two different news outlet sources. Compare how the topic is presented in the two articles. What are the similarities and differences and how do these affect the reader? Consider at least three of the elements presented in Reading Strategies, Recognizing Media Bias on page 123. Summarize the important information about your news item (including the 5 Ws: who, what, why, when, and where) and state the findings of your comparison. Use some of the transitional expressions for making comparisons from page 134.

 Go to Explore Online for a list of appropriate news sources for this activity.

 **Field-specific activity**

Writing

Choose one of the following activities.

1. Find an article related to your field of study or future career from a valid source (see Research Strategies, Evaluating Sources, page 116). Annotate the text, then create a visual summary of the article. See page 128 for information about summarizing and visual summaries.

2. Write a news article related to your field of study or future career.

You can find information about the structure of a news article with an online search.

 Field-specific activity

 Go to Explore Online to download a template for creating a personal vocabulary list.

Vocabulary

Fill in the chart below with useful words that you learned in this unit. Transfer these words to your own personalized digital vocabulary list that you can organize and add to.

Field-specific vocabulary			
Word	**Part of speech**	**Definition**	**Example sentence**

Theme-specific vocabulary			
Word	**Part of speech**	**Definition**	**Example sentence**

If at first the idea is not absurd, then there will be no hope for it.

—Unknown

Stephanie Kwolek, mentioned in the introduction below, invented Kevlar, a material stronger than steel that is used in products like tires, shoes, and bulletproof vests.

What do Leonardo da Vinci, Stephanie Kwolek, and Elon Musk have in common? Their innovations have affected our lives in numerous ways. Innovation is not just in the domains of computer science and medicine; great innovators are found in all fields. Employers in your field will also be looking for individuals who can think outside the box. In this unit, you will explore the concepts of creativity and innovation and how they drive change in all aspects of our society.

Warm Up

1. In small groups or with a partner, discuss and then write your own definition for

    a) creativity _____

    b) innovation _____

2. Reread the quote on page 43. What do you think it means? Write your own interpretation and be prepared to share it with the class.

    _____

    _____

    _____

Speaking

Innovations often stem from a desire to solve a problem. Look at the following oddball products that made millions of dollars. Try to imagine the situation in which the inventors of these innovations came up with the ideas, then guess what problem they were attempting to solve.

1. Pet rock

    The inventor got the idea listening to his friends complain about the cost and trouble of taking care of their pets. He thought of the perfect pet: a rock.

    _____

    _____

2. Doggles (goggles for dogs)

    The inventors (husband and wife) noticed when they took their dog for a walk that the dog's eyes were highly sensitive to sunlight.

    _____

    _____

3. Slanket (the blanket with sleeves)

    The inventor (a university student) was always cold while watching TV in his dorm room at night, but when he wrapped himself in a regular blanket, he couldn't use the remote control.

    _____

    _____

4. Heelys (the shoe with wheels)

    The inventor (a psychologist) was having a mid-life crisis and saw young kids skateboarding and running and he wanted to just forget his problems by rolling away like them.

    _____

Reading

The world is changing at an incredible pace. Read "Four Innovations Changing Our World" about new innovations in the fields of health care, transportation, agriculture, and business.

Pre-Reading Activity

Think of an innovative new product or service that you either already own or use or would like to own or use. Share the following with your classmates:

- What is the name of product and what does it do?
- What features make it innovative?
- What problem(s) does it solve?
- Can you think of a way it might be improved?

Annotate the article as you read to help you complete the chart in the comprehension and analysis section that follows the reading.

Four Innovations Changing Our World

Our societies are constantly evolving, and technological innovations play a big part in this evolution. We strive to improve and simplify our lives through technology. Take a look at four interesting innovations of today, three of which involve new technological advances.

This futuristic water bottle is an edible, gelatinous blob

1   In the future, rehydrating on the go might not mean chugging from a bottle, but inhaling a gelatinous, edible blob that looks like water floating in the space station.

2   That's the messed-up vision of the folks at London's Skipping Rocks Lab, anyway. They've devised a method for home cooks to whip up servings of water encased in algae-based gel. People consume the squishy balls by biting them and sucking out the liquid or—if they have great gag reflexes—swallowing them like oysters.

3   The H_2O orbs are called Ooho!, perhaps from the sound drinkers make when the orbs explode and drip water on your shirt.

4   Though they might raise eyebrows, the globs have an honourable and pressing purpose: to battle the worldwide epidemic of plastic pollution. Here's a bit more about that from Ooho!'s nomination at the 2015 "Design to Improve Life" competition (apologies for the weird grammar).

> When we drink bottled water we throw away plastic, [and] 80% of the bottles are not recycled. . . . Ooho! uses the culinary technique of sphereification, the water is encapsulated in a double gelatinous membrane. . . . The final package is simple, cheap (2 cents per unit), resistant, hygienic, biodegradable, and even edible.

5   Customers make their own orbs. Preparing these things at home also has a climate benefit, as it doesn't involve the fossil fuels and CO_2 emissions of the bottle-manufacturing process.

Hyperloop

6   Picture this: a brilliant billionaire designs an innovative all-electric car, founds a company to supply the International Space Station, and invents a super-successful alternative banking system. It may sound like the next summer blockbuster, but it's real life. Elon Musk is the founder of Tesla Motors, SpaceX, and PayPal, and now he's revolutionizing public transport. He recently unveiled his idea for an ultra-fast, city-

to-city transportation system that could get you from San Francisco to Los Angeles in just 35 minutes. Hyperloop is described as an elevated steel tube containing aluminum capsules that would travel at speeds over 1200 kilometres per hour (760 miles per hour), ferrying cars as well as people. And it would all be powered by solar energy.

7   The major drawback? The price tag. Musk estimates that Hyperloop would cost $70 billion just to get started. The final expenditure could be a mind-boggling $100 billion. But Hyperloop also has its critics. Many complain that the system is too expensive, too impractical, even too slow.

8   Nevertheless, the plan is rolling ahead. A startup named Hyperloop Transportation Technologies, Inc. has published a timeline projecting the completion of a Hyperloop prototype. Only time will tell if this is actually feasible, but who knows? The future could be here sooner than we think.

grafted (v) joined together and grown as one

Art professor grows tree that bears 40 types of fruit

9   The first time Sam Van Aken saw tree branches being **grafted** and grown onto other trees, he likened it to Frankenstein. Yet when the process became a full-time fascination, the Syracuse University art professor did not seek to create a monster but a piece of art.

10 The "Tree of 40 Fruit" is Van Aken's creation, a single tree that can produce 40 different stone fruits, or fruit with pits, including peaches, apricots, plums, cherries, and nectarines. "I look at the Tree of 40 Fruit as an artwork, a research project and a form of conservation," Van Aken said in a 2014 TEDxManhattan talk.

11 He uses chip grafting to create the trees, which involves cutting the buds off a fruit tree and having them heal to the lateral branches of a rootstock tree. Branches from the different fruit trees grow off of the rootstock, which is typically a tree variety natural to the area's climate and soil. This allows fruit to be grown in areas that might not otherwise support that type of tree. Van Aken has planted 16 trees in seven states across the United States. Van Aken's trees can be found in Arkansas, Kentucky, Maine, Massachusetts, New Jersey, New York, and Pennsylvania.

The preschool inside a nursing home

12 For the elderly residents, interacting with the kids is a jolt back to the world of the living.

13 Giggles and the pitter-patter of little feet echo through the halls of Providence Mount St. Vincent in Seattle—not exactly the sounds you'd expect to hear in a living-care community for older adults.

14 Five days a week, residents and staff share the 300 000 square-foot facility with up to 125 children, from newborns to five year olds. The program was designed to counterbalance the loneliness and boredom that so often characterize life in a nursing facility.

15 Numerous studies have linked social interaction with decreased loneliness, delayed mental decline, lower blood pressure, and reduced risk of disease and death in elders. Socializing across generations has also been shown to increase the amount of smiling and conversation among older adults, according to one Japanese study from 2013.

16 While it's unclear what kind of impact such social interaction has on children, research suggests it may come with a variety of benefits for them as well. For example, kids who have early contact with older people are less likely to view them as incompetent—and simply exposing children to positive depictions of elders makes them less likely to exhibit ageism.

17 These incredible innovations are only the tip of the iceberg. Imagine how future innovations will continue to change our world!

Comprehension and Analysis

Complete the chart with information from the text.

You can also take a communicative approach to this comprehension exercise by making it a jigsaw reading. The text can be divided into four parts and a group of four students can read one part each (one innovation) and then share their answers orally to complete the chart together.

Questions	Innovation			
	Ooho!	**Hyperloop**	**Tree of 40 Fruit**	**Preschool inside nursing home**
1. What are the innovative features of this product or service?	−no container −can be made at home −cheap, resistant, hygienic, biodegradable, edible −manufactured without using fossil fuels or creating CO_2	−super fast −can carry cars and people −runs on solar energy	−one tree can grow many types of stone fruit −allows fruit to be grown in areas/climates that might not otherwise support that type of tree	−young children interact with the elderly in nursing home
2. Who created it? Where is it located or being used?	−Skipping Rocks Lab in London −can be made at home and used anywhere (not clear who is currently using it)	−Elon Musk −to be located between San Francisco and Los Angeles	−Sam Van Aken, Syracuse University art professor −trees located in Arkansas, Kentucky, Maine, Massachusetts, New Jersey, New York, and Pennsylvania	−Providence Mount St. Vincent nursing facility in Seattle
3. What problem was it made to solve or what kind of impact will it have on society?	Answers will vary; may include: reduce plastic pollution, make water bottles obsolete	Answers will vary; may include: reduce pollution, increase speed of public transport, increasing its use worldwide	Answers will vary; may include: allow people to grow the fruit they consume at home; may reduce transportation costs and pollution	Answers will vary; may include: a new model for nursing homes; better health outcomes for nursing home residents; less ageism among children
4. What role could someone in your field of study have played in the development of this product or service? Field-specific activity				

Question 4 may be challenging for students in certain programs. They will have to think outside the box to complete the chart. For example, consider all aspects of the development: research, design, production, and promotion. Students are working in a group and can share ideas and be creative when responding.

 Field-specific activity

Teachers can choose to define the time period (e.g., in the last 100 years) or leave the choice to students.

 GG

For more information about using the active or passive voice, see Grammar Guide, page 186.

Speaking

1. As a group, discuss the innovations you just read about on page 45 and decide which one you find most interesting and useful. Support your opinion.

2. Brainstorm a list of important historical innovations, positive or negative. Each of you must include innovations from your own field of study or future career. Choose the five most important innovations. Your group must reach a consensus. Support your choices.

Grammar

Active voice and passive voice

Each pair of sentences in the chart below is based on information from the reading on innovations. The first sentence in each pair is written in the *active voice* and the second sentence is in the *passive voice*. Read the sentences and answer the questions that follow.

Active voice	Passive voice
People call the H_2O orbs Ooho!	The H_2O orbs are called Ooho!
Elon Musk describes Hyperloop as an elevated steel tube containing aluminum capsules.	Hyperloop is described by Elon Musk as an elevated steel tube containing aluminum capsules.
People can find Van Aken's trees in seven states.	Van Aken's trees can be found in seven states.
Studies have shown socializing across generations increases smiling and conversations among older adults.	Socializing across generations has been shown to increase smiling and conversation among older adults.

1. In the active voice sentences, highlight the subject and circle the object of the verb.

2. In the passive voice sentences, circle the subjects.

3. What do you notice about the relationship between the object of the active voice and the subject of the passive voice?

   The objects in the active voice sentences become the subjects of the passive voice.

4. What happens to the subject in the active voice when the sentence is transformed into the passive voice?

   It is omitted or can be added in with a by phrase after the verb (e.g., by people, by Elon Musk).

5. What is the form of a verb in the passive voice?

   be* + past participle of main verb (conjugated for person and tense)

Writers also use the passive voice to be polite (to avoid assigning blame to a specific person) or to introduce known information before new information.

6. Why would a writer choose to use the passive voice? List three possible reasons.

   a) *There is no specific agent of the action (i.e., the agent may be people in general).*

   b) *The focus is on the action or result, not the agent.*

   c) *The agent is unknown, unimportant, or obvious.*

Listening

Playing with games or toys can be more than just for fun. Playing can have many positive effects and teach us valuable skills. In this section, you will listen to an audio clip about the link between creativity and a famous game.

Vocabulary

Make sure you know the meaning of the following words before you listen.

revel (v)   to take great pleasure or delight

ill-defined (adj)   not having a clear description or limits

convergent thinking (n)   the ability to get to an answer in the most efficient way

cognitive (adj)   related to intellectual mental processes, such as thinking, reasoning, or remembering

Pre-Listening Activity

Artist Michael Johansson's work was inspired by his favourite game. Looking at the examples of his art installations below, what game do you think that is?

In a small group, discuss the following questions:

1. What were your favourite games or toys when you were a child? Why?

2. Do you play with any games or toys now? If so, which ones and why?

3. What skills did (do) each of those games help you to develop?

Listening Strategy

Predicting

When you predict, you anticipate the kind of information you are likely to hear. Predicting before a listening exercise helps activate your background knowledge and vocabulary related to the topic, which helps you better understand the ideas from the listening. Predicting also helps you focus on the type of information you'll need to listen for and recognize the essential ideas. To help you predict

- look at the title and read the introduction to the audio
- ask yourself what you already know about the topic
- think about your purpose for listening and read the comprehension questions
- listen carefully to the introductory and concluding sections of the audio clip
- listen for transition words and questions that indicate a new point or aspect is being introduced

S For more information on transition words, see Writing Strategies, page 134.

Students can discuss these questions in small groups or as a class before listening.

The host is equating coding and engineers with analytical thinking, and poetry and artists with creative thinking.

Because playing with Lego involves both analytical and creative thinking.

Before you listen to the interview, read the host's introduction (below) and make some predictions.

> "Should you take coding or poetry? Should you think like an engineer or like an artist? Is it possible for your brain to do both? It turns out the answer may be found here, in a pile of Lego."

1. What distinction is the host making between coding (computer programming) and poetry? Between an engineer and an artist?

2. How might the answer to her questions be found in a pile of Lego?

Lego Kits and Your Creative Soul [10:12] 🔊

Manoush Zomorodi, WNYC Note to Self

Comprehension and Analysis

Answer the following questions in your own words.

1. What does Professor Moreau say about the new Lego kits and how they differ from the original, traditional Lego sets?
   a) They are harder to assemble.
   b) There is a correct way to assemble them.
   c) They are more attractive on the store shelves.

2. In Professor Moreau's experiment, how did the initial task differ between the two study groups?

   One group assembled a Lego kit (well-defined problem) and the other built freely
   with Lego bricks (ill-defined problem).

3. a) Fill in the blanks: Professor Moreau assessed the students' creativity using the
   ____unfinished____ drawing task, in which students were given a piece of a
   paper with a squiggle and asked to ____complete____ the drawing.

   b) What criteria were used to assess the title and drawings?
   how abstract the title was, how original and how elaborate the drawing was

4. a) What were the results of Professor Moreau's Lego study?

    Building with Lego kits made students less creative.

    b) How does Moreau explain the results of her Lego study—and what caused those findings?

    The brain has trouble switching between creative and non-creative tasks.

5. What did the study from the research paper titled "The Creativity Crisis" find?
    a) Kids are scoring better on standardized tests and their creativity is increasing.
    b) Kids are scoring the same on standardized tests and their creativity is decreasing.
    c) Kids are scoring better on standardized tests and their creativity is decreasing.

6. Fill in the blanks. The study of how sports affect adulthood creativity found that:

    a) children who spent two hours per week doing informal sports were ___more___ creative as adults.

    b) doing more than three hours of highly organized sports per week ___decreased___ creativity as adults.

7. The head of Lego's educational branch mentions that building Lego kits can develop skills related to what three fields of study?

    a) ___engineering___   b) ___architecture___   c) ___math___

8. What advice does Professor Moreau give about how to get into a creative mindset?

    Prime your brain by doing exercises like free associations.

9. What do you think is the connection between uncertainty and creativity?

    Answers will vary.

10. Do you agree that Lego kits stifle kids' creativity? Support your answer.

    Answers will vary.

Field-Specific Practice

When people think about their future careers, more often than not, they think about the technical skills needed to do a specific job. However, research shows that creativity is as important in today's job market as technical skills.

For example, scientists might need creativity to come up with ideas for new experiments. A nurse might use creativity to find ways to help patients remember when to take their medication. Police officers might find creative ways to defuse a tense situation.

Imagine three situations related to your future career that might require creativity and write them in the second row of the chart below. Then survey two classmates and add their answers to your chart. Be prepared to share your findings with the class. An example has been provided for you.

	Situation 1	Situation 2	Situation 3
Miguel: personal trainer	**developing a marketing plan to attract clients**	**coming up with interesting training exercises**	**finding creative ways to motivate clients to meet their goals**
1. You			
2.			
3.			

Reading

Years ago, if you worked in an office you might have spent eight hours a day sitting in a little cubicle surrounded by partitions. Today, companies are experimenting with innovative work spaces, as described in the text entitled "Innovative Ways Companies Are Changing the Workplace."

Pre-Reading Activity

"You are a product of your environment. So choose the environment that will best develop you toward your objective. Are the things around you helping you toward success—or are they holding you back?" —Unknown

Work with a partner or a small group. Think about where you work or study. Does that environment help you toward success or hold you back? Consider your purpose and then consider whether it is served by the realities of the space, such as lighting, furniture, décor, physical set up, location, noise, and busyness. Support your answer with examples. Be prepared to share your answer with the class.

busyness (n) how crowded or busy a space is; includes how cluttered or messy it is

Innovative Ways Companies Are Changing the Workplace

Lindsay Kolowich, HubSpot.com

1   Facilities managers and office managers around the world are asking themselves about the office spaces they're responsible for organizing. How can they set up a space that's not just a place to shelter employees, but one that's a strategic tool for productivity, collaboration, and growth?

2   What makes an office environment great is different for every company. A lot of it has to do with a company's culture and how its employees like to work. The right office environment can provide employees with the right ambience and motivation to tackle the challenges of their work.

3   Thanks to wireless Internet, laptops, and tablets, employees are finding they don't necessarily need to be chained to a single desk. Instead, they can move around their space, technology in tow. Some companies have taken this to the next level by eliminating personal desks and opting for a configuration called "hot desking."

4   Hot desking simply means no one in the office has an assigned desk or seating area. Instead, when you come in to work in the morning, you can sit anywhere you please—from open tables or desks set up with cables and monitors, to more public spaces like couches and chairs. For this to work, a company must take special care to create spaces in the office that can easily be reconfigured for different tasks and evolving teams.

5   The financial services and mobile payment company Square has done some experimentation with hot desking. In an Inc interview, Maja Henderson, Square's global facilities manager explains why hot desking has worked for them.

> We don't want our employees sitting in one chair all day, because that's not good for them and it's not good for collaboration. We just get these really great intersections of people and ideas. . . . Suddenly and randomly, we'll have these conversations with people from finance, legal, design, and you get these collaborations that wouldn't otherwise occur. I love how flexible it is, and that there are always different people sitting at my desk. It makes me feel more in touch with my co-workers and what's going on in the company.

6   But be aware that hot desking may not be an effective way to create movement in the office. One study found that when people didn't have an assigned desk, they didn't move around more; instead, they would find a place to work and then stay there for the rest of the day. Thus, while interaction among employees did increase by 17 percent in the study, the number of individuals' encounters during the day actually dropped by an average of 14 percent. As a result, team communication actually dropped by 45 percent. In such a case, you could keep teams together but change their assigned seating area every few months.

7   Another alternative to help encourage spontaneous collaboration among employees is designing your space to allow for "overlap zones," which make it more likely your employees will run into each other.

8   Research from the University of Michigan showed that when scientists worked in a space where they ran into one another—in areas known as "zonal overlap"—they were more likely to collaborate. The data suggests that creating opportunities for unplanned interactions among employees both inside and outside the organization actually improves performance.

9   "The most creative ideas aren't going to come while sitting in front of your monitor," said Scott Birnbaum, a VP of Samsung Semiconductor. That's why the folks at Samsung made plans to build an office that includes large outdoor areas sandwiched

between floors that encourage employees to hang out and mingle in shared spaces. According to Birnbaum, the new space is "designed to spark not just collaboration, but that innovation you see when people collide."

10 One way to boost employee productivity at the office is to foster a positive company culture. To give employees a place to blow off steam at work, why not add a music room to the mix? For the musically inclined, going into the company music room to play music alone or with co-workers is one way to do it. (And for the non-musically inclined, let's hope that music room is super soundproofed.)

11 "While the benefits (of a music room) to employees are obvious, we have uncovered many benefits to the company as well," said Michael Oliver, the former engineering director at LinkedIn who helped build the room. "Musicians perform, which improves the office culture. The program improves the company's marketability to potential employees, especially musicians, both as a specific perk and also as a 'think different' means of demonstrating our commitment to fun."

12 Whether or not allowing pets in the office boosts or hinders productivity is often debated. But there are a lot of companies that *do* allow folks to bring their pets to work, and they have good things to say about it—it reduces dog-walking expenses, improves work-life balance, serves as a social catalyst, and helps people de-stress.

13 A Virginia Commonwealth University study found that employees who bring dogs to work produced lower levels of the stress hormone cortisol. In the study, as the workday progressed, the employees who'd brought their dogs to work experienced a decline in stress levels of 11 percent, while those who didn't bring their dogs saw their stress levels rise by up to 70 percent by the end of the day. Finally, office pets—especially dogs—give owners a reason or excuse to take a break, which has been shown to be restorative and boost productivity later on.

14 Researchers found that adding plants and greenery in an office can help increase employee productivity by 15 percent. "A green office communicates to employees that their employer cares about them and their welfare," said psychology professor Alex Haslam, who co-authored the study. "Office landscaping helps the workplace become a more enjoyable, comfortable, and profitable place to be."

15 Some companies have started investing in installing plants and greenery around the office to help make their employees happier and healthier (and to boost productivity at the same time). For example, Google's office in Tel Aviv, Israel has an indoor orange grove that makes you feel like you're sitting outside on a park bench.

16 Live plants in the office need natural light—and natural light helps reduce monitor glare and eye strain, says Teri Ianni Driscoll, director of marketing for a company called KA Inc. Employee productivity went up even in offices with landscape imagery (such as wallpaper mimicking the outdoors) or large windows with views of the outdoors.

17 There are other health benefits of decorating with plants and greenery. NASA reported that live plants can significantly reduce toxic chemicals in the air emitted from furniture, rugs, and so on.

18 And that's it: a collection of the latest office designs sweeping the business world. Now, over to you: What designs do you think companies should implement in the future? [1147 words]

Comprehension and Analysis

Answer the following questions in your own words. If the answer to a True or False question is False, rewrite the sentence to make it true.

The speaking activity in the Wrap Up section is a good follow-up to this reading. The speaking activity has students design their own office space.

1. What are some potential benefits of hot desking? Support your answer with information from the reading.

   It encourages collaboration and connection between workers and causes
   employees to move around, which is good for health.

2. What problems do you think hot desking could create in an office?

   Answers will vary.

3. a) Give two or three examples of overlap zones in your work or school.

   Potential answers: hallways, cafeterias, libraries, break rooms, lawn

   b) Do you think these spaces effectively encourage collaboration? Explain your answer.

   Answers will vary.

4. The only reason LinkedIn added a music room was to attract employees who were also musicians.　☐ True　☑ False

   The music room showed potential employees the company was different and fun.

5. What do you think is the greatest benefit for a company that welcomes pets at work? Explain your answer.

   Answers will vary.

6. Adding nature to an office increases employee productivity and therefore increases the company's profitability.　☑ True　☐ False

7. According to the author, which of the following is *not* a way that office landscaping can benefit the workplace?
   a) it improves the air quality in the office
   b) it reduces eye strain
   c) it encourages collaboration between employees
   d) it increases employees' sense of well-being

8. What sources are referenced in this article? Are they objective and reliable? What other sources might you add if you were writing this article?

Credibility Check

When you hear or read information, it is important to apply critical thinking skills and analyze the source. Do you find the information to be reliable?

Support your answer using criteria from the Evaluating Sources Checklist on page 117.

Writing

To help students develop their paraphrasing skills, consider having students share and compare their answers. Have some students write their answers on the board or display them on the projector and then examine and analyze the paraphrases as a class.

For information about how to cite sources, see Research Strategies, page 118.

For more about plagiarism and paraphrasing, see Research Strategies, page 118.

Writing Strategy

Students can compare their summaries to the summary of this reading in the Revising and Editing section on page 61.

Avoid plagiarism by paraphrasing

Plagiarism is when you use another person's words or ideas without stating the source. Even if you paraphrase the ideas in your own words, you must still cite the source. If you use more than a few consecutive words in a row from the original source, you must use quotation marks.

To paraphrase (express the information differently from the original source), use synonyms and alter the sentence structure.

Key words	Synonyms
easily	readily
reconfigure	rearrange
different tasks	various projects
evolving teams	changing groups

Note that the synonyms maintain the same tone (level of formality) as the original.

EXAMPLE

Original   For [hot desking] to work, a company must take special care to create spaces in the office that can easily be reconfigured for different tasks and evolving teams.

Paraphrase   Companies that use hot desking must be able to rearrange their space readily to accommodate changing groups and various projects.

Notice the change in key words and sentence structure.

1. Paraphrase the following sentence from "Innovative Ways Companies Are Changing the Workplace" on page 53). Underline the key words and find synonyms for these words if possible. Then rewrite the sentence in your own words. Check the original passage to see if you kept the original meaning and all the essential information. If not, revise your paraphrase as needed.

    Some companies have started investing in installing plants and greenery around the office to help make their employees happier and healthier (and to boost productivity at the same time).

    _____

    _____

    _____

    _____

    _____

For details on how to write an informative summary, as well as an example, see Reading Strategies, page 126.

2. Now use paraphrasing to write an informative summary of the entire article "Innovative Ways Companies Are Changing the Workplace."

Field-specific activity

For information about giving an oral presentation, see Speaking Strategies, page 145.

Speaking

Imagine a company that offers headstand courses to employees, where there are free convenience stores on every floor, where company bikes and umbrellas are available for employees to use and where employees can bring their pets to work. Well, this is what it can be like working at some of the most innovative companies in the world.

Research a company with an innovative workplace. Try to find one related to your field of study or future career—it could be a company you want to work for. What makes that workplace innovative? Prepare a short oral presentation to describe the company, the ways in which the workplace fosters creativity and innovation, and how this approach benefits the company and its employees.

Watching

Historically, certain places were at the centre of extraordinary innovation and advances. What is it about those places that created, encouraged, or supported creative genius? Can we simply create the right environment for genius to flourish?

Eric Weiner addresses these questions as he discusses ideas from his book *The Geography of Genius: A Search for the World's Most Creative Places*.

Pre-Watching Activity

In a small group, discuss the following questions.

1. What makes a country innovative? List as many factors as you can.

   _____

   _____

   _____

   _____

You might want to mention that Canada placed number 20 on the list of most innovative countries.

2. Which countries do you think Bloomberg ranked as the top five most innovative countries in 2019?

☐ Canada	☐ France	☑ Israel	☑ Switzerland
☐ China	☑ Germany	☐ Japan	☐ United Kingdom
☑ Finland	☐ India	☑ South Korea	☐ United States

The factors used in determining the list of countries include
1. government spending on research and development; number of researchers
2. number of high-tech companies
3. number of people enrolled in post-secondary education
4. number of patent filings

3. Imagine you are standing in the middle of an office with four white walls, no windows, a brown desk, and black chair. Now imagine standing in the middle of the Sistine Chapel, looking up at Michelangelo's masterpiece. Which place would inspire you to be more creative? Are there some spaces that spur your creativity more than others? Discuss as a class.

You may find it useful to first discuss what and where the Sistine Chapel is and perhaps show some pictures. Some students will find the Sistine Chapel more inspiring, but others might feel more creative in a space with fewer distractions or influences. The key is that surroundings can affect our creativity—with each place inspiring one individual differently from another.

Sistine Chapel

Vocabulary

The following sentences are adapted from the video. Use word and context clues to match each bolded word or expression to the correct definition in the box below. An example is provided.

Bureaucracy is **antithetical** to creative genius. [adj]

You need more than comfort or interesting neighbourhoods; you need **hardship**. [n]

He pieced together a list of ingredients that he believes played a **vital** role. [adj]

All creative **breakthroughs** are preceded by this state. [n]

A number of places all around are trying to create the **Silicon Valley** of blank. [n]

Its product is technology, but the **means** by which it reached success is social and cultural. [n]

Both were **moochers**—they borrowed, or stole, from other places. [n]

Even if you do **buck the trend** and become very good . . . [exp]

Vocabulary	Definition
1. **Silicon Valley**	a region in San Francisco, California, considered the technology centre of the world
2. moocher	a person who takes something from or is financially supported by someone else and doesn't intend to return or repay it
3. buck the trend	to do something differently from the way others are doing it
4. antithetical	directly opposed to, contrasted with, and mutually incompatible with something
5. vital	essential, absolutely necessary, or important
6. hardship	severe suffering or a lack of things essential to human well-being (such as food or warmth); difficult living conditions
7. breakthrough	an important discovery or development in a particular field or activity
8. means	a system, method, or way by which a result is achieved

The Frank Lloyd Wright-designed SC Johnson Administration Building, Racine, WI

The Geography of Genius [9:14] ▶

Reason TV

Comprehension and Analysis

Answer the following questions in your own words. If the answer to a True or False question is False, rewrite the sentence to make it true.

1. Author Richard Florida developed a theory that places that are attractive to the "creative class" do better economically, and he developed a formula to attract those creative people.

   a) What part of Florida's theory does Weiner agree with?

   Place is important.

   b) What does Weiner disagree with?

   He doesn't agree that a place needs technology and talent in order to foster and attract creativity.

2. According to Weiner, what unexpected factor plays a role in driving creativity?

difficult places; constraints and hardships; chaos

3. According to Weiner, what state precedes all creative breakthroughs?

chaos/the I-don't-know state/disruption

Apple Park, Cupertino, CA

You may want to ask your students what the metaphor of Silicon Valley stands for here.

4. How does Weiner describe all of the geniuses he looked at throughout history?

They were all outsiders, not part of the status quo.

5. Weiner believes there is a formula for building the next Silicon Valley.   ☐ True   ☑ False

Weiner believes there is no formula for building the next Silicon Valley.

6. To what does Weiner attribute Silicon Valley's success? Circle all the correct answers.
   a) creative ecology
   b) cultural factors
   c) social factors
   d) technological factors

7. What does Weiner say Silicon Valley has in common with ancient, creatively successful societies, such as Athens?

They were moochers—they borrowed ideas from others and perfected them.

8. Weiner believes that government innovation programs are effective.   ☐ True   ☑ False

Weiner believes government intervention to encourage creativity doesn't work.

9. Weiner says that "we get the geniuses that we want and that we deserve." What does he mean?

Geniuses go where the recognition is; therefore, societies generate genius in the

areas they value. (Currently our geniuses are in the field of technology.)

10. What is the main idea of the video?

Place and societies have an effect on the creation and fostering of genius.

Speaking

In a small group, discuss the following questions.

1. Do you agree with Weiner that the "best and the brightest" people today end up in finance and in technology? Explain your answer.

2. The Quebec government spends money supporting the arts. Do you think this funding will have any effect on fostering artistic genius or a creative society? Support your answer.

Writing

Weiner speaks about the influence of place on creativity. Write a paragraph in which you describe a place that makes you feel creative or affects you in some other positive way (e.g., motivates you to do something or makes you feel joyful). Use descriptive language that includes many vivid sensory details.

Credibility Check

When you hear or read information, it is important to apply critical thinking skills and analyze the source. Do you find the information in the video to be reliable?

Support your answer using criteria from the Evaluating Sources Checklist on page 117.

ARE YOU ACHIEVING YOUR GOALS?

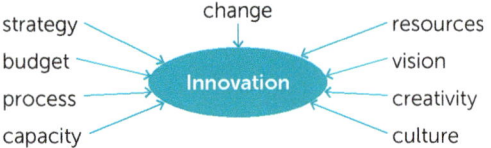

strategy
budget
process
capacity

change

Innovation

resources
vision
creativity
culture

Innovation is recognized as a business priority

CEOs surveyed by PricewaterhouseCoopers say it's essential that their organizations systematically generate and develop new ideas, products, and processes.

61% of CEOs say that innovation is a priority or an essential element for their businesses.

61%

Innovation efforts are random and inadequate

Although innovation is considered critical to success, more than half the CEOs surveyed by Accenture don't have innovative strategies, and when they do, they are not effectively implementing them.

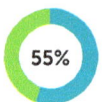 **55%** 55% don't effectively seek innovation opportunities

 66% 66% don't have well-defined innovation strategies

What prevents innovation?

Top 3 Challenges to Business Innovation (according to Forrester)

1 Resource constraints (time and people)
2 Budget constraints
3 Lack of structured innovation processes or procedures

THE KEY COMPONENTS OF INNOVATION

Robust processes and organization-wide support are essential for successful innovation. A PricewaterhouseCoopers survey asked CEOs for the "most important ingredients for successful innovation."

5 most important ingredients for successful innovation

1 **57%** the right culture to foster and support innovation
2 **44%** strong visionary business leadership
3 **37%** willingness to challenge norms and take risks
4 **31%** ability to capture ideas throughout the organization
5 **31%** capacity and capability for creativity

Successful innovation boosts revenue

Successful innovation has a direct impact on the bottom line. According to Bain, companies that innovate effectively grow much faster than companies with sluggish innovation programs—showing a three-fold difference in growth in 5 years.

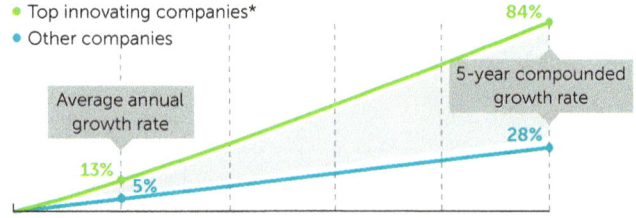

- Top innovating companies*
- Other companies

84%

5-year compounded growth rate

Average annual growth rate

28%

13%
5%

* "Top innovating companies" refers to companies with top quartile scores in the Bain Innovation Assessment Survey of executives at enterprises around the world.

Hoping that innovation will occur is not enough. Data shows that innovation is the result of strategy and structure, supported by processes and company culture.

Sources: Accenture, Bain, Forrester, PricewaterhouseCoopers

Interpreting Data

"Innovate or die!" Research indicates that most enterprises agree with this statement. The question is whether companies practise what they preach. Answer the following questions using support from the chart on the left.

Comprehension and Analysis

Answer the following questions in your own words. If the answer to a True or False question is False, rewrite the sentence to make it true.

1. Is innovation seen as important by most companies?
   Yes: 61 percent of CEOs say that they value innovation and it is a primary focus of their business activity.

2. What are the consequences of *not* being innovative?
   Non-innovative companies grow more slowly than innovative companies, with the top innovating companies growing by 84 percent in five years, as compared to other companies, which grow only 28 percent over the same period.

3. Do most companies foster innovation?
   No, not effectively: 55 percent don't effectively seek opportunities and 66 percent don't have well-defined innovation strategies.

4. Respondents considered visionary leadership more important than having the right culture to support innovation. ☐ True ☑ False
   Of respondents, 57 percent considered having the right culture to be a key to supporting innovation, while only 44 percent identified having visionary leadership as a key factor.

5. After five years, innovative companies grow three times as fast as lesser performing companies. ☑ True ☐ False
   _____
   _____

6. After one year, what is the average annual growth rate (percentage) for . . .
   a) innovative companies ____13____ percent
   b) less innovative companies ____5____ percent

7. Of the five ingredients for innovation listed on the chart, which do you think is the most important and why?
   Answers will vary.
   _____

Pronunciation

Word stress and the *schwa*

In English, some syllables are emphasized and pronounced for a longer time. These are called stressed syllables. A syllable may have primary stress (strong stress) or secondary stress (weaker stress) or may be unstressed (no stress). When learning a new word, it is important to learn which syllables are stressed because pronouncing a word with the wrong stress pattern can result in miscommunication.

In dictionaries, primary stress is often indicated by a short vertical line at the top left of the stressed syllable and secondary stress with a short vertical line at the bottom left of the syllable. Sometimes the syllable with primary stress is capitalized.

EXAMPLES   ˌsit-u-'A-tion   'PHO-to-ˌgraph   'COM-pli-ˌca-ted

The *schwa* (ə)

In English, any vowel that occurs in an unstressed syllable is pronounced as a *schwa*. The closest sound to a *schwa* is the short /u/ (as in *cup*). In the phonetic alphabet, the *schwa* is represented as **ə**. Note, however, that schwa followed by an /r/ sounds like the *er* sound in the word *her*.

> A **long vowel** sounds like it is pronounced when you say the alphabet. The **short vowels** are pronounced as in the following words: /a/ as in *hat*, /e/ as in *bed*, /i/ as in *it*, /o/ as in *not*, /u/ as in *bus*.

1. Listen to the following words and underline the stressed syllable in each word. Also, circle the vowel that is pronounced as a *schwa*.

    (a)-bout   e-n(e)-my   fa-m(i)-ly   free-d(o)m   (u)n-der-stand

2. a) Circle the vowels in the following words that are pronounced as a *schwa*. Use the stress marks (') as a guide (both primary and secondary stress (ˌ) have been marked).

    ˌau-t(o)-'ma-tion   ˌau-'ton-(o)-mous   de-'sign-(er)   de-'vel-(o)p-m(e)nt

    i-'ni-tia-ˌtive   ˌin-n(o)-'va-ti(o)n   ˌop-p(o)r-'tu-n(i)-ty   so-'lu-ti(o)n

    sus-'tai-n(a)-ble   ˌtech-'no-l(o)-gy

    b) Now go to Explore Online, listen to the words and check your answers.
    c) Say the words out loud. Be careful to pronounce them correctly.

Revising and Editing

Read the following summary of the article from page 53. Underline the eight verbs in the passive voice and correct any that are formed incorrectly.

> Recall that the passive voice is formed by conjugating the auxiliary *be* + the past participle of the main verb.

In the article "Innovative Ways Companies Are Changing the Workplace," Lindsay Kolowich states that the productivity, collaboration, and growth of a company can be affected by a workspace. She then gives examples to demonstrate how work environments can be set up by companies to bring about positive results.

One way is by "hot desking," which means that desks and seating areas are not assign. Instead there are open tables and desks and public spaces with couches and chairs. Employees can sit where they like, which leads to more interaction between employees from different departments and levels. However, if more specific team interaction is the goal, then it might be better to keep the team together in the same workspace, but change their work area every few months. Companies can also use movable desks that can be move around and fitted together in different ways. To increase spontaneous collaboration, zones can be created that cause colleagues to bump into one another more frequently throughout the day.

assigned

moved

To increase productivity and decrease stress, employers can make a music room where employees can play music or they can allow employees to bring their pets to work.

Finally, it has been shown that adding sunlight, plants, and greenery in an office can help increase employee productivity by making them feel happier, healthier, and cared for. Even installing windows or landscape imagery, such as wallpaper with an outdoors scene, can boost productivity. Additionally, toxic chemicals in the air can be reduce by adding live plants to the workspace.
reduced

Kolowich concludes by saying that these innovative office designs are being adopt by more and more businesses.
adopted

Wrap Up

Alternatively, you can have students write an essay, a blog post, or a testimonial or have them present the information as a poster.

Field-Specific Practice

 Field-specific activity

Research and write a 450-word text about a great innovator or innovation (past or present) from your field of study or future career. Include information about the importance or influence of time and/or place on the innovator or innovation.

Speaking

This can be done as a fun group speaking activity, or students can be required to give a more formal oral presentation.

Field-specific activity

Working individually or in a group, imagine that you are starting a business linked to your field of study or future career and you must design a workspace. Prepare an oral presentation to present your workspace to the class.

- Choose the name of your company.
- Choose the product or service you offer.
- Determine the approximate number of employees and the type of work they perform.
- Design your company's workspace.

As you design the workspace, remember to consider how to divide the space, who will sit where, where essential supplies and facilities should be placed, how each person and department will interact, and how to adapt the environment to enhance the work experience.

Below, you will find an example organigram of the hierarchy of a company.

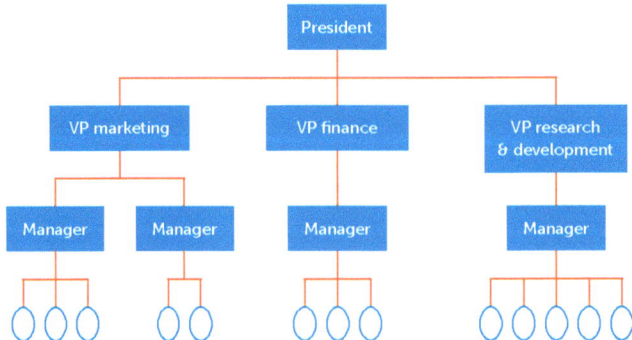

Writing

 Field-specific activity

Create a 300-word pamphlet to promote one of the following:

- an innovative product or service related to your field of study
- a conference or event related to your field of study
- an innovative company related to your field of study trying to attract potential employees

Be sure to consider both audience and intent. Be creative and incorporate images into your pamphlet where appropriate.

Vocabulary

 Field-specific activity

Fill in the chart below with useful words that you learned in this unit. Transfer these words to your own personalized digital vocabulary list that you can organize and add to.

 Go to Explore Online to download a template for creating a personal vocabulary list.

Field-specific vocabulary			
Word	Part of speech	Definition	Example sentence

Theme-specific vocabulary			
Word	Part of speech	Definition	Example sentence

Power does not corrupt. Fear corrupts,
perhaps fear of a loss of power.

—John Steinbeck

When we make choices, those decisions are guided by our values and beliefs—which are often informed by our society's laws and institutions. In this unit, you will have the opportunity to explore several ethical issues and perhaps question your own values.

Warm Up

Speaking

1. In a small group, discuss the difference between unethical behaviour and corrupt behaviour.

2. Together, complete the chart below. In the left column, write five different professions. In the right column, identify a corrupt or unethical action that could be committed by someone in that profession. Identify the action as corrupt or unethical.

Profession	Corrupt or unethical action
Teacher	accepting money for giving a student a better mark (corrupt)
a)	
b)	
c)	
d)	
e)	

3. How serious a problem is corruption in our society? Discuss and be prepared to present your ideas to the class.

It may be helpful to review the answer to question 1 with students before they continue the Warm Up activity. Ensure students recognize the following differences between corrupt and unethical behaviour.

Corrupt behaviour is dishonest or illegal behaviour, committed especially by people in positions of power. Behaviour can be judged corrupt according to existing laws, facts, and objective truths.

Unethical behaviour goes against a set of core values and principles held by a specific group. The question of whether or not something is ethical is more subjective. What is considered unethical may vary depending on a person's personal, cultural, or religious experiences or beliefs.

Discuss the responses to question 3 with students. You can expand this discussion with recent examples from corruption scandals in the news.

Reading

It sometimes seems that political and economic corruption is everywhere. Why should we care? Can we stop it? If so, how? Read the article "Why Corruption Should Matter to Everyone" to see what solutions it offers.

Pre-Reading Activity

1. Skim the article and predict what it will be about.

    a) What does the title tell you about the content of the article?
    Answers will vary.
    _____

    b) Does the source of the article give you any clues about its content? If so, what can you infer?
    Answers will vary.
    _____

2. What do the two subheadings (shown below) suggest about the content of the text?

    a) "Corruption remedy not the same for all situations"
    Answers will vary.
    _____

For more information about skimming, see Unit 1, page 5 and Reading Strategies, page 124.

b) "Technological innovation an important part in anti-corruption efforts"

Answers will vary.

_____

_____

3. Read the first paragraph. What did you learn?

Answers will vary.

_____

_____

4. Read the concluding paragraph. What more did you learn?

Answers will vary.

_____

_____

_____

_____

5. After skimming the article, write a short paragraph (30–50 words) to predict the main ideas of the article.

Answers will vary.

_____

_____

_____

_____

_____

_____

Vocabulary

Use the appropriate word or phrase from the box below to complete the sentences. You may use a dictionary to look up the definition of words in the box whose meaning you cannot guess from word or context clues.

cripples	gangrene	mitigate	touching off
cronies	high-handed	pilfered	
decried	leverage	squandered	

1. Jonathan's foot was removed when he got ____gangrene____ and all the tissue died.

2. There is so much bureaucracy in municipalities. This often ____cripples____ local mayors, preventing them from meeting campaign promises.

3. The goalie insulted the forward, ____touching off____ a huge bench-clearing brawl.

4. The president has been very ____high-handed____ in her decisions since crushing her opponent in the election.

5. My boss used his ____leverage____ in the company to have the vice-president fired.

6. Because of Maxwell's planning, he was able to ____mitigate____ a lot of the financial problems his company faced.

7. Many gifted people have ____squandered____ their talents with a lack of effort.

8. The criminal ____pilfered____ millions of dollars from senior citizens.

9. The mafia boss always has his ____cronies____ around him.

10. The employees ____decried____ the bad treatment they received from some clients.

Why Corruption Should Matter to Everyone

William J. Burns and Michael Mullen, *Project Syndicate*

1   Pope Francis has called corruption "the **gangrene** of a people." Former US Secretary of State John Kerry has labelled it a "radicalizer," because it "destroys faith in legitimate authority." And former British Prime Minister David Cameron has described it as "one of the greatest enemies of progress in our time."

2   Corruption, put simply, is the abuse of public office for personal gain. As leaders increasingly recognize, it is a menace to development, human dignity, and global security. At the upcoming anti-corruption summit in London, world leaders—together with representatives from business and civil society—will have a critical opportunity to act on this recognition.

3   Corruption is **decried** across cultures and throughout history, yet it has existed as long as government has. Like other crimes, it has grown increasingly sophisticated over the last several decades, with devastating effects on the well-being and dignity of countless innocent citizens.

4   For starters, corruption **cripples** prospects for development. When, say, public-procurement fraud is rampant, or royalties for natural resources are stolen at the source, or the private sector is monopolized by a narrow network of **cronies**, populations are unable to realize their potential.

5   But corruption also has another, less-recognized impact. As citizens watch their leaders enrich themselves at the expense of the population, they become increasingly frustrated and angry—sentiments that can lead to civil unrest and violent conflict.

6   Many current international security crises are rooted in this dynamic. Indignation at the **high-handed** behaviour of a corrupt police officer helped to drive a Tunisian fruit seller to set himself on fire in 2010, **touching off** revolutions across the Arab world. Protesters demanded that specific ministers be arrested and put on trial, and they called for the return of **pilfered** assets—demands that were rarely met.

7   In places where government officials enjoy (and often flaunt) their enrichment and impunity, extremist movements—including the Taliban, Boko Haram, and the Islamic State—exploit citizens' outrage. The only way to restore public integrity, these groups assert, is by means of a rigidly applied code of personal conduct. With no viable recourse—and no avenue for peaceful appeal—such language has grown increasingly persuasive.

Corruption remedy not the same for all situations

8   It is clear that corruption must be combated. What is less clear is how to do it. In a world of competing demands, corrupt governments may seem to serve vital purposes. One deploys soldiers to the fight against terrorism; another provides critical energy supplies or access to raw materials. Leaders must inevitably contend with difficult trade-offs.

9   To determine the best approach in each specific case, governments must analyze the problem more effectively, which means improving the collection of intelligence and data. As security expert Sarah Chayes argues in *Against Corruption*, the volume of essays that the British government will publish to accompany the summit, corruption today is structured practice. It is the work of sophisticated networks, not unlike organized crime (with which corrupt agents are often integrated). Governments must study these activities and their consequences the same way they study transnational criminal or terrorist organizations.

10   Armed with such assessments, donor countries must structure assistance in a way that **mitigates** corruption risks. Military or development assistance is not apolitical. Programs must be tailored to ensure that funds are not captured by **kleptocratic** elites. This means that anti-corruption efforts can no longer be **shunted** off to under-

Syndicate in English is a false cognate. You may want to point this out to students before they begin.

syndicate (n) a group of people or organizations working together to promote a common interest (often to maintain good working conditions and workers' rights)

kleptocratic (adj) characterized by corruption in the interest of personal profit for government leaders or high-ranking officials at the expense of the people

shunted (v) moved from one place to another, diverted

resourced specialists; they must be central to the planning of major development initiatives or the sale of costly weapons systems. Recipient governments must understand that funding will dry up if they continue to **squander** or steal it.

11 In fact, corruption and its implications must inform the way Western officials interact with their counterparts in the developing world. The departments that we spent our careers serving—the US State Department and the US Department of Defense—set great store by building relationships. Diplomats depend on these relationships to advance their national interests, and professional ties between military officers are sometimes the only channels that weather political storms. But diplomats and **military brass** alike should be willing to take a step back when appropriate, condition their interactions, and make use of available **leverage**—even at the risk of a counterpart's **wrath**.

12 But, as recent revelations about **purveyors** of shell companies or bribery by intermediaries demonstrate, much of the real leverage is to be found at home—in the domestic financial and property industries, in public relations and law firms that **burnish** kleptocrats' images, and in universities that educate corrupt officials' children and solicit their donations. The application of the US Racketeer Influenced and Corrupt Organizations Act to indict officers of FIFA, soccer's international governing body, shows how focusing on Western service providers can curb corruption among foreign officials.

Technological innovation an important part in anti-corruption efforts

13 Another important tool in the fight against corruption will be technological innovation, which can reduce opportunities for wrongdoing, empower citizens to highlight illegal practices, and enhance government transparency and accountability. Strides have already been made in a number of areas, from electronic voter registration to electronic payments for civil servants. While technology is no panacea, when paired with wise policy reforms, it can make a meaningful contribution to the fight for good governance.

14 None of these suggestions will be easy to implement. But, to address many of the crises currently besetting the world, a strong focus on combating corruption is vital. Our hope is that the upcoming conference in London demonstrates the unity of purpose and commitment to action that is so badly needed.   **[914 words]**

military brass (n) high-ranking members of the military

wrath (n) anger

purveyors (n) people or organizations that promote, provide, supply, or sell ideas or goods

burnish (v) to polish

Comprehension and Analysis

Answer the following questions in your own words. If the answer to a True or False question is False, rewrite the sentence to make it true.

1. Pope Francis calls corruption, "the gangrene of a people." What do you think he means by this?
    Corruption is destructive to people and society.
    _____

2. Corruption is a fairly recent phenomenon.   ☐ True   ☑ False
    Corruption has existed as long as governments have existed.

3. What are two effects of corruption the article mentions?
    a)   It prevents economic development in countries.
    b)   It can lead to conflict and civil unrest.

4. Why do people turn to extremist organizations when corruption occurs?
    When governments are corrupt, people may become angry and turn to organizations
    that tell them a rigid personal code of conduct will help restore public integrity.

The article defines corruption as "the abuse of public office for personal gain" (para. 2). Corruption is more generally defined as dishonest conduct of any person in power, which includes business leaders. This disparity might be interesting to bring up when discussing the article's bias.

5. Why might some Western governments not want to fight corruption in developing countries?

Western governments may ignore corruption because they do business with these

governments or the governments are useful in some other way.

6. What link do the authors make between corrupt governments and terrorist organizations?
   a) They both involve complex and highly organized networks.
   b) They both involve corrupt agents of the government.
   c) They both operate internationally.

7. What do the authors say donor countries should do if a corrupt government steals aid?

Donor countries should cut off future funding.

8. In paragraph 12, the author lists three ways that the United States helps support corruption. Explain how these three things might support corruption.

   a) "domestic financial and property industries"

   Answers will vary: allows corrupt governments to steal and hide money in the

   US and potentially profit further from these corruptly acquired funds

   b) "public relations and law firms that burnish kleptocrats' images"

   Answers will vary: legitimizes corrupt governments; masks corruption; makes it

   less likely corrupt governments will face consequences on the international stage

   c) "universities that educate corrupt officials' children and solicit their donations"

   Answers will vary: legitimizes corrupt leaders; profits from corruption, making it

   less likely anyone will confront it

You may want to explore whether electronic voting, which the authors appear to embrace, is truly a remedy for anti-corruption efforts or whether it could be co-opted to uphold corrupt governments.

9. How could electronic voter registration help combat corruption?

   _____

   _____

10. a) What part of this article did you find most interesting, revealing, or surprising? How did this information make you feel? Compare your answers with those of your classmates.

    _____

    _____

For more information on connotative language, see Unit 2, page 25 and Reading Strategies, page 123.

   b) Look through the article for examples of connotative language. What do these examples of connotative language tell you about the authors and their purpose in writing the article?

   Answers include: menace to development (para 2), devastating effects (para 3),

   cripples prospects (para 4)

For more information on connotative language, see Unit 2, page 25 and Reading Strategies, page 123.

Credibility Check

When you hear or read information, it is important to apply critical thinking skills and analyze the source. Do you find the information from this text to be reliable?

Support your answer using criteria from the Evaluating Sources Checklist on page 117.

Speaking

1. As a class or in small groups, discuss the following questions: What do you know about the person/people who wrote this article? Where do they live and where did they work? What biases do you see in the article? In your opinion, does this article tell the whole story about corruption? Explain why or why not.

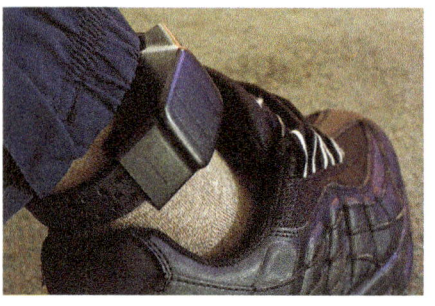

Given the noticeable bias in this article, you may want to spend time as a class on the Credibility Check. Points of discussion might include: the existence of right-wing extremism in Western countries; corruption in Western countries, including local governments; the perpetuation of stereotypes about developing countries; and the fact that bias might lessen the article's effectiveness.

2. The authors argue that the remedy for corruption is not the same for all situations. Think of an example of corruption that does or could exist in your field of study or future career. (You can use examples from the speaking activity on page 66 if necessary.) Think of a solution to remedy the situation and write it in the first row of the box below. Survey two of your classmates and write their responses in the next two rows.

 Field-specific activity

Field of study or future career	Corrupt situation	Solution
1.		
2.		
3.		

Listening

The sports world has always grappled with the ethical issue of how far athletes should be allowed to go to gain a competitive advantage, whether it's related to doping or equipment. Today, athletes and athletic organizations are faced with a new ethical dilemma—body enhancement. Listen to the audio to learn more.

Pre-Listening Activity

1. Should Paralympic athletes—for example, athletes with prosthetic limbs—be allowed to compete in the Olympic Games? Explain your answer.

2. List three examples of sports scandals involving corrupt or unethical behaviour.

Listening Strategy

Create a visual summary (bubble style)

Visual summaries may take a variety of forms. The bubble style uses boxes, ovals, arrows, and images to show how essential ideas are organized and to demonstrate the connections and relationships between ideas.

detail — Supporting idea — detail — MAIN IDEA — Supporting idea — detail — Supporting idea — detail — Supporting idea — detail

The Paralympic Games is an international multi-sport competition for athletes with disabilities. The Paralympics are held immediately following the winter and summer Olympic Games.

You may want to start this activity by asking students to identify some Paralympic athletes. Although Quebec has many well-known Paralympians, students may find it challenging to name them. This may prompt the question *Why?* and bring the discussion back to the Unit 2 question, *Who decides what is news?* Don't Paralympians deserve the same recognition as Olympic athletes?

There are several examples of male and female athletes with prosthetic limbs who have competed in running, swimming, archery, gymnastics, table tennis, and other Olympic events. Students may not be aware of this and may find it interesting to research these athletes and share information with the class. Extensive research is unnecessary—this is relevant to the pre-listening discussion but not specifically to the audio that students will hear.

S   For more information on and examples of different styles of visual summaries, see Unit 2, page 36 and Reading Strategies, page 128.

Vocabulary

Before listening to the interview, familiarize yourself with the following words and expressions.

IOC (n)	International Olympic Committee
cadaver (n)	a dead body, corpse
hack (v)	1. to cut up, to mutilate; 2. to find a quick, clever solution to a problem

Now listen to the audio. As you listen, fill in the note-taking template to capture the essential ideas and examples. You will use this template to create a visual summary.

Should Athletes Be Allowed to Hack Their Bodies to Get an Edge? [11:04] 🔊

CBC Radio, Day 6

Comprehension and Analysis

1. As you listen, fill in the table.

Ethical issue	Technological enhancements of athletes' bodies
Examples (sport / type of enhancement)	Track and field: prosthetic limbs
	Fighting sports: shave down bones or use cadaver skin in face to prevent bleeding
	Weightlifting: put carbon tubes around knees to lift heavier weights
	Baseball: replace ligaments with tendons
	Baseball/tennis/golf/shooting: laser eye surgery to improve vision above 20/20
Why athletes do it	Overcome disability (allows athletes to compete)
	Improve performance (for a chance at fame and fortune)
Difference between the cases of Pistorius and Rehm	Pistorius → Sports Federation had to prove that blades gave him an advantage; results were inconclusive, so he was allowed to compete in the Olympics.
	Rehm → Rehm had to prove he did not get an advantage (burden of proof had been changed). Again, results were inconclusive, so he was not allowed to compete in the Olympics.
	Pistorius wasn't good enough to win a medal at the Olympics and was allowed to compete; Rehm could potentially have won an Olympic medal (and broken records) but was not allowed to compete.
Future scenarios (possible enhancements and categories for competition)	Possible enhancements: • synthetic ligaments or tendons • prosthetic limbs that look more human Possible categories for competition: • athletes who dope/don't dope • athletes with/without technological enhancements
Questions raised by body enhancement (within the sports world and beyond)	Within sports world: • Should we accept Paralympic athletes in the Olympic Games? • Will athletes have to augment themselves to compete at the highest levels? Outside realm of sports: • What does it mean to be human? • Should there be limits to how people can enhance themselves?
How to regulate body enhancement	Athletic organizations are going to have to decide on some general principles for regulation rather than dealing with individual cases on a case-by-case basis.

2. Using the information you noted in the table on page 72, create a visual summary of the essential ideas and examples using bubble style.

3. Compare your visual summary to a partner's and to the example in Explore Online. Discuss what you did well and what you will do differently next time you create a visual summary.

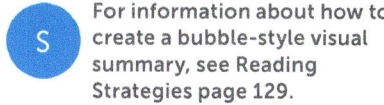

For information about how to create a bubble-style visual summary, see Reading Strategies page 129.

Alternatively, you may work together as a class to create a visual summary.

Speaking

In a small group, discuss the following questions.

Do you agree with the IOC's decision to let Oscar Pistorius compete in the Olympic Games but not Markus Rehm? Would you have made the same decisions in each case? Explain.

Field-Specific Practice

 Field-specific activity

You may want to use this field-specific question as a research and writing topic.

Identify some new and interesting technologies currently being used or developed for future use in your field of study. Provide a brief (one- to two-sentence) description of each one and explain its applications in your field.

Are there any negative aspects to these technologies? Are there any ethical issues to be resolved? Choose one technology and write a paragraph (150–200 words) in which you identify and describe potential ethical issues related to its use.

Writing

Writing Strategy

Persuasive writing

When writing an opinion and trying to persuade a reader to agree with a particular point of view, you must offer logical support for your opinion. To do this, you can use a number of rhetorical techniques:

- include facts (e.g., statistics, scientific data)
- refer to an authority or expert
- provide examples
- use anecdotes (a short story about a particular event or experience)
- refute opposing arguments (respond to arguments from the other side)
- state consequences (to be effective, the statements must not be exaggerated)

For more information about how to write a persuasive essay—and to see an example essay—see Writing Strategies, page 135.

Research a performance-enhancing technology and write a 450-word persuasive essay supporting your position regarding the use of the technology. You may use one of the examples below or choose your own.

- bionic prosthetics (e.g., to create stronger limbs)
- brain-computer interfaces and neurotechnology (e.g., facilitating information flow from the brain to a computerized device, such as a prosthetic hand)
- nootropics / cognitive enhancers (e.g., substances that improve brain function)
- gene editing (e.g., to create designer babies)

You can also choose to have students research these technologies and discuss in small groups or write about their findings or opinions in a report.

Reading

Our society can be very cynical. We often lack trust in our institutions, and with the rise of fake news and new technologies, we doubt more and more the truth of what we are told. In our search for truth we need to ask questions, do research, seek out opposing views, and come to our own conclusions. In our quest for information, it is important to recognize the points of view expressed in the articles we read and the reports we watch or hear. Understanding the speaker or writer's tone tone can help to identify point of view.

For more information on recognizing and creating tone, see Reading Strategies, page 122.

Reading Strategy

Recognizing tone

Tone indicates the author's attitude or feelings about a subject. Recognizing the tone helps you identify the author's purpose for writing—for example, whether the writer is trying to persuade or simply inform. A text can have more than a single tone; examples of tone include alarmist, annoyed, condescending, critical, cynical, excited, humorous, optimistic, outraged, puzzled, sarcastic, and skeptical.

A writer can create tone through many rhetorical techniques, including the use of

1. highly connotative language (i.e., words with positive or negative associations) rather than strictly denotative language

2. colourful, emotionally charged language and content

3. hyperbole—exaggerated language

4. satire—humour used to ridicule, criticize, or discredit

5. allusions with negative associations

6. direct address or appeal to the audience

7. first-person references and pronouns

8. purposeful mechanics (creative sentence structure, formatting, punctuation, etc.)

Pre-Reading Activity

1. Read the short text below. What is the author's tone? Provide examples.
   Answers will vary: critical, annoyed, cynical, sarcastic

2. Underline all the words or phrases that contribute to the tone of the text. Above the underlined words or phrases, write the number of the technique (from the box above) used to create tone.

³
Corruption is everywhere. It has been allowed to flourish because of the
²
inaction of successive governments. It would be nice if politicians did
^{2 and 3}
something about it; however, it seems like they are useless when it comes to
^{2 and 6}
curtailing corruption. Isn't that a surprise?
^{2, 3, 4, and 8}   ²
Last year, the "geniuses" in government finally decided to do something about corruption in the construction industry, and they created a law intended to solve the problem. Unfortunately, after working for weeks,
⁵
like Sisyphus pushing a rock up a hill, they came up with a law so weak that
²
it was really a waste of time.

^{2 and 3}
Maybe one day, government workers with more than half a brain will be able
⁷
to figure out how to decrease corruption. We can only hope.

3. Based on the title of the reading below, what do you think the author's point of view is toward the subject?

_____

_____

It's Silly to Assume All Research Funded by Corporations Is Bent

Tracey Brown, *The Guardian*

Technique 8

1 Corporate funding of multiple vaccine research was "exposed" again recently. This time it was in the latest round of **MMR**-causes-autism allegations, which we exported to the US. We've seen the same "exposés" in the UK, on **fracking**, on genetically modified plants, and on sugar. Last year, some of the best-regarded nutrition researchers were taken out and given a public beating when it was revealed that the food industry funds research in their institutes. ³

2 Well, it wasn't revealed¹ exactly so much as noted from the researchers' clear and public funding declarations. A "sugary web of shame" piece in the *BMJ* (formerly, the *British Medical Journal*) found no indication that the funding had caused bias and, indeed, it was clear to anyone who looked at the researchers' publications that their conclusions about sugar were the very opposite to what the industry hoped. The beating went ahead anyway.

3 It was then that the Academy of Medical Sciences took a step that the academies and government should have taken a long time ago, and held a meeting to ask what to do when accusations of vested interests derail important research that relies on corporate funding. It published its report of that meeting last week, with an invitation to all of us to express a view.

4 We shouldn't¹ just lazily¹,²,⁷ assume that all opportunities to influence research turn out the same way.

5 It's important we talk about this because in the media and the public consciousness, corporate funding has become shorthand for bad. Crooked deals (you write this, I'll pay for your holiday) are presented as on par with well-structured research agreements (we need vaccines to test vaccines, so the pharma company provides them gratis, no results guaranteed). Researchers are being hung out to dry³ because their institutes take corporate funding, even while government is pressuring them to do so. Meanwhile, terrible problems of bias, such as the failure to publish all clinical trial results, attract far too little attention.

6 What's especially annoying² is that the "who funded it?" question—often by people with axes to grind²,³—overrides the inquiries that the public rightly ask. "What do we actually know?" "Do scientists agree on this?" "Is this a proper study and how can I tell?" These are good questions that show us whether the research is actually biased and what we should trust.

7 We need to get used to asking them, because corporate funding accounts for more than half of our research base. In some areas, including areas of engineering that are no less matters of public safety, there is hardly any public funding. That's not likely to change: can you imagine⁶ popular support for a research tax to replace corporate funding? We need⁷ a lot of money to maintain research infrastructure and programs. Where would we rather see those corporate funds—put into research, or given to shareholders to make the richest 2 percent richer?²

8 So what's to be done?⁶ An open discussion about the good and bad ways to run corporate and academic partnerships would be a start. An acknowledgement of the potential for interference in independent research and a laying out of the protective

---

Comprehension question 1 asks you to underline examples of techniques used to create tone. The quotation marks around *exposed* is an example of technique no. 8—use of mechanics.

bent (adj) crooked or not straight; corrupt

MMR (n) a vaccine that protects against measles, mumps, and rubella

fracking (n) a method of getting oil and gas from underground rocks by injecting liquid into the rocks so that they break apart

processes that can be put in place to prevent it. Contracts and codes are what matter, and they should protect research from all funders, corporate or not.

9   We also shouldn't just lazily assume that all opportunities to influence research turn out the same way. (Nor should we assume that those opportunities are limited to companies. Advocacy groups and government departments fund research, too. I've spent many years questioning researchers and working out reliable sources for helping the public with difficult issues. I am sure we're far better off with research teams who are able to attract company funding and handle it with good governance than we are with the complacency of those who have never been put to this test and who have never thought to question their own standards and objectivity.

10   If we accept that commercial funding of research is necessary, we need to decide the right way to do it. There is huge variation in institutions' contracts with external funders. Surely the research academies and government have a duty to draw up a standard and a code, and talk to the public about it. We must encourage everybody with a concern about commercial influence to test research against that standard, instead of indulging in this episodic outing and bloodying of researchers.   **[735 words]**

Comprehension and Analysis

When reviewing the answers, the goal is for students to perceive the tone, recognize the article as an argumentative text on a debatable ethical issue, and note that the text includes research and gives both sides of the issue (with one side presented in a sarcastic tone with the intent of using it to argue for the other side). In the Wrap Up, students will research an ethical issue and write an argumentative text of their own.

Answer the following questions in your own words.

1. Underline examples in the text of the various techniques discussed in the Recognizing Tone strategy box on page 74, then write the number of the technique above the text. The first one has been done for you.

2. What point is the author making in the following sentence from paragraph 2?

    "Well, it wasn't revealed exactly so much as noted from the researchers' clear and public funding declarations."

    Researchers were not hiding where the funding comes from—it was noted in their research. There was nothing hidden to "expose."

3. What event caused the author to write this article?

    The Academy of Medical Sciences' report on a meeting to discuss how public distrust of corporate funding can interfere with important scientific research.

Correct answer, question 4: It is important to talk about corporate funding of research because without that funding important research would not get done (public funds are not available).

4. The author thinks it is important to talk about the issue of corporate funding of research because
    a)   corporations are too powerful.
    b)   all assume corporations are corrupt.
    c)   political parties are funded by companies.
    d)   none of the above

5. According to the text, what are three problems with seeing all corporate funding as unacceptable?

    a)   Researchers often have no other avenues to get funding for their research.

    b)   Governments are pushing researchers to take corporate funding as there are no public funds available.

    c)   It takes attention away from real problems with some research, such as unreported trials.

6. In the author's opinion, what is wrong with the "Who funded it" question?

    The problem is that the question is often asked by people with ulterior motives and distracts from other, more relevant questions. If the answer to "Who funded it?" is a corporation, it tends to automatically, perhaps unfairly, discredit the research.

7. What is one potential ethical issue the author identifies about corporate funding?

The author acknowledges there is potential for interference when corporations

provide funding.

8. What does the author propose in regards to commercial funding? Choose all that apply.
   (a) setting up regulations to govern it
   b) limiting the extent of it
   (c) publicly examining how it should be regulated
   d) more openly acknowledging when it occurs

9. What is the main idea of the article?

The main idea is that we need corporate funding for research, but we need

regulations to govern it.

10. What overiding tone does the author take to argue his point?

His tone is annoyed, critical and sarcastic.

Speaking

In a small group, discuss the following situations and determine the best approach to resolving each one. You may consider punishment, rehabilitation, or a more creative method of resolution. Be prepared to justify your choices.

1. The leader of a country has appointed her son-in-law as her chief adviser. The son-in-law does not have much political experience. Key politicians who were hoping for the position are claiming that this nepotism is unethical—maybe even illegal—and are demanding that the son-in-law be removed from the position.

2. A PhD student is troubled by her research results that indicate potential dangers of a chemical used in a product that is about to be released to the public. The company that sells the product is a major financial donor to the university, and her academic adviser tells her to focus on the results that do not indicate a problem. Soon after the product is released, a child is seriously injured by the chemical. The child's family is suing the company, the university, and the PhD student.

3. A weightlifter wins an Olympic gold medal shortly after having had knee surgery following an injury. It is discovered that the biotechnology used in the surgery had made his knee stronger than it was before the injury. Other athletes are calling for him to be disqualified and stripped of his medal.

You may want to discuss the idea of creative sentencing and have students research specific examples.

You may want to discuss the difference between white-collar and blue-collar crime and whether students consider white-collar crime to be as serious as blue-collar crime.

Scenario	How the case should be resolved	Factors considered in your decision
1. Political appointment		
2. Potentially dangerous product		
3. Surgically enhanced athlete		

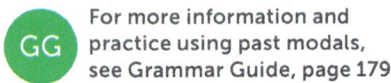

For more information and practice using past modals, see Grammar Guide, page 179.

Grammar

Past form modals

Modals are auxiliary (helping) verbs used to express permission, ability, possibility, obligation, and so on. Common modals include *can, could, may, might, must, should,* and *would.* Modals are always used with a main verb.

The following example shows modals used in the past (underlined).

> I <u>could not believe</u> what I heard on the news yesterday! The CEO of my cousin's company was arrested for accepting a bribe. He <u>should not have accepted</u> the bribe. The company also <u>had to pay</u> a huge fine when he was caught. He <u>could have bankrupted</u> the company, which <u>would have cost</u> all the employees their jobs.

1. Examine the past form of the modals used in the above paragraph, and complete the following chart.

Modal (present tense)	Meaning	Modal (past tense form)
1. can	ability	could not believe
2. should	advice/suggestion	should not have accepted
3. have/has to	necessity/obligation	had to pay
4. can/could	possibility	could have bankrupted
5. would (conditional)	conditional	would have cost

2. Based on your observations, complete the rule about how to form a past modal (Note that the modals *can*—when it refers to ability—and *has to/have to* are exceptions): modal + *have* + _____past participle_____

3. Using the clues in brackets (modal / main verb), write the correct form of the past modals in the following paragraphs.

   a) Marie plagiarized part of her essay. She received a failing grade. She _____should not have plagiarized_____ (should / not / plagiarize). She _____should have referenced_____ (should / reference) her sources. She _____could have researched_____ (could / research) how to cite sources properly.

   b) Stan had a successful fashion company. He stole a competitor's ideas for one of his clothing lines, which destroyed his company's reputation. He _____should not have stolen_____ (should / not / steal) the ideas. Having been in the business for so long, he _____must have known_____ (must / know) the risks.

Watching

People are becoming increasingly concerned about the power and influence of social media companies. Their concern has not been helped by revelations that some social media companies are experimenting on their users. Is this ethical? Consider this question as you watch the video on social media ethics.

Pre-Watching Activity

In a small group, choose a social media company and go online to scan its terms of service (TOS). Then have each person in your group read one section of the TOS closely. Discuss the following questions.

1. What topics are covered in the TOS?

2. Search for the term *research*. What do you think the term covers? Is it clear?

3. Did you learn anything that surprised or concerned you while examining the TOS? If so, what? Why did it concern you?

4. Do you think what you see on social media can affect your feelings or behaviour? Explain your answer.

Not all social media apps will include references to research in their TOS.

Vocabulary

Cognates and false cognates

English and French share many cognates (i.e., words that share a common origin and have a similar meaning in both languages). Recognizing English/French cognates will help you understand the meaning of English words that might be unfamiliar.

For more about cognates, see Vocabulary Strategies, page 149.

The following words from the video are English/French cognates.

aggregate (n)	the whole or total
arrogant (adj)	having a high opinion of one's own abilities or importance
contagion (n)	the spreading of an idea, practice, or disease; usually negative
explicit (adj)	stated clearly
reputable (adj)	respectable

Be wary of false cognates—words that look the same but have different meanings in English and French. Here are some false cognates to be aware of when discussing ethical issues. Define each word in French, then look up its English definition.

English word	French word/definition in English	English definition/example sentence
deception (n)	déception/**disappointment**	**the act of tricking someone into believing something untrue** **Denying his gambling addiction was his greatest deception.**
demand (v)	demander/ to ask	to insist forcefully The irrate customer demanded to speak to the manager.
proper (adj)	propre/ clean or belonging to	appropriate You must use the proper level of formality in a cover letter.
sensible (adj)	sensible/ emotional	rational Be sensible and study for the exam.
sympathetic (adj)	sympathique/ nice	understanding of somebody else's feelings I felt very sympathetic toward Ann when she lost her job.

Now write a sentence using as many of the above cognates and false cognates as possible.

_____

_____

non-partisan (adj) not associated with any political party or philosophy

Students can practise making a visual summary by creating a summary that shows the arguments given in the video for and against Facebook's experiment. An example is available on Explore Online.

As you watch the video, pay attention to the two sides speakers take regarding Facebook's experiment.

Social Media Ethics [8:33] ▶

Lucky Severson, PBS

Comprehension and Analysis

Answer the following questions as you watch the video.

1. a) Describe Facebook's emotional contagion experiment.

    Facebook filtered out negative or sad news and posts to see if it made people

    happy, and filtered out positive messages to see if it made people sad.

    b) What were the results?

    It worked; happier messages prompted people to post happier updates, and

    sadder messages prompted people to post sad messages and fewer updates.

2. What is the primary concern of James Grimmelman and Danah Boyd?
    a) Social media companies are spying on their users to sell them products.
    b) Users don't know they are being experimented on.
    c) Social media companies may be able to affect people's feelings and behaviour.

3. a) Describe OK Cupid's human experimentation project.

    OK Cupid told people they were good matches on its online dating site when

    they were not.

    b) What were the results?

    Some people dated their mismatches.

4. What does Danah Boyd suggest might improve the ethics within social media companies?
    a) improve how Institutional Review Boards function
    b) teach engineers about ethics and making ethical decisions
    c) apply stricter regulations to social media companies

5. What are the implications of Facebook's "get out the vote" experiment?

    Facebook might be able to influence election results.

6. a) What has Facebook done to address concerns about its emotional contagion experiment?

    The company apologized for how information about the study was

    communicated and agreed to a stronger internal review process. Facebook did

    not apologize for conducting the study.

    b) What has Facebook not done?

    stopped the experiment

7. Why do you think it be difficult to regulate social media companies?

Answers will vary.

_____

_____

8. How do you think the journalist, Lucky Severson, feels about the behaviour of social media companies? Explain your answer. Consider tone, bias, and what you know about Severson.

Answers will vary.

_____

_____

_____

Credibility Check

When you hear or read information, it is important to apply critical thinking skills and analyze the source. Do you find the information in the video to be reliable? What do you know about the three sources in the video? What biases might they have?

Support your answer using criteria from the Evaluating Sources Checklist on page 117.

Writing

Write a letter to the editor of your local newspaper (100–150 words) expressing your view on the ethics of Facebook's experiment on its users. State your opinion, give two supporting points, and explain what you think should be done. Use tone and persuasive rhetorical techniques to make your point.

Speaking

In a small group, you will debate an ethical issue. You may choose a resolution (statement) from the list below or come up with one of your own. If possible, choose an issue related to your field of study or future career. Once you have chosen your topic and come up with a resolution, follow the steps for the debate.

Possible resolutions

1. Police officers should wear body cameras at all times while on the job.

2. Selling organs for money should be legal.

3. Children who are not vaccinated should not be allowed to attend school.

Debate process

Step 1: Assign roles   Divide your group in half. Half of your group will argue *for* the issue (answer *Yes* to the resolution) and the other half will argue *against* (answer *No* to the resolution).

Step 2: Research   Research your side of the topic. Make sure you have enough information to debate the issue for at least five minutes. You should have a minimum of three different arguments.

Step 3: Presentation   First each team will make a two-minute presentation of its point of view and main arguments. This presentation should include a very short introduction (stating your point of view on the topic), a brief summary of your arguments, and a conclusion (a sentence reaffirming your position). While the other side is presenting its arguments, you may take notes, but you may not interrupt.

Step 4: Debate   Each team tries to convince the other that their position is the right one by restating their main arguments and rebutting their opponents' arguments. The teacher will moderate to ensure order and that each student has the opportunity to participate.

Step 5: Conclusion   Each team will have one minute to make a final pitch for its point of view.

The length of the debate depends on the number of participants. Usually, each person is allowed about three minutes.

Teachers may want to assign students to listen to a specific group instead of the whole class taking notes for every group.

Interpreting Data

Acts that are against the law are considered crimes. Crimes are committed by people of all ages; however, when a crime is committed by a young person, it is particularly worrisome. Understanding youth crime is the first step to reducing it.

Rates of youth and young adult accused, selected offences, by age of accused, 2014

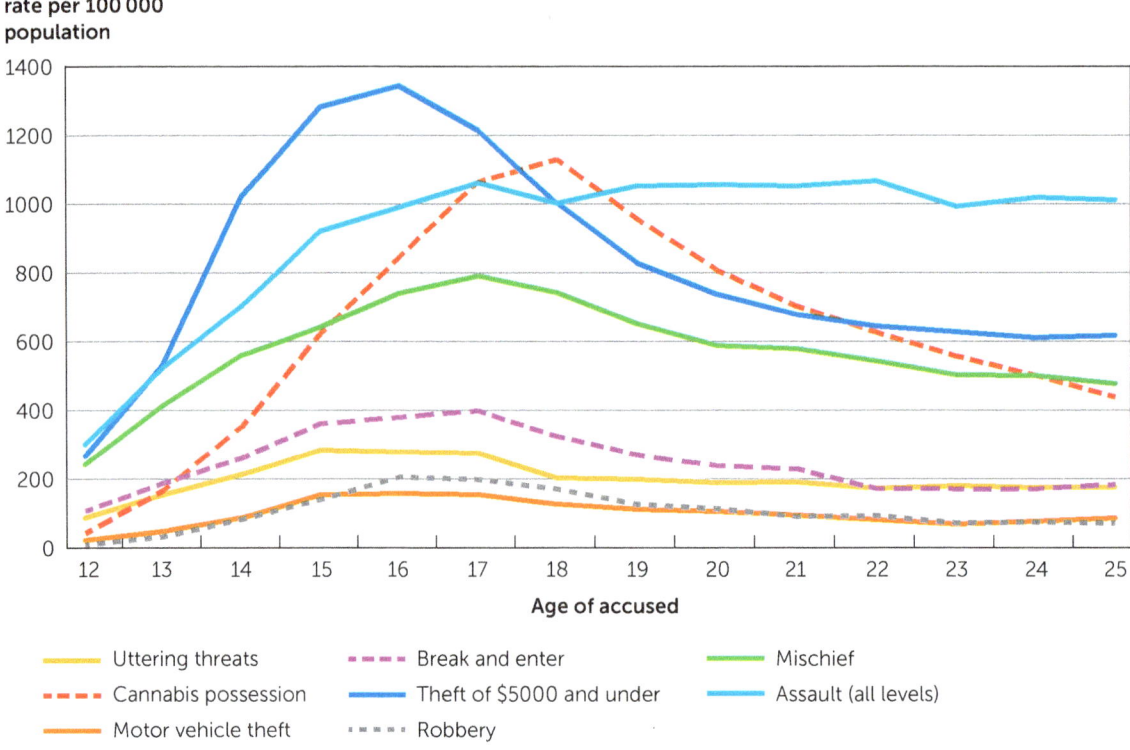

rate per 100 000 population

Uttering threats	Break and enter	Mischief
Cannabis possession	Theft of $5000 and under	Assault (all levels)
Motor vehicle theft	Robbery	

Recreational cannabis use was illegal in Canada until October 2018 and continues to be illegal for children and teens.

Comprehension and Analysis

Answer the questions based on your interpretation of the data in the line graph.

1. What crimes are most likely to be committed by a person of the following ages: 12, 15, 18, 21, 24?

12	15	18	21	24
assault	theft under $5000	cannabis possession	assault	assault

2. Which crime rate has the least variability between the ages of 12 and 25? Which crime rate is the most variable during that time period?

    least variable—motor vehicle theft and robbery; most variable—assault

3. What overall conclusion can you make about the crimes shown and the offenders' age?

    Overall, for the crimes shown, people 15 to 18 were accused more often than people in their mid-20s.

4. Are there any statistics in the chart that surprise you? If so, why do you find them surprising?

    _____

    _____

Pronunciation

English stress patterns

In English, stress is placed on individual syllables of single words, unlike some languages (such as French) in which the stress pattern is based on entire phrases with the final word in each phrase receiving the stress. In English, the primary stress within a word is determined by the structure of the word and its parts (the root, prefixes, and suffixes).

Work with a partner. Read each sentence out loud and pay particular attention to how you pronounce the words in bold. Use the information on Speaking Strategies page 147 to help you. Your partner will tell you if you pronounced the bolded words correctly in terms of word stress. Student A reads the sentences in Student A's List and Student B reads the sentences in Student B's List.

Use the answer key on page 86 to see if your partner is stressing the correct syllable in the target words. You may also listen to the recorded sentences online.

It is highly recommended that you read the section Word Stress and the *Schwa* (Unit 3, page 61) before you do this pronunciation activity.

Tell students not to give the correct answer when their partners get a wrong answer. Let the students find their own errors and self-correct.

Student A's List

1. My boss gave me a **present**: I have to **present** something at the next meeting.

2. The students reacted with **enthusiasm**. Their reaction was **enthusiastic**.

3. In the **psychology** course, students learn **psychological** theory.

4. The specialized language of the **legal** profession is called **legalese**.

5. They were not to **express** emotion, so the jurists' faces had no **expression**.

6. You always **exaggerate**. That was an **exaggeration**.

7. There are a lot of **dropouts** from school. How many **drop out** every year?

Student B's List

1. He specializes in **engine** design. He is an **engineer**.

2. Video editing allows a person to **create**. It requires a lot of **creativity**.

3. Most of my **neighbours** have no cars. There are few cars in our **neighbourhood**.

4. Who do the police **suspect**? The son-in-law is the prime **suspect**.

5. The guidelines come from the **ministry**. They are **ministerial** guidelines.

6. The accused is innocent; it was a **setup**. Somebody **set** him **up**.

7. That professor has interesting **ideas**. I like her **ideology**.

Revising and Editing

It is fun to have students share and compare their revised versions.

With a partner or in a small group, revise the following paragraph to create a specific tone. (You choose the tone.) You cannot add or delete any sentences and you must retain the the main words from the paragraph, the basic meaning, and the words in bold. However, you may replace words with synonyms and add words or phrases to the existing sentences. Use the techniques from page 74 for creating tone. Then share your revised paragraphs with another group to compare the differences in tone. Your goal is to demonstrate how the writer is feeling and to show the attitude the writer has toward his job and the new employee.

A Day at Work

I walked **out of my office** and went to get a coffee from the common room. While I was getting my coffee, I saw a person looking at me **from across the room**. It was the new employee. I looked back at the new employee and **I had a feeling** that this person was going to be a unique employee.

Sample revision: I trudged out of my drab office and plodded over to get an extra strong coffee from the common room. While I was sluggishly preparing my coffee with a great lack of enthusiasm, I spotted a bizarre-looking person peering at me with a strange but friendly look from across the room. It was the new employee. I stared back at my new colleague with raised eyebrows and I had a feeling that this latest staff member was going to be an interesting addition to our otherwise boring company.

_____

_____

_____

_____

Wrap Up

Field-Specific Practice

 Field-specific activity

Encourage students to be creative in their selection of the source. They may want to choose a blog, a rant, slam poem, etc.

Find a printed text, audio, or video related to your field of study or future career and do the following:

- identify the overall tone of the piece
- identify at least three examples of words or phrases that contribute to the tone
- identify the technique(s) used to create tone

 Field-specific activity

Speaking

You may opt to have students complete this activity as a group speaking activity or as a writing activity.

Research a case of corruption or unethical behaviour in your field of study. What corrupt or unethical action was committed and by whom? What was the impact of the action? If it is a past case, what was the punishment or outcome? If you agree with the punishment or outcome, explain why. If you disagree, explain what you think the punishment or outcome should have been. If you chose a current case, state what you think the outcome should be. Present your findings about the case and your opinion about the outcome to a small group or in front of the class.

Writing

Write a persuasive research essay (450 words) about a debatable issue in your field of study or future career. For information on persuasive research essays—and to see an example of one—see Writing Strategies, page 135.

 Field-specific activity

Vocabulary

Fill in the chart below with useful words that you learned in this unit. Transfer these words to your own personalized digital vocabulary list that you can organize and add to.

 Field-specific activity

 Go to Explore Online to download a template for creating a personal vocabulary list.

Field-specific vocabulary			
Word	Part of speech	Definition	Example sentence

Theme-specific vocabulary			
Word	Part of speech	Definition	Example sentence

Answers to Pronunciation activity on page 83.

Answers for Student A's list

1. **pre**sent, pre**sent**
2. en**thu**siasm, enthusi**as**tic
3. psy**cho**logy, psycho**lo**gical
4. **le**gal, legal**ese**
5. ex**press**, ex**pre**ssion
6. ex**ag**gerate, exagge**ra**tion
7. **drop**outs, drop **out**

Answers for Student B's List

1. **en**gine, engi**neer**
2. cre**ate**, crea**ti**vity
3. **neigh**bour, **neigh**bourhood
4. sus**pect**, **sus**pect
5. **mi**nistry, minis**te**rial
6. **set**up, set (him) **up**
7. i**de**as, ide**o**logy

Coming together is a beginning; keeping together is progress; working together is success.

—Edward Everett Hale

How important is it to work together in collaboration? Think about something as simple as building a house. You need an architect to design it, a framer to put up the walls and roof, an electrician to power it, a plumber to bring water to it. As you move through this unit, consider the benefits of collaboration, your own collaborative skills, and the role they will play in your life and future career.

Warm Up

Speaking

As a wrap up activity for this section, you can have a class discussion on the following question: How important is teamwork in a professional environment?

In a small group, conduct the survey below. Each member of your group must ask the survey questions to two students from a different group and write their answers in the chart. When you have completed the survey, share the responses with your group. Then compile your answers and prepare a brief summary of the results. Be prepared to present your results to the class.

Questions	Student A	Student B
1. Generally speaking, do you like working on a team? Why or why not?		
2. Describe a time when you worked as part of a team—what challenges, if any, did you encounter?		
3. What qualities do you bring to a team and how might those qualities affect a team that you are part of (in positive or negative ways)?		
4. In your future career, in which situations might you have to work as part of a team?		

Reading

In your career, you may find yourself on various teams in which each person will bring his or her own personality, ideas, expectations, goals, skills, and knowledge to the project. Working on a team can be extremely beneficial, but it is not always easy. Sometimes team members do not work well collectively, but other times teams come together and triumph! What role will you play in building an effective team?

Pre-Reading Activity

The reading on page 89 discusses how to work effectively with others. Discourage students from looking at the text beforehand to find ideas for this activity.

Whether at school, at work, on a sports team, or in other situations, we have all had to work with other people. For a team to work effectively, it often helps to establish rules. For example, you may have a rule requiring everyone to come to meetings prepared and on time. What other rules do you think are necessary for effective teams? Fill in the chart below.

Rules for an effective team
Answers will vary and may include the following:
Define clear roles for team members.
Establish goals for the team and for individuals.
Choose a leader and decide how decisions will be made.
Be respectful, open to self-examination, and responsive to constructive criticism.
Establish guidelines for clear, regular communication.
Regularly assess progress against goals.

Vocabulary

The vocabulary in the chart below come from the text you are about to read. Find the vocabulary in the reading and use word and context clues to match each word or phrase with the correct definition.

Vocabulary	Definition
__d__ 1. solopreneur (n) (para. 1)	a) confident and firm (but not aggressive)
__f__ 2. reap (v) (para. 1)	b) to copy
__g__ 3. mutual benefits (n phr) (para. 1)	c) useful suggestions or advice
__e__ 4. synergy (n) (para. 2)	d) a person who owns and runs a business alone
__a__ 5. assertive (adj) (para. 6)	e) the interaction of two things (people or objects) that results in a better product than would have been produced by either of the two things working alone
__b__ 6. replicate (v) (para. 7)	f) to profit from something
__c__ 7. constructive feedback (n phr) (para. 9)	g) a situation in which all parties profit

Together We Succeed. Divided We Fail!
Carthage Buckley, Coaching Positive Performance

1 We all have to work with others if we want to fulfill our potential and meet our objectives. Even those of us who are **solopreneurs** have this requirement. Just because other people do not work in the same company, it does not mean that we do not have to cooperate with them. If you can work effectively with others, you are already halfway toward your goal. When you work effectively with others, together, you achieve more than you could by working only for your own needs. You do not have to like everybody in order to work effectively with others. Just look at some of the world's greatest sports teams; they often contain two or more players with egos the size of small countries. Yet they succeed; why? Because they understand that when they work effectively together, they can **reap** the **mutual benefits** that will help each person achieve their own personal goals.

2 When I started my journey in the working world, it was popular to say in interviews that you were a team player. You wanted to portray the image that whenever the company called, and whatever it asked you to do, you would be ready to jump and obey its commands. I always hated the idea of saying that I was a team player. I am not and I don't believe that there are many people who are. I am not prepared to sacrifice my own needs and goals to pursue the objectives of an organization. However, I do believe that I work effectively with others because I am prepared to work together in a manner that helps us to both achieve our goals. And that is what a team really is—a group of individuals **harnessing** the power of **synergy** to achieve their own objectives and, in the process, helping others to achieve their objectives too.

harnessing (v) taking control of something

How to work effectively with others

3 We all have to work with others to achieve our goals. There will be some people that you enjoy working with and others that you'd rather not know. However, achieving your goals does not require universal popularity but it does require you to be able to

work effectively with others, even those whom you do not like. These tips will make this task a little easier.

Tip 1: Everyone has their own goals

4   Being part of the same team does not mean that you all have the same goals. When you understand this, you understand one of the best ways to create positive relationships. Take the time to get to understand the goals and objectives of others and find a way to help them achieve these. When you do that, you will have allies who will want to return the compliment.

Tip 2: Everyone has a job

5   Each person has their own area of expertise and their own job. Take the time to get to understand each other's strengths and weaknesses. Also, if there are job descriptions, make sure that you know each other's role. When you do this, you can achieve the following benefits:

- you know what to expect of each other
- it is easier to divide up work
- **delegation** is much easier
- you don't offend anybody by asking them to do something that is not their job

delegation (n) the act of distributing work to other people

You cannot work effectively with others unless you know each other's jobs.

Tip 3: Be assertive

6   When you adopt an **assertive** communication style, you are better able to work effectively with others. You respect your own rights while also respecting the rights of others. For example, a colleague may ask you to complete a task for them. While you respect their right to ask this of you, you also have the right to say *No*. An assertive communication style allows you to form better relationships because, even when they do not get their way, people understand that you are not being cruel to them; you are simply doing what is right for you. Assertiveness allows you to set clear boundaries with others, including:

- your right to prioritize your own tasks
- your right to decline requests
- your right to make requests of others
- your right to privacy and confidentiality

These are just some of the many rights that you are entitled to in the workplace. When you defend your rights and respect the rights of others, you build relationships based on respect, which will reap greater rewards.

Tip 4: Set the example

7   If you want people to work with you in a particular manner, the best way to do this is to provide a clear example of the behaviour that you are looking for. If you want people to improve their time management, then you must be an example of an effective time manager. If you want people to communicate more openly, you must communicate openly. As Gandhi said, "Be the change you wish to see in the world." Don't wait for others to work out how you want them to behave; show them. All it takes is one person to initiate the desired behaviour and the rest are more than likely to **follow suit**. When you demonstrate how to work effectively with others, they are far more likely to **replicate** your behaviour.

follow suit (phr. v) to do the same thing as somebody else

Tip 5: Display the right attitude

8   The majority of communication does not take place in the form of words. Regardless of what words you are saying, the message that your body language is communicating is far more powerful. You may think that you can hide your attitude with fancy words but rest assured that your body language will betray you.

9 If you want to work effectively with others, your attitude and body language must communicate that. When people see that you genuinely want to build a positive relationship, where you help each other to achieve your goals, they will be more open to the prospect. There are many ways that you can demonstrate your desire to work effectively with others.

- Be willing to trust others.
- Be prepared to give the benefit of the doubt when things go wrong.
- Rather than complain when things go wrong, offer **constructive feedback**.
- Don't just wait for things to go wrong before you communicate. Every time that someone does something right, praise them with positive feedback.
- If you are having a bad day, try not to dwell on it for too long. See what actions or steps you need to take to rectify it.

10 If you want to achieve your goals and objectives, in any area of your life, you must learn to work effectively with others. When you work effectively with others, you harness the power of synergy and achieve more together than you ever could apart. The old ideal of the team, where people sacrifice their own needs and goals to work solely for the benefit of the team, is no longer relevant. People may be prepared to make these sacrifices for a short period but if a job is not allowing them to fulfill their own objectives, they are likely to move on, sooner rather than later. Rather than focus on building a team, it is far better to build mutually beneficial relationships where you work effectively with others to achieve better results for all. **[1210 words]**

Comprehension and Analysis

Answer the following questions in your own words. If the answer to a True or False question is False, rewrite the sentence to make it true.

1. Why does the author believe most people are not team players? Support your answer with a quote from the text.

    The author says that, like him, most people are not willing to sacrifice their "own
    needs and goals to pursue the objectives of an organization." People may set aside
    self-interest for a short time but ultimately, they want to "fulfill their own objectives."

2. Does the author believe he is a good team player? Support your answer with examples from the text.

    The author says he is not a team player. "I always hated the idea of saying that I was a team
    player. I am not and I don't believe that there are many people who are. I am not prepared
    to sacrifice my own needs and goals to pursue the objectives of an organization."

3. Why does the author say it is important to be assertive?

    Being assertive allows you to set clear, reasonable boundaries at work and develop
    respectful relationships with co-workers.

4. According to the author, words are the most important
    form of communication.   ☐ True   ☑ False

    According to the author, most communication does not take place through words,
    but rather through what body language is communicating.

5. According to the author, there are many ways to show that you want to work effectively with others. Check all that are mentioned.

    ☐ Do not trust others.   ☐ Communicate only about problems.

    ☑ Offer constructive feedback.   ☑ Take steps to improve a situation.

6. Do you agree with the author's point of view that most people are not team players? Why or why not?

_____

_____

_____

_____

7. Do you agree with the author that it is important for you to know the goals and objectives of your colleagues? Why or why not?

_____

_____

_____

_____

8. Tip 4 is about setting an example. Think of a specific type of team you might be on. What example would you want to set for your teammates? How would it benefit your team?

_____

_____

_____

_____

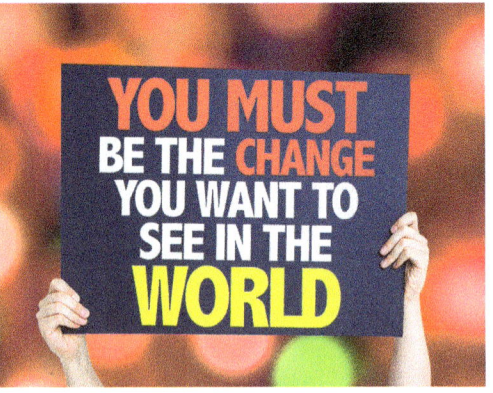

Field-specific activity

Speaking

In a small group, discuss the following questions.

1. In Tip 2, the author lists four benefits of understanding team members' expertise. Which of these points is the most important in your field of study or future career? Why?

2. The author suggests five tips for working effectively with others. What advice would you add to the author's list? Explain how your advice is important to your field of study or future career.

Watching

Collaborating is sometimes the best way to find innovative solutions. Working in isolation, we may not be able to see a problem from different perspectives. Think about how the same food can be made differently depending on where it is from. Asian pork ribs are completely different from Kentucky ribs. Imagine what an Asian chef and American chef can create when they work together. Listen to Tom Hulme talk about the importance of innovation and collaboration.

Field-specific activity

scarcity (n) short supply; not easily available

These questions may be challenging for students so working in groups will be helpful.

Pre-Watching Activity

In a small group, discuss the following questions.

1. In his presentation, Tom Hulme says, "Scarcity breeds innovation." What does he mean? Provide an example from your own field of study or future career that would prove this.

2. Hulme believes that diversity and collaboration are essential for success. What do you think he means by this? Explain why you agree or disagree with his opinion.

Vocabulary

Before you watch the video, familiarize yourself with the words below.

queue (v)   to line up

swabbing (v)   to take a specimen with an absorbent pad similar to a Q-tip

lurk (v)   to read posts on a social network platform without commenting

grant (n)   money given, often by a government, for a specific purpose

The Importance of Open Innovation and Collaboration [15:33] ▶

Tom Hulme, OpenIDEO

Comprehension and Analysis

Answer the following questions in your own words. If the answer to a True or False question is False, rewrite the sentence to make it true.

1. According to Hulme, breakthroughs are usually made by geniuses working alone.   ☐ True   ☑ False

    According to Hulme, collaboration allows us to achieve more.

2. Many people believe that technology makes us antisocial. Does Hulme believe this to be true? Explain.

    No, Hulme does not believe technology makes us antisocial. Technology is just a tool that allows us to meet needs in new ways.

3. What are some of the problems Hulme identifies with suggestion boxes?

    Generally people don't contribute to suggestion boxes, often because they don't know the purpose. In cases when people do contribute to such boxes, the result may be a bottleneck with too much information to process. Overall, suggestion boxes are not collaborative, but rather results in duplication of effort.

4. What is often the simplest incentive for getting people to participate? Does Hulme think that this simple incentive is good for encouraging diversity of perspective?

    Money is often the incentive, but Hulme does not consider money to be ideal for getting diverse participation.

5. What was the goal of OpenIDEO?

    to create a more open space to share suggestions and encourage participation in solving complex problems related to the social good

6. What does Hulme says is the first step in solving problems?

    The first step is to understand the problem and the context.

7. How many members are part of the OpenIDEO community?
    a) 6000
    b) 60 000
    c) 16 000
    d) 160 000
    e) none of the above

8. List two things OpenIDEO has accomplished.

    110 000 bone marrow registry applicants; developed social apps such as Panic
    Button (for Amnesty International); 1800 patients treated in Colombia; Knight
    Foundation gave away millions of dollars in grants.

9. What did one airline company do with the software from OpenIDEO?

    The airline asked 12 000 cabin crew staff what type of meals to put on flights and to
    recommend ways to help flyers sleep better.

10. Can technology enable diversity? Explain your answer.

    Answers will vary. If only rich people can afford technology, then technology does
    not create diversity. But if even the poorest person can go to a university virtually, at
    little cost, then technology may enable diversity.

Speaking

At the end of the presentation, Hulme says that to solve complex problems we need to collaborate. To do that, he says there are three questions we need to address:

If students find this activity challenging, you can provide some prompts to help them. You may want to mention some of the following: climate change, urban sprawl, or health care in remote areas. You can also nudge students to think about problems that may exist in their respective fields of study.

a) Who can help us resolve the problems that we have?
b) How can we involve those people (inside or outside an organization)?
c) How do we motivate those people to help us solve the problem?

In a small group, identify a problem that exists in our society. Discuss how to solve that problem by answering Hulme's three questions.

EXAMPLE

The problem: A teacher wants to improve her course to make it interesting and relevant for students.

Who can help address this issue? students (current students or former students)

How can the teacher involve them? ask students in class or create an online forum where students could share ideas and make recommendations about the class

How do we motivate the students to help? give rewards to students who respond or promise to modify the class based on students' responses

Field-specific activity

Field-Specific Practice

In multi-disciplinary groups of three or four, read the case study on page 95 and prepare a persuasive five-minute oral presentation along with a slide presentation (6–10 slides). Use the tips from "Together We Succeed. Divided We Fail!" to help you work together effectively as a team. Your objective is to redesign the learning environment in a school. You must demonstrate both hard skills—technical abilities (preparing a slide presentation) and knowledge of your field—and soft skills (your ability to work well with others).

Your slide presentation should include a title page, an outline or overview of the presentation, clear identification of the problem(s), proposed solutions clearly linked to your—and your teammates'—fields of study or future careers, and a conclusion.

S For information about preparing slide presentations, see Speaking Strategies, page 146.

Encourage students to be creative and think about how technology and the physical environment can be used to create an ideal learning space. For example, they could consider using headphones and interconnected technology to reduce sound.

Case Study

A small private school in Quebec City employs eight teachers and two administrators. Approximately 100 students, ages seven to sixteen, attend the school. The classes are multi-level.

The problem is that having so many teachers and students in the same area creates a noisy, challenging learning environment. There is no budget to expand the school. The school is willing to invest but only in certain areas. There are three main problems that must be resolved.

- **Space**—The school rents a small building (the layout is shown in the margin). There are only two classrooms (400 square metres each). Make suggestions to improve the physical environment.
- **Technology**—The administrators will invest in technology but want to use money wisely. Suggest how technology can be used to improve the physical environment.
- **Physical environment**—The school must invest in new equipment such as desks, chairs, boards, and other tools. The administrators want to create an environment conducive to learning. The school needs areas that work for students studying many different subjects such as science, math, languages, or history. Suggest new products and equipment for the school.

Go to Explore Online to download a full-page version of the diagram showing the layout of the school. Use it as a reference for your redesign.

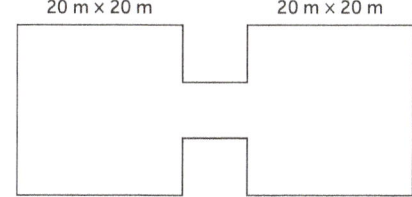

20 m × 20 m   20 m × 20 m

Layout of the school to be redesigned

All three problems are related and your team must prepare a proposal to solve them. Redesign the classrooms to create a better learning environment. Your field of study must be represented in your proposal. For example, a health sciences student may invest in ergonomic workstations, or an electrical engineering student may suggest special lighting.

Reading

In many cities, summer is orange cone season. Drive around and you will see not only orange cones but also cranes, dug up roads, and the skeletons of buildings under construction. We complain about construction because of the resulting traffic problems, but it does create jobs. Have you ever considered the extent of the collaboration necessary for those complex projects? Construction is a specialized field that involves different types of professionals, and it illustrates the diversity of roles and expertise in a workplace as well as the necessity of working together effectively for success.

Pre-Reading Activity

In a small group, look at the photo on the right and make a list of all the different professions that may have been involved in construction of the building and its environment. Look beyond the construction of the building itself and consider the individual tasks that would have been required. One profession has been listed for you.

Examples of the professions that may have been involved in the construction include general contractor, electrician, plumber, interior designer, graphic artist, construction worker (framer, plasterer, roofer, general labourer), painter, engineer, accountant, urban planner, landscaper, sod grower, plant grower, brick mason, glass manufacturer, marketer, lawyer (e.g., dealing with legal issues involving city governments), project manager, administrative professionals, and security guard (prevent theft during construction). Students may think of other professions—any that can be explained or justified are valid.

1. _____architect_____   6. _____
2. _____   7. _____
3. _____   8. _____
4. _____   9. _____
5. _____   10. _____

Vocabulary

The following words are used in the text you are about to read. Read the definitions and then complete the sentences below with the appropriate word from the chart.

emergence (n)	the process of becoming visible or exposed after being hidden or concealed
procurement (n)	the act of acquiring something
mitigate (v)	to make less serious or less painful
fragmented (adj)	broken into pieces; isolated; not whole or complete
amendments (n)	minor changes in wording to improve a document
subcontract (v)	employ a business or person outside one's company to do work as part of a larger project

1. The contractor made several ___amendments___ to the contract when it decided to ___subcontract___ the work to other companies.

2. The salesperson made an error in the contract and now has to try to ___mitigate___ the damage it caused.

3. The frequent ___emergence___ of new innovations makes it hard for companies to keep up to date.

4. The ___procurement___ of new equipment is done by the purchasing director.

5. Traditional media is not as influential as it used to be because today's audiences are increasingly ___fragmented___—there is no longer one way that everyone accesses the news.

Better Together: Why Construction Needs Collaboration to Work Efficiently

Mike Scott, *The Guardian*

1 Communication failures between architects, designers, contractors, and **procurement** teams compromise the construction industry. How can this be **mitigated**?

2 For centuries, the building trade has been a hugely **fragmented** industry, with lots of different companies coming together for a particular building and then moving on to different projects.

3 Typically, a client will commission an architectural team or design team, then engineers will become involved, explains Graham Watts, chief executive of the Construction Industry Council. Building services consultants and structural engineers get the call next, before a separate building contractor finally arrives to undertake the actual work itself. "And that contractor won't directly employ many of the people working on site. He will **subcontract** out various parts of the work," Watts says.

Breaking out of "little bubbles"

4 Such fragmentation means that it takes a long time for best practice to filter through, he continues: "A particular project may see some innovation that is a better way of working that could benefit the whole industry, but that team disintegrates at the end of the project and that innovation is lost."

5 In addition, there is a lot of waste in the system. Some owners, architects, or designers insert certain criteria into the building specifications, such as environmental product declarations that require certain sustainability standards, explains Heather Gadonniex, head of the building and construction team at PE International, a consultancy that

specializes in life cycle assessment. Yet procurement teams or contractors often **ride roughshod** over such requirements in their pursuit of short-term cost reduction.

ride roughshod (idiom) to ignore anything that gets in the way of one's one desires or vision

6   "There is a common understanding that there needs to be greater collaboration and better integration between the various parties in the design and construction process," she says.

7   That is beginning to happen. The **emergence** of national Green Building Councils and building standards such as Breeam and Leed v4 are providing **incentives** to follow more integrated design processes. But such approaches remain fairly **niche** in the building sector.

incentive (n) something that motivates someone to do something

niche (n) specialized; in this context, *niche* means rare

8   "It's not just about particular products—it's about the entire design process," says Gadonniex. "If you want to build a net-zero building or just a beautiful and functional building, you have to have the contractors interacting with the mechanical contractors interacting with the designers and the architects. In the past, everyone worked in their own little bubbles and that separation made it a challenge to meet common goals."

Modelling collaboration

9   New technology and ways of working are helping to break down barriers between the different players in the construction process. Integrated Project Delivery (IPD), which advocates the collective harnessing of all project participants' talents and insights, is one approach that many in the industry think can make the process more collaborative.

10   "IPD allows discussion at the start of the project to create stronger links between all the various stages. It's extremely important to break down the silos that exist in the industry," says Gadonniex. "A lot of the **siloed** nature of the industry goes with the fear of losing one's territory and not accepting the benefits of this type of collaboration, particularly when it comes to saving time and money."

siloed (n) isolated (especially from other departments or people working on the same project)

11   A central aspect of IPD is Building Information Modelling (BIM), which Watts describes as "a real force for collaboration, because it can't really operate unless you have the entire team on board at the earliest possible stage—which encourages much earlier contractor involvement."

12   BIM is a single digitally enabled integrated model of a building's designs and specifications that allows all the various people involved in a project to see what has gone before and what needs to be done. "The biggest enemy of the construction industry was the arrival of email," says Watts. "Two parties would make **amendments** to the drawings but they wouldn't tell anyone else. With BIM everyone can see what has happened."

13   BIM makes projects much quicker, smoother, and cheaper, he adds, which is why the government requires that, as of 2016, all new public sector buildings must be developed using the technology.

14   However, BIM is only being used properly on the largest projects, says Barry Connolly, a director at real estate consultancy JLL. "There is still a big disconnect within the industry. Architects and designers generally collaborate well, but even if they develop a project in BIM, the contractor will often do nothing with it because its own supply chains have not invested in BIM."

15   There is a further disconnect between a building's developer and its end-occupier. If the tenant knew that a developer could save him 30 percent on energy costs by specifying certain equipment or materials, a different decision might be made, Connolly reasons: "But because the developer mostly does not know who the tenant will be, they can't justify the extra expense."

16   Change will come as best practice filters down from the largest players to the rest of the industry. But the pace is unlikely to be lightning quick, unfortunately. In the building industry, as Connolly ruefully concludes, "things don't change overnight."   **[815 words]**

Comprehension and Analysis

Answer the following questions in your own words. If the answer to a True or False question is False, rewrite the sentence to make it true.

1. Historically, has collaboration between construction trades been the norm? Explain.

   No. Historically, the construction industry has been highly fragmented. Many companies work together on a project then disperse to work with other companies on different projects.

2. How does the traditional approach to construction projects hurt innovation?

   Such fragmentation means best practices are not shared among companies or across the industry as a whole—and may be lost altogether—when teams dissolve without sharing the knowledge and innovations that facilitate better ways of working.

3. Why don't contractors always respect environmental requirements?

   When short-term cost reduction is the primary goal, businesses often ignore environmental requirements that will slow them down or increase a project's cost.

4. Why does Gadonniex think there needs to be greater collaboration in the construction industry?

   She says that "If you want to build a net-zero building or just a beautiful and functional building," it's essential that the individual specialists—for example mechanical contractors, designers, and architects—work together to achieve the best results.

5. According to Gadonniex, why would some contractors be afraid to share information?

   Contractors who work indep endently may fear that sharing information puts them in a vulnerable positon, at risk of losing control of their work or their part of the project.

6. Watts says that email has made collaborating much easier.   ☐ True ☑ False

   Watts says that "the biggest enemy of the construction industry was the arrival of email" because it allowed some parties to amend plans without telling others.

7. What are some of the problems associated with BIM? Circle all the correct answers.
   a) Only the largest projects use it properly.
   b) Not all suppliers have invested in BIM.
   c) It is a very complicated program.
   d) Most companies don't know about BIM.

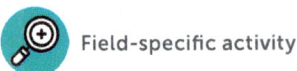 Field-specific activity

Speaking

With a partner, discuss what you learned from the article. How does that insight apply to collaboration in your field of study or future career? Be prepared to share your ideas with the class.

Listening

Humans have encountered many challenges throughout history, including deadly diseases that have devastated populations. In the 14th century, the bubonic plague is estimated to have killed between 30 and 50 percent of Europe's population. More recently, HIV has killed an estimated 35 million people. Periodically governments and health officials deal with outbreaks of highly infectious diseases such as SARS or Ebola. We must be prepared to face unexpected events and deal with crises of an unfamiliar nature. Would you be prepared if there were a worldwide crisis that threatened human life? How would you apply your knowledge and skills to survive?

Pre-Listening Activity

Imagine that a virus has caused a zombie apocalypse. You and your classmates survived the first few days, but now you must think about the future. You decide to find a safe place to stay and to bring some people with you. Fill in the chart below with professionals from your fields of study that you would bring with you and explain what role they would play.

Field of study	Professional	Role that professional would play
Health science	Doctor	provide medical treatment

Vocabulary

The words and phrases below are used in the audio. Before you listen, write a short horror story (one paragraph) in which you use as much of the vocabulary from the chart as possible. Be creative and be prepared to share your paragraph with the class.

stockpile (n)	an accumulation of goods for emergency use
fighting chance (n)	the possibility of winning if one puts in the hard work
striking out (phr v)	to start moving forward; begin doing something new or going in a new direction
basher (n)	an object used to hit something or someone; in this context a shovel is a "zombie basher" for hitting zombies
dispose (v)	to throw something away
thoroughfare (n)	a main road or route between two places
double back (v)	to go back in the direction you came from
well (n)	a hole dug into the earth to reach a supply of water
kerosene (n)	fuel often used in camping lamps, camp stoves, and jet engines
infrastructure (n)	the physical structures required to operate a city or town (e.g., sewers, buildings, roads, power supply)
artillery (n)	large guns used in war
transcend (v)	to go beyond the limits of something
hypothermia (n)	the condition of having dangerously low body temperature
prepper (n)	a person who believes a disaster will occur in the future and makes preparations by accumulating food, ammunition, and other supplies

The zombie apocalypse can be seen as a metaphor for any life-threatening cataclysmic event that human civilization may face. Allow students to be as creative as possible, but they must be able to justify the choices that they make.

Fun Fact: Apparently, the American military has a manual to prepare troops for a zombie attack. The manual is entitled *CONOP 8888*.

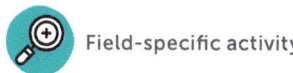 Field-specific activity

A zombie apocalypse is an imaginary scenario in which a catalyst (possibly an infection or event) transforms humans into zombies, creating widespread chaos and threatening human survival.

Students can decide what their groups' ultimate goals are: to stay alive until help arrives, actively work to stop the zombies from taking over, rebuild civilization, etc.

You could also allow students to write a short graphic comic strip using the vocabulary.

Is Mount Washington Observatory the Ultimate Zombie Fortress? [12:59] 🔊

Taylor Quimby, New Hampshire Public Radio

Comprehension and Analysis

Answer the following questions in your own words.

1. Narrator Taylor Quimby says we don't enjoy fantasizing about life after a nuclear war or a worldwide pandemic, but talking about a zombie apocalypse is fun. Why?

   When you know there is no real danger, it's fun to consider the possibilities. He says "it's fake, so it's safe."

2. According to Quimby, do you need specific qualifications to survive a zombie apocalypse? ☐ Yes ☑ No

   What two things does Quimby say you need to survive a zombie apocalypse?

   There are no special qualifications required to survive—anybody sensible can do it.

   It's about good planning and the ability to make do with limited resources.

3. Max Brooks identifies characteristics of a good zombie fort. Circle any of the following that he mentions.
   - (a)) has a source of water
   - (b)) has a way to get rid of sewage
   - (c)) is isolated
   - d) has a strong fence
   - e) has an underground bunker
   - f) has a lookout tower

4. Where does the water come from at Mount Washington?

   There is a well that goes down about 600 to 800 feet to the freshwater aquifer.

5. How long would the food last if food deliveries stopped (based on the current number of staff members at the observatory)?
   - a) 1 month
   - b) 2 months
   - (c)) 3 months
   - d) 4 months
   - e) none of the above

6. How many feet above sea level is the Mount Washington observatory?
   - (a)) 6228 feet
   - b) 16 228 feet
   - c) 60 228 feet
   - d) 628 feet
   - e) none of the above

7. What does Brooks say is the most important element in establishing a zombie fortress? Based on this answer, why would Mount Washington not be a good zombie fortress?

   The most important attribute is anonymity. Desperate people are more dangerous than zombies. After the broadcast, humans will be aware of the observatory and will go there in a crisis. The site will be overwhelmed.

8. What is the narrator's opinion of Brooks's novel *World War Z*?

   The narrator says the author achieved a difficult task. He wrote a serious literary zombie novel that goes beyond the "silliness of the genre." He became an expert on a make-believe topic.

9. The narrator concludes that Mount Washington would not be a good place to go during a zombie apocalypse. Do you agree with this analysis? Why or why not?

_____

_____

_____

_____

_____

_____

Speaking

For information on creating a slide presentation, see **Speaking Strategies, page 146.**

In a small group, create a short slide presentation explaining how you would survive the apocalypse. You should consider

- location
- supplies
- security
- social structure
- how a person in your field of study could contribute to the community

This activity offers a chance for students to really think about their future career and what role they may end up playing in society. Encourage students to reflect on this as they create their presentations.

You may also refer students to the Writing Strategy on page 102 if you want them to practise making a checklist to itemize requirements and responsibilities for group members.

You may include your own ideas. Your presentation should have at least five slides, be grammatically correct, use appropriate vocabulary, and include visuals.

Pronunciation

Voiced and voiceless /*th*/

There are two ways to pronounce /*th*/ in English:

1. as a **voiced dental fricative** /ð/. This sound is sometimes mistakenly pronounced like a /d/.

    EXAMPLE   then   than   there   this   mother   father   brother   farther

2. as a **voiceless** dental fricative /θ/.

    EXAMPLE   thank   think   thick   path   faith   death
    thieves   youth   Thanos   thimble   bathroom

To practise the pronunciation of the /*th*/ sound, read the sentences below out loud. Work with a partner who can listen to you practise, or record yourself on your computer or phone and listen to your recording.

1. I think I know what path my brother will follow in life.

2. My mother has a lot of faith in Matthew.

3. My business partner and I were thick as thieves in our youth.

4. Johnathan thinks the sinks need to be farther apart than the ones in his bathroom.

5. Thanos' thimble broke and that put him behind in meeting his orders.

You may also listen to the online recording to check your pronunciation.

A voiced sound is one that makes the vocal cords vibrate when the sound is made. To see if a sound is voiced or voiceless, put your fingers on your throat and make a sound. If the sound is voiced, you will feel the vibration. Try it with the word *this*.

Note that in the phrase "voiced (or voiceless) dental fricative," *dental* refers to teeth and *fricative* means friction.

Go to Explore Online to listen to a recording of the sentences and check your pronunciation.

 **Field-specific activity**

S For tips on creating your own checklists, see Writing Strategies, page 133.

Essay

An essay is a structured academic text that can take many different forms. For this activity, you will write an argumentative essay in which you try to convince the reader of your point of view.

For information on how to write an essay, see Writing Strategies, page 135.

Blog

A blog is a regularly updated online journal hosted on a web page. A blog post is a creative piece of writing, which can be formal or informal, but the tone is often conversational. A blog may be written by an individual or a group to share information or personal stories, or to keep track of observations.

For information on how to write a blog, see Writing Strategies, page 144.

Both students and teachers can be creative with this activity. You may make it as simple or as complex as you choose. You may want students to use vocabulary linked to their field of study. You could have them detail how they are going to do something (e.g., repair a generator or design a sewage system). Students can do this as a group or individually.

Students can also write using third-person perspective. For example, the person who repairs the generator (or performs some other task) can be someone other than the writer.

Consider extending the blog writing activity. When students have finished writing, ask them to complete a revision grid (available on Explore Online) for their own blog post, then exchange blogs and revision grids with a partner. While reading a partner's post, students circle the errors they find but do *not* correct the errors. Instead, they fill in the revision grid for the partner's blog post, indicating with *Yes* or *No* whether their partner has fulfilled all the requirements. Students return the blog and completed revision grid to their partners. Then each student can revise his or her own blog based on their partner's assessment.

Writing

Writing Strategy

Using checklists

Checklists are practical tools that you can use to make sure you have included everything required by your teacher for an assignment. Sometimes, your teacher will give you a checklist with an assignment. If not, create your own.

For this writing assignment, your teacher will assign either an essay or a blog post. If a checklist is not provided, create your own. Remember that a checklist is not a substitute for an outline.

Write an essay

You can also have students work in a group and create the outline for the essay together. Then students can write their essays individually.

Choose one of the topic statements below and write an essay agreeing or disagreeing with the statement.

Topic Statements

1. Collaboration is the key to success.

2. ". . . the people who are crazy enough to think they can change the world are the ones who do." (Steve Jobs)

As much as possible, use examples from your field of study to support your point of view. Before you begin, note the three requirements below.

1. Start by developing an essay outline (download a template from Explore Online). Add more paragraphs if you wish. Your teacher will tell you how many words you are permitted to have on the outline. Any examples you plan to include in your essay must be written in point form. The only complete sentences allowed in the outline are your thesis statement, topic sentences, and quotations (if you choose to include any).

2. Use an external source to provide support (examples, statistics, or quotations) for your argument. You may use any of the readings, audio clips, or videos used in class.

3. Your essay should be approximately 450 words and should include

    *   an introduction, body paragraphs, and conclusion
    *   a clear and concise thesis statement
    *   topic sentences
    *   support: examples, statistics, quotations
    *   precise, rich, and varied vocabulary

Write a series of blog posts

1. Imagine that there has been a zombie apocalypse and you and a small group of people made your way to the observatory on Mount Washington. Read the Day 1 blog post on page 103 then continue to write daily posts about the ongoing challenges.

2. Relate the information in your posts to your field of study or future career. For example, if you are studying to be a lawyer, think about how a lawyer would contribute to a post-apocalyptic community. If you are in nursing, you could write about how your community will set up a medical clinic.

3. The blog post for each day must be a minimum of 350 words. Each entry must show collaboration between the people at the observatory and include at least three field-specific words.

Surviving the Zombie Apocalypse

Day 1

We finally arrived at the observatory. I have decided to keep a record of our time here to keep track of what has been done, what we have to do, and the challenges I know we will face.

It is really cold up here and it is not even winter yet. We will have to start prepping for the colder months immediately. Right now, there is no electricity and very little security, so this is definitely a priority. There are also a lot of repairs to be done. I don't know how we are going to do it all before zombies begin to wander up the hill.

I've decided to list all the issues because right now, everything seems overwhelming. Making a list of things to do will make me feel better. I like lists!

- Finding food and organizing food distribution is critical.
- Getting the generator working to power the observatory must be completed quickly.
- Establishing a secure perimeter and security protocol for people coming and going should be done quickly to ensure safety.
- Creating some form of government and legal system may not be the first priority but has to be on the list. We can't live in a lawless community!
- Finding a place for entertainment is important: we need to be able to relax in a stressful time or we will go crazy.
- Building a medical clinic is going to take time. We may not have a doctor, but we need to have a clinic at least. Medical care should include physical and mental health care.

That is all I can think of now, but I am sure the list will grow as time goes on.

You can refer to this list to introduce gerunds if you would like. The discovery activity for gerunds is below.

Grammar

Gerunds

A **gerund** is the *-ing* form of a verb which functions as a noun.

EXAMPLE

Finding food is very important.
In this sentence, *finding* is a gerund.

We are looking for food.
In this sentence, *looking* is not a gerund; it is part of a verb.

Read the sentences below and identify whether the words in bold are gerunds or part of a verb.

1. **Finding** food and organizing its distribution is critical. ☐ verb ☑ gerund
2. Jonathan is **waiting** for someone to save him. ☑ verb ☐ gerund
3. We should start **bashing** the zombies before they eat Grandma. ☐ verb ☑ gerund
4. I wonder if the zombies enjoy **eating** brains. ☐ verb ☑ gerund
5. **Getting** the generator working to power the observatory must be completed quickly. ☐ verb ☑ gerund
6. Look! Stuart is **running** away from the living dead. ☑ verb ☐ gerund

GG For more information about gerunds and how to use them, see Grammar Guide, page 197.

WHAT IS A ZOMBIE?

The three factors that are the foundation of a zombie survival plan are referred to as the Zombie Knowledge Triangle. All zombie survivalists must understand how a zombie is created, be able to recognize the different types, and deal with the walking dead.

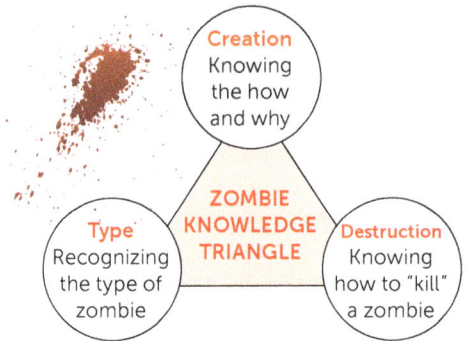

Creation
Knowing the how and why

ZOMBIE KNOWLEDGE TRIANGLE

Type
Recognizing the type of zombie

Destruction
Knowing how to "kill" a zombie

ZOMBIE CREATION MYTHS

In a recent survey by GeoPol, fewer than 23% of Canadians realized that zombism is caused by a virus. Here is a breakdown showing the level of misunderstanding of the root cause of zombies.

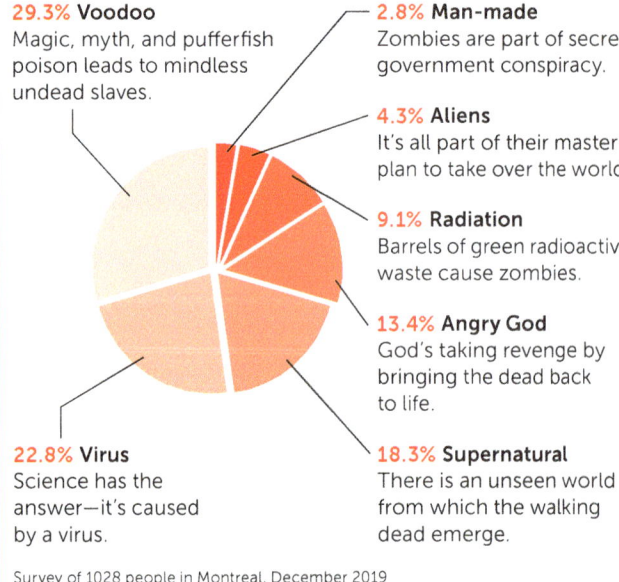

29.3% Voodoo
Magic, myth, and pufferfish poison leads to mindless undead slaves.

2.8% Man-made
Zombies are part of secret government conspiracy.

4.3% Aliens
It's all part of their master plan to take over the world.

9.1% Radiation
Barrels of green radioactive waste cause zombies.

13.4% Angry God
God's taking revenge by bringing the dead back to life.

22.8% Virus
Science has the answer—it's caused by a virus.

18.3% Supernatural
There is an unseen world from which the walking dead emerge.

Survey of 1028 people in Montreal, December 2019

ZOMBIE CHARACTERISTICS

The zombic condition is characterized by the slow stagger, lumbering walk, and violent appetite for the flesh of the living. There is nothing supernatural or superhuman about the walking dead. They are simply humans transformed into very different creatures. But once a human has become infected with the virus, typically by a bite from an infected zombie, then the transformation will begin.

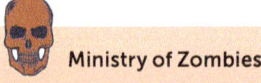

Ministry of Zombies

Interpreting Data

The infographic on the left explores information about zombies, including how zombies are created and what you need to know to survive a zombie plague. Review the infographic with a partner and answer the following questions. If the answer to a True or False question is False, rewrite the sentence to make it true.

Comprehension and Analysis

1. More people believe that zombies are caused by radiation than by a virus. ☐ True ☑ False

   More than twice as many people (22.8 percent) believe a virus creates zombies, not radiation (9.1 percent).

   _____

2. According to the survey, what is the least popular theory of zombie creation?
   a) alien intervention
   b) supernatural forces
   ⓒ man-made
   d) virus

3. The Zombie Knowledge Triangle identifies four key factors essential to survival. ☐ True ☑ False

   Identify the survival factors.
   Three factors are essential to survival: knowing how a zombie is created, recognizing the type of zombie, and knowing how to kill a zombie.

4. Is a slow, lumbering walk a sign that someone might be a zombie? ☑ Yes ☐ No

5. Zombies, or the walking dead, are supernatural beings. ☐ True ☑ False

   There is nothing supernatural about the walking dead.

   _____
   _____

6. A person bitten by a zombie must get treatment immediately in order to be cured. ☐ True ☑ False

   Once a human has been infected with the virus, the transformation begins and cannot be reversed.

   _____

7. Why is it important to understand the Zombie Knowledge Triangle?
   Understanding the triangle will help you know how to deal with the walking dead.

   _____

Speaking

There has been a zombie outbreak. In a small group, create an informative, coherent news bulletin to inform people about the event. Each person in your group should speak for approximately two minutes. Include information from the infographic on page 104 in your presentation.

Start by brainstorming ideas about the topic. Ask yourself the questions *who*, *what*, *when*, *where*, *why*, and *how*. Answer these questions, then ask further questions to develop your bulletin script. Be sure to paraphrase any information you take from the infographic, and interpret the data for your audience, explaining what the information means and why it is significant.

Students can record their news report on their cellphones, create a slide presentation, or use any other visual aid to enhance the news report. If you choose, you can tell students that the news studio was attacked and they have to create a makeshift news bulletin. Creativity is the key here.

Revising and Editing

Note that it is possible for students to rewrite this paragraph without using gerunds. For example, "Dr. Smith believes *collaboration* is essential. . ." "He started *to treat* patients. . ." ". . . while he *relaxed*. . ." ". . . staff started *to collaborate*. . ."

Although the paragraph would still be grammatically correct, the intent of the exercise is to have students differentiate between verbs and gerunds. Students should be encouraged to use gerunds where possible.

Read the text below. Correct any verbs that are formed incorrectly and identify all the *-ing* words as either gerunds or verbs by writing either V or G above the word.

> Dr. Smith believes <u>collaborate</u> is essential for the protection of society. Last year, while he was <u>worked</u> overseas, he realized how important teamwork is. There was a terrible disease outbreak and as soon as he arrived, he started <u>treated</u> patients. In his second week, while <u>relaxed</u> after a long shift, he noticed that all the doctors were <u>struggle</u> to treat patients on their own. No one was <u>work</u> together. Dr. Smith decided to change this. He consulted the doctors and created a new protocol. From that point on, the staff started <u>collaborate</u> as a team.

collaborating (G)

working (V)

treating (G)

relaxing (G)

struggling (V) working (V)

collaborating (G)

Wrap Up

Field-Specific Practice

 **Field-specific activity**

1. In a small group, create a pamphlet, brochure, or advertisement about a process, innovation, or experience related to your field of study of future career that involves collaboration. You must include information that highlights or demonstrates the collaborative elements of what you are describing. Keep the content simple and well organized and include an introductory and concluding statement. Make it visually appealing. The following are examples of possible topics.

   - How to protect yourself from a disease or health risk (nursing/medicine)
   - How to invest your money (business/finance)
   - How to prepare for a trip to another country (hospitality/travel)
   - The importance of voting (sociology/political science)

Students can use a template in Word to create a brochure.

2. Write a checklist to use when completing a task that you might have to perform in course work or a professional task in your field of study or future career. For example, a student studying in computer science may want to explain how to create a bootable USB drive. Include vocabulary specific to your field of study.

Field-specific activity

Speaking

Choose one of the following activities.

1. Research three situations where collaboration is important in your field of study or future career. It could relate to an idea, a process, or a particular type of job. Describe three common situations in which collaboration is important and the purpose of collaborating in these situations: the problem it solves, its benefits, and so on. Consider finding examples from specific companies where you may want to work. Use your research to support your ideas. Prepare a short oral presentation (2–3 minutes) on the role of collaboration in your field. Include a short slide presentation to support your ideas.

S For more information about giving oral presentations and creating effective slide presentations, see Speaking Strategies, page 145.

2. In a small group, take turns leading a group discussion. Choose a task linked to your field of study, present the problem to your groupmates, and ask them how they would accomplish it. Your groupmates should come up with the steps to complete the task. You may come up with your own task or choose one of the following:

    *   How to give CPR
    *   How to write a book
    *   How to conduct an experiment
    *   How to build a house

Field-specific activity

Writing

Choose one of the following activities and write a text of approximately 450 words.

1. Create a journal detailing a project or experiment you completed in one of your courses. For example, if you conducted a week-long experiment in a chemistry course, imagine what a daily journal would chronicle as you moved through the experiment. You may be creative with the information to make the journal more exciting. Remember to use field-specific vocabulary.

2. Write a short story about a zombie apocalypse or a similar disaster. Write it in the first person as though you are chronicling the events as they happen. Link the events to your field of study and make sure you include field-specific vocabulary.

S For information about writing an essay see Writing Strategies page 135.

3. Write a research essay on a topic of your choice. The topic must be linked to your field of study and must be approved by your teacher before you begin.

Vocabulary

Fill in the chart below with useful words that you learned in this unit. Transfer these words to your own personalized digital vocabulary list that you can organize and add to.

Field-specific activity

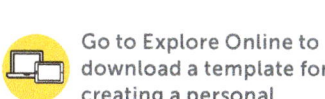
Go to Explore Online to download a template for creating a personal vocabulary list.

Field-specific vocabulary			
Word	**Part of speech**	**Definition**	**Example sentence**

Theme-specific vocabulary			
Word	**Part of speech**	**Definition**	**Example sentence**

Projects

Project A

Job Search

The objective of this project is to research your future career, prepare a tailored resumé and cover letter, and participate in a mock interview for an advertised position.

Step 1: Choose a career

Identify the occupation that you plan to have in the future or one that you would like to explore (e.g., aircraft mechanic, computer technician, elementary school teacher).

Step 2: Conduct job-specific research

Research the occupation you have chosen. You can find useful information with an online search using the following key words:

- *explore careers* (Then click on the jobbank.gc.ca link.)
- *occupations guide*
- *occupation + job description* (e.g., *veterinarian job description*)
- *what skills are needed to be a* [insert your own key words, e.g., *mechanical engineer*]

During your research, find and note key information about the following.

1. official job title

2. definition of the occupation and basic job description

3. activities or duties of the job that interest you the most

4. tools and equipment used

5. hard and soft skills necessary to succeed

6. average wage or salary

7. list of professional associations, organizations or regulatory bodies related to that career

Step 3: Select and annotate a job posting

1. Find an English job posting related to the occupation you have chosen. Ideally, find an ad that provides a lot of information about qualifications, skills, job requirements, work environment, and so on.

2. Print the job posting.

3. Highlight or underline essential information from the job posting that you need to and want to refer to in your cover letter, resumé, and job interview.

Step 4: Write a resumé

Write a professionally formatted resumé in response to the job posting you chose. (Imagine that you have all the requirements for the job described in the ad.) Remember to include key requirements and skills mentioned in the job posting in your resumé.

Step 5: Write a cover letter

Write a tailored, well-formatted cover letter in response to the job posting you chose. (Imagine that you have all the requirements for the job.) In your cover letter, it is important to include references to key requirements and skills mentioned in the job posting. You should also include information that shows that you are a good fit with the company culture.

Read "Writing a Cover Letter" before you write your own cover letter.

Step 6: Role play a job interview

In a group of three or more students, role play job interviews. Each of you will take a turn being one of the job interviewers and the candidate being interviewed.

Interview instructions

1. Each interview should be approximately 10 minutes.

2. As an interviewer, ask questions from the list of common job interview questions (see page 142). Also include one question from the list of the top 10 weird job interview questions (see page 12).

3. As an interviewer, be sure to customize the interview to the specific job (i.e., to the occupation chosen by the student candidate).

4. After each interview, discuss how each candidate felt about his or her performance (including strong points and lessons learned for future interviews).

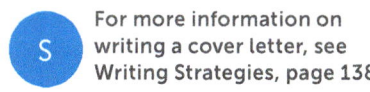 **For more information on writing a cover letter, see Writing Strategies, page 138.**

Instead of a cover letter, you could have students prepare a professional job summary for an online site (e.g., LinkedIn) or a video cover letter.

Project B

Field-Specific Research

Go to Explore Online for a list of good, stable academic search engines that you may want to download for students. The list is organized according to expressed student preference. You may reorganize or revise it if you wish.

The objective of this project is to research a topic related to your field of study or future career. In the space below, note any specific instructions your teacher gives you regarding the role your research project will play in your course assessment.

_____

_____

_____

_____

_____

You may wish to use the field-specific research project as the basis of your students' final writing or speaking exam.

You may want to have students complete all or only some of the steps in this research project.

Go to Explore Online for a research project template that includes validation of sources, annotation instuctions, a Kahoot quiz, and a works cited page.

Go to Explore Online for a Research Project Topic Proposal template and an example of a completed form.

Step 1: Choose a research topic related to your field of study or future career

Topic: _____   Your field of study: _____

Write five questions you would like to investigate concerning your topic. The purpose of these questions is to narrow your topic and guide you in your research. Your questions may change or become more focused during the research process.

1. _____

2. _____

3. _____

4. _____

5. _____

Step 2: Research

Find articles written in English related to your chosen topic (750–1500 words each). (Your teacher will specify how many articles you must find.) Your teacher may also ask you to include audio or video material.

Be sure that

- all of the articles and any audio/video content come from a valid source
- you record all necessary information to write a Works Cited entry for each source

In the space below, note your teacher's instructions about how many articles or audio/video sources you must include in your project:

_____ articles   _____ audio or video sources

You may want to have your students find some articles on a general topic and some on a more specific topic within their fields of study (e.g., two articles on general psychology and three articles on depression).

S For more information on evaluating sources and citing them correctly, see Research Strategies, page 116.

S For more information on annotating a text, see Reading Strategies, page 124.

S To avoid plagiarism, use your own words and always acknowledge where your information came from. For more information about avoiding plagiarism, paraphrasing, and citations, see Research Strategies, page 118.

Step 3: Annotate the articles

After you have become familiar with the information in each article, underline or highlight the main idea(s) in each paragraph. You should also write notes in the margins that identify the main idea or subtopic of each paragraph. Your annotation will help show how the ideas in the article are organized and connected.

If you teacher asked you to include audio or video material, take notes of the essential ideas in each item. Use good note-taking strategies. Hand in your notes along with your completed research project.

Step 4: Summarize your research

You will be required to write a summary of some type (descriptive, informative, or visual) for at least one of your articles or audio/video content. Note any specific instructions from your teacher here.

_____

_____

_____

 For more information and examples of different types of summaries—informative, descriptive, and visual—see Reading Strategies, page 126.

Step 5: Prepare a Works Cited page

Prepare a Works Cited page that lists all the sources you referenced in your research project. Use proper MLA format (unless your teacher requests a different style).

 For information about how to prepare a Works Cited page and examples of MLA-style Works Cited entries, see Writing Strategies, page 119.

Step 6: Create a vocabulary list

Create a list of key words that are new for you from the articles and audio or video sources you used for your research project. Your teacher will specify the required number of words. Try to include as many vocabulary words as possible that are specific to your field of study, but some of your words can be general vocabulary. For each word, identify the article, audio clip, or video from which it was taken, write down the sentence in which it was used, its part of speech, and a definition, and use the word in a new sentence (or context) of your own. Be sure that you know how to pronounce each word properly (with proper stress). You can check pronunciation on most online dictionaries.

 Go to Explore Online to download a vocabulary list template.

Required number of words: _____

Submission requirements

Submit your completed research project to your teacher in an organized manner on the due date. Your project must contain

- a title page
- a table of contents
- a copy of your articles (They must be annotated.)
- your required summaries
- your vocabulary list
- a Works Cited page

 Go to Explore Online and download the Research Project: Evaluating Sources template.

Project C

Survey

Individually or with a partner, you will conduct a survey to investigate a subject, issue, or problem related to your field of study or future career. You will conduct the survey, analyze your findings, then interpret the results. You will present your findings in an oral and/or written report. (Your teacher will provide specific instructions.)

Step 1: Choose a topic

Select the subject and purpose of your survey. For example, if you are studying the social sciences, you may want to investigate students' beliefs and behaviours regarding community engagement. If you are studying administration, you may want to question students about their knowledge and practices regarding financial investing.

Step 2: Identify survey subjects

Select whom you want to survey: college students, teachers, general population. You may want to compare different groups of respondents (e.g., high school versus college students, people of various age groups (people between 15 and 25 versus those over 25), or males versus females, and so on.

Step 3: Devise your hypothesis

A hypothesis is a prediction about what your survey findings will reveal. For example, your hypothesis might be that college students believe that being involved in one's community is important or that college students have limited knowledge about investing.

Come up with one or two testable hypotheses.

Step 4: Prepare the survey

Write 10 survey questions. You may include a variety of question types: multiple choice, *yes/no*, true/false, rating or ranking, or short answer questions. Remember that short answer questions can be informative, but they are more difficult to quantify.

Step 5: Conduct the survey

You can decide how you want students to conduct the survey. You may want to use an online survey site such as SurveyMonkey.

Administer the survey in person or use an online tool to conduct your survey. Your teacher will tell you how many people you should survey.

Step 6: Analyze the data

Collect and analyze the data, then draw conclusions. How did the respondents answer the questions? What generalizations can you make based on the results? Were your hypotheses confirmed or disproved? How did the results and hypotheses differ? What findings are the most important, the most interesting, or the most surprising? What are some possible interpretations of the results? What were the limitations or weaknesses of your study? Could your results have been more valid and reliable? If so, how? What are your overall conclusions and recommendations based on your research?

You may want to specify whether you want students to include charts, graphs, or visuals within the report itself or as appendices.

Step 7: Write your report

 For more information on writing a survey report and to see a model report with these sections, see Writing Strategies, page 142.

Prepare a report based on your survey. Your report should include the following sections: abstract, introduction, method, results, discussion, limitations of the study, and conclusion. Include any necessary charts, graphs, or visuals.

Learning Strategies

Research Strategies

Go to Explore Online for a list of good, stable academic search engines that you may want download for students. The list is organized according to expressed student preference. You may reorganize or revise it if you wish.

Research is important to develop a better understanding of a topic and find solutions to problems. Throughout college or university, you will need to research topics related to your field of study. In the workplace, you will also need to do research for a variety of purposes. This section deals with types of sources, how to evaluate the validity of a source, how to avoid plagiarism, and how to cite sources correctly.

Types of Sources: Primary, Secondary, and Tertiary

A **primary source** is the original source of information or a first-hand account of an event by a participant or witness. A **secondary source** explains, interprets, analyzes, judges, or discusses information from a primary source. **Tertiary sources** contain and organize information.

Primary sources	Secondary sources	Tertiary sources
official records original research a novel	a politician's speech quoting official records a news report discussing original research a critique of a novel	indexes databases

When you include information in your work from external sources, you may use primary or secondary sources. Whenever possible, you should consult the primary source.

Evaluating Sources

When you do research, it is essential to evaluate your sources. You must know where the information comes from and if it is valid (i.e., reliable) and recognize if it could be biased. When conducting research, ask yourself the following questions to evaluate your sources.

Audience and purpose

For whom is the article written: experts, the general public, or a specific group of people?

What is the purpose of the information: to inform, describe, entertain, persuade, or sell?

Publisher

Who published the information?

- What do you know about the publisher? Is it a known and reliable source?
- Does this publisher have a bias or a vested interest? For example, is the publisher a company or a partisan of a particular group or cause?

For more information on domain extensions, see page 117.

For online sources, what is the domain extension (e.g., .com, .org)?

When was the information published? Is it recent?

In the case of a printed text, is it a reprint or an original publication?

In the case of a research study, was it peer reviewed?

Author

Who is the author?

- What are the author's credentials (educational and professional)?
- Does the author have a bias?

Content

Does the author support his or her ideas with reliable facts, statistics, or examples? Can the information be verified with other sources?

Does the information presented appear to represent a balanced view?

Does the author cite his or her sources? Are those sources reliable? Does the information come from a primary or secondary source?

Does the container (i.e., website, newspaper, video, etc.) from which the information was taken contain advertising? If so, does that have an influence on the content?

Is the information written in grammatically correct language?

Domain extensions

With online sources, be aware of domain extensions. You cannot decide if a website is reliable based on the domain extension alone and domain extensions are not assigned as strictly as they used to be; however, being aware of the purpose of these extensions may help you assess a website's reliability and whether or not the information on the website may be biased.

Evaluating Sources

Audience and Purpose

- ❑ Is article written for experts, general public, a specific group?
- ❑ Is the purpose to inform, describe, entertain, persuade, sell?

Publisher

- ❑ Is the publisher known and reliable?
- ❑ Does the publisher have a bias or vested interest?
- ❑ Online: what is the domain extension?
- ❑ Is the information recent?
- ❑ Research study—was it peer reviewed?
- ❑ Printed text—is it original or a reprint?

Author

- ❑ Who is the author?
- ❑ What are author's educational credentials?
- ❑ What are author's professional credentials?
- ❑ Does the author have a bias?

Content

- ❑ Are ideas supported with reliable facts, statistics, or examples?
- ❑ Can the information be verified with other sources?
- ❑ Does the information represent a balanced view?
- ❑ Does author cite sources? Are those sources reliable?
- ❑ Is information from a primary or secondary source?
- ❑ Does container (website, newspaper, video, etc.) contain advertising?
- ❑ Does advertising influence the content?
- ❑ Is the language grammatically correct?

Extension	Intended use	Actual use
.biz	Businesses	Meant to relieve the demand for .com names. Must be for business or commercial use.
.ca	Canadian entities	Limited to Canadian entities: citizens, permanent residents, organizations, Indigenous groups, governments, etc.
.com	Commercial	Used by all types of entities (e.g., non-profits, schools, individuals). Many of these sites exist to sell a product or service. Any person or entity can register. This is the most common domain name.
.edu	Education	Limited to accredited higher educational institutions and used almost exclusively by American colleges and universities. These sites can be useful and reliable; however, many schools offer free .edu websites to their students. You would not want to use a student paper as a source.
.gov	US government agencies	Limited to American governmental entities. These can be useful especially for up-to-date information such as medical news, statistics, and information about laws and legislation.
.info	Unrestricted	Open for any purpose similar to those of the .com, .net, and .org domains. Explicitly created for unrestricted use.
.net	Network	Originally intended for domains pointing to a distributed network of computers, or "umbrella" sites that act as the portal to a set of smaller websites. Any person or entity can register.
.org	Organization	Originally intended for non-profit organizations. These can be useful, but remember that many organizations have a specific mission, and the information on their sites is not always objective. Any person or entity can register.

Using Wikipedia

Wikipedia is an open source site, meaning that anybody can contribute information to the site. The information on Wikipedia is not always reliable and should not be used as a primary reference. However, this site can be useful as a starting point to obtain general information about a subject and for the links it offers to other, more reliable references. Check with your teacher before using Wikipedia.

Citing Sources

For information about evaluating sources, see page 116.

When you include information from external sources, you must acknowledge where that information comes from. That is to say, you must **cite your sources**; if you do not, you will have committed academic fraud or plagiarism.

Citing your sources, whenever you use somebody else's ideas, words, or images in your own work, requires both in-text citations and a Works Cited page (or Bibliography) at the end of your work. There are many different citation styles; two of the most common citation styles that you may use in college or university are MLA and APA.

Modern Language Association (MLA) style is most often used by those studying language and literature or the humanities, whereas American Psychological Association (APA) style is most often used in the social and behavioural sciences. As in most English courses, MLA style is used in this textbook.

Always check with your teacher regarding which style you should use. The rules and examples given below for creating a Works Cited page are for MLA format.

Avoiding plagiarism

Plagiarism is a serious offence. It is considered fraud and can have significant consequences for your academic career. You must avoid plagiarism at all times, and the information that follows will help you do so.

When you produce written or oral work, you must cite your sources—whether you use another person's exact words or you paraphrase their words or ideas. In academic writing, using more than a few consecutive words in a row from an external source without citation is considered plagiarism.

Quoting directly

Be sure to use the proper style for quotation marks in English: two rounded marks at the top left and right of the quotation. The punctuation mark at the end of a sentence is usually placed inside the closing quotation mark.

Direct quotation is copying the exact words of another person without making any changes to the words or their order. When using direct quotation, use quotation marks (" ") to clearly identify the person's original words.

> **EXAMPLE**   Dr. Durcharme said, "Hard work is what will lead to success."

Paraphrasing

For more information on paraphrasing, see the example summaries on page 126.

Paraphrasing means taking the ideas or words of another person and rewriting them in your own words. You must cite your source when you paraphrase, but you do not use quotation marks (because you are not quoting directly). When you write a summary, paraphrase the ideas from the original work and mention the source at the beginning of the summary.

When you paraphrase, you must do the following:

- preserve the original meaning of the passage
- keep all essential information
- maintain the style and level of formality of the original text

Strategies for paraphrasing

1. Identify key words in the original text and find synonyms to replace them.

2. Change the sentence structure.

   EXAMPLE

   Original text: Thanks to wireless Internet, laptops, and tablets, employees are finding they don't necessarily need to be chained to a single desk (Kolowich 55).

   Paraphrased text: Workers are no longer confined to their desks thanks to wireless technology (Kolowich 55).

   Paraphrased text: In "Innovative Ways Companies Are Changing the Workplace," Kolowich notes that workers are no longer confined to their desks thanks to wireless technology (55).

Key words	Synonyms
wireless Internet, laptops, tablets	wireless technology
employees	workers
chained	confined to

Using in-text citations

When you include information or refer to ideas taken from an external source in your work, you must identify the source of the information or ideas with an in-text citation.

Here are two examples of how to write an in-text citation using MLA style:

1. Scott mentions that "Communication failures between architects, designers, contractors and procurement teams compromise the construction industry" (98).

2. "Communication failures between architects, designers, contractors and procurement teams compromise the construction industry" (Scott 98).

In the first example, the author's name is mentioned within the sentence and the page number is given in parentheses at the end of the sentence. For online sources with no page number, just mention the author's name within the sentence.

In the second example, both the author and page number are noted in parentheses at the end of the sentence. For online sources with no page number, just put the author's last name in the parentheses (or the first word from the title of the text—between quotation marks—if the author is unknown).

For more information on citation styles, see the Purdue University Online Writing Lab (OWL) website.

Preparing a Works Cited page

Whenever you use somebody else's ideas, words, or images in your own work, you must cite the source not only with an in-text citation but also in a Works Cited section on a separate page at the end of your work. Remember that there are different citation styles. The rules and examples given below for creating a Works Cited page are for MLA style.

- Use the title "Works Cited." Centre the title in the middle of the page.
- List entries in alphabetical order according to the author's last name. If a document has no author, alphabetize it according to the first word of the title (not including articles, prepositions, and conjunctions).
- Double space the information in each entry, but do not double space between entries.
- Start the first line of the citation at the left margin and indent the following lines by half an inch (1.27 cm).
- Capitalize all words (except articles, prepositions, and conjunctions) in the title of the article book, or other work.
- Include the following information in your citation: author(s), title (italicized if it's a book; in quotation marks if it's an article), title of the container (e.g., name of the magazine, journal, online publisher [in italics; underline if handwritten], publisher, publication date, location (page number, paragraph, URL/DOI), date of access (for online sources).

The Purdue OWL website is a useful reference for MLA style.

Notice the abbreviated form for dates and the punctuation used within the entry in the following example Works Cited entries.

Example Works Cited entries—DIGITAL or ONLINE sources

Individual page on a website

"Autism and Pets: More Evidence of Social Benefits." *Autism Speaks*, 15 Apr. 2014, www. autismspeaks.org/science-news/autism-and-pets-more-evidence-social-benefits. Accessed 2 Oct. 2018.

Online newspaper or magazine article

Kluger, Jeffrey. "The Sixth Great Extinction Is Underway—and We're to Blame." *Time*, 24 Apr. 2017, time.com/3035872/sixth-great-extinction. Accessed 9 Nov. 2018.

Online scholarly journal article

Jensen, Eric. "How Poverty Affects Classroom Engagement." *Educational Leadership*, vol. 70, no. 8, 2013, pp. 24–30, www.ascd.org/publications/educational-leadership/ may13/vol70/num08/how-poverty-affects-classroom-engagement.aspx. Accessed 7 Feb. 2018.

If you find the electronic version of a journal on an **electronic database** (such as ProQuest, Academic Search Premier, etc.), it is important to cite this information. Articles in journals online are often assigned a Digital Object Identifier (DOI). If your source includes a **DOI**, use that instead of a URL.

Ferguson, H.B., et al. "The Impact of Poverty on Educational Outcomes for Children." *Paediatrics & Child Health*, vol. 12, no. 8, 2007, pp. 701–706. *Academic Search Premier*, doi: 10.1093/pch/12.8.701.

Online video or audio

Cornett, Mick. "How an Obese Town Lost a Million Pounds." *YouTube*, uploaded by TED, 2 Jan. 2014, www.youtube.com/watch?v=raCIUeGUr3s. Accessed 9 Aug. 2018.

Podcast radio or television program

Young, Marcia. "Should Athletes Be Allowed to Hack Their Bodies to Get an Edge?" *Day 6*, 5 Aug. 2016, *CBC Radio*, http://www.cbc.ca/radio/day6/should-athletes-be-allowed-to-hack-their-bodies-to-get-an-edge-1.3709675?autoplay=true. Accessed 31 Mar. 2017.

Example Works Cited entries—PRINT sources

Book

Atwood, Margaret. *Oryx and Crake*. McClelland & Stewart, 2003.

Newspaper or magazine article

Kirkey, Sharon. "Another Medical Marvel: Montreal MDs 'Shrink' Girl's Head." *Montreal Gazette*, 14 Dec. 2018, p. NP1.

Scholarly journal article

Crane, John. "This Summer, What You Should Know about West Nile Virus." *Courtlands Forum*, vol. 16, no. 6, 2003, pp. 35–38.

Remember that if you use MLA style in your Works Cited page, each line of an entry must be double spaced.

Reading Strategies

Reading is one of the primary ways to learn new information, build vocabulary, and engage with the world. Improving your reading skills will save you time and make you more successful in English at school and work.

Understanding the Main Idea, Supporting Ideas, and Details

The **main idea** is the key message of a text. It is the speaker's or writer's overall conclusion (i.e., main message) about the subject.

Supporting ideas help to explain and back up the validity of the main idea. **Supporting details** expand upon and clarify the supporting ideas. Supporting ideas and details may include facts, statistics, examples, quotations, and anecdotes.

NOTE The term *essential ideas* refers to all the ideas in a text or audio that are necessary for you to extract in order to complete a specific task. This may include only the main idea and supporting ideas, or it may include more minor details: it all depends on what task you need to complete and the type of information you need to complete it successfully.

You may want to show students an example paragraph in Unit 1, page 19, that demonstrates clearly the main idea, supporting ideas, and supporting details.

Understanding the Author's Purpose

When reading a text, ask yourself why the author wrote it. Check to see which of the following the author had as a goal:

- to inform
- to describe
- to entertain
- to persuade
- to sell

To determine the author's purpose, ask yourself the following questions:

- What does the author want to accomplish?
- What effect does the author want to have on the reader?
- What is the author's tone?

For information about tone, see page 122.

Differentiating between objective and subjective writing

One clue to the author's purpose is whether the text is written from an objective or subjective perspective.

Objective writing refers to a text in which the author's purpose is to inform, explain, or describe. The author is not trying to make an argument or persuade the reader and does not express personal feelings about the subject.

Subjective writing refers to a text in which the author's purpose is to persuade or entertain. In this case, the author does express an opinion or personal feelings about the subject.

Objective writing	Subjective writing
• information presented does not vary from person to person or day to day • remains neutral and impersonal • does not use first-person pronouns (*I* or *me*) • refers to facts and observable data without adding personal analysis or commentary • does not use emotionally charged language or techniques • gives both sides of the issue **EXAMPLES** The exam lasted 60 minutes. Twenty-two people were killed by the bomb blasts.	• information presented can vary from person to person or from day to day • expresses the author's opinion or personal feelings • can include first-person pronouns (*I* or *me*) • includes personal analysis or commentary • uses emotionally charged language and techniques (e.g., asking rhetorical questions) • does not give both sides of the issue **EXAMPLES** I thought the exam was really difficult. Terrorists murdered 22 innocent people.

Tone is the way a writer expresses his or her attitude in writing—how the writer feels about the subject. Recognizing the tone helps you identify the author's purpose for writing—for example, whether the writer is trying to persuade or simply inform. The tone of a text can be formal, informal, serious, humorous, sarcastic, critical, supportive, reasoned, alarmist, optimistic, pessimistic, bored, enthusiastic, and so on. A text can express more than one tone.

A writer can create tone through many rhetorical techniques, including the use of

For information about denotative versus connotative vocabulary, see page 123.

- highly connotative language (i.e., words with positive or negative associations)
- colourful, emotionally charged language and content
- hyperbole—exaggerated language
- allusions with negative associations
- direct address or appeal to the audience
- first-person references and pronouns
- purposeful mechanics (creative sentence structure, formatting, punctuation, etc.)

Identifying bias

When you read a text, ask yourself if the writing shows bias. Bias is when the author does not present a balanced view or fails to offer all the available information or evidence. To detect bias, ask yourself: What evidence is provided? Does the text favour one perspective more than another? Objective writing does not contain bias.

Recognizing media bias

Media bias occurs when a news story is presented in a one-sided or unobjective way. When evaluating for bias, there are many factors to be considered, including

- the placement of news stories (i.e., front page versus back page; first versus last item in a news lineup)
- the wording of the headline, subtitles, and captions
- the selection of information to include or not include
- the placement of particular information within the news story (e.g., the positive perspective of an issue mentioned at the beginning rather than the end)
- word choice (neutral, positive, or negative connotation)
- the choice of references or experts mentioned or not mentioned (e.g., layperson versus scientist versus professional with biased opinion)
- the way in which numbers and statistics are interpreted (optimistically or pessimistically)
- accompanying photos (flattering versus unflattering, the selected focus of the image, etc.)
- whether any sponsors or research funding are mentioned (could affect content)

Recognizing and using denotative and connotative vocabulary

Denotation refers to a word's objective or literal meaning—the meanings you find in a dictionary. *Connotation* refers to the associations and emotional sentiments attached to particular words that add shades of meaning.

Words can have positive, negative, or neutral connotations. For example, the words *well-known*, *famous*, and *notorious* all have a similar denotation—to be familiar to others, widely known. However, *well-known* has a fairly neutral meaning, *famous* has a positive connotation (i.e., to be known for good reasons), and *notorious* has a negative connotation (i.e., to be known for bad reasons).

When you are writing and have a word in mind but want to use a more precise word or more varied vocabulary, look up the word in a thesaurus or check the list of synonyms given for that word in standard dictionaries. Always try to find examples of words used in context.

Sometimes a word can have either a positive or negative connotation depending on the context in which it is used. Consider, for example, the word *whimsical* used in two different sentences.

> She has a **whimsical** sense of humour.
> Here *whimsical* means unusual or imaginative in a positive way.

> The **whimsical** decisions of the administration frustrated the other employees.
> In this case *whimsical* means changeable and unpredictable in a negative way.

The use of connotative words helps to

- make writing more precise
- create a specific tone
- incite interest or emotions in the audience
- reveal a writer or speaker's bias

To see examples of the use of connotative words in context, see the Pre-Reading Activity on page 25.

Skimming

Skimming is doing a quick examination of a text before reading deeper: going over a text quickly focusing only on certain parts to get the *gist* of the text—an overall idea of what information it contains and the main idea. When researching, skimming can help you determine whether a text will be useful and decide if you want to spend more time reading it more thoroughly. Research shows that skimming a text before deeper reading helps you read more effectively. Skimming helps prepare you for reading, allowing you to absorb and understand the information better when you start to read the text more closely.

Use these key steps when skimming a text:

- Read the title, subtitle, and any headings. Note how long each section is. Look for any visuals, charts, or graphs. These features will give you an idea of the topics covered, how the subject matter is organized, and the focus or main idea of the text.
- Read the introduction (first paragraph) and the conclusion (last paragraph). The main idea of a text is usually stated in these sections.
- Read the first sentence of each paragraph in the text. The first sentence often states the main idea or focus of the paragraph.

Scanning

Scanning is looking quickly over written material to find a specific fact or piece of information. Scanning is useful when looking up a word in a dictionary, checking suggested links during an Internet search, trying to find an answer in a text during an exam, or locating specific information (a date, statistic, or name) in a report. Scanning is essential to save time while performing many academic and workplace tasks.

Annotating

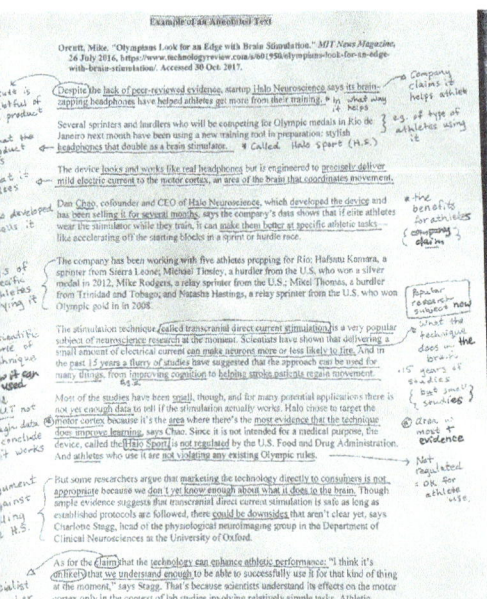

Annotating involves actively engaging with a text by responding to it and marking it up as you read. Annotation helps you to pick out the essential ideas in a text and see how they are organized and connected. The process can improve your comprehension and analysis of the ideas presented in a text and foster deeper understanding of the material. It allows you to analyze those ideas in relation to prior knowledge or future use.

Annotation may include any or all of the following:

- highlighting or underlining essential ideas
- noting (in the margins) the subtopics covered in each paragraph
- making marginal notes, comments, or images regarding essential ideas
- connecting different parts of the text with arrows
- summarizing difficult concepts
- putting a box around important technical terms
- noting emotional reactions
- circling unfamiliar words or references
- noting questions about the material
- jotting down thoughts connecting ideas in the text to prior knowledge, possibilities of future research, or future use
- noting any bias or interesting use of language

Annotated text example

Olympians Look for an Edge with Brain Stimulation

by Mike Orcutt

[margin: Orcutt is doubtful of the product—reason why]

Despite the lack of peer-reviewed evidence, startup Halo Neuroscience says its brain-zapping headphones have helped athletes get more from their training. *[margin: *in what way?]*

[margin right: Company claims it helps athletes.]

Several sprinters and hurdlers who will be competing for Olympic medals in Rio de Janeiro next month have been using a new training tool in preparation: stylish headphones that double as a brain stimulator. *[margin: *Called Halo Sport (H.S.)]*

[margin right: e.g. of type of athletes using it]
[margin right: what the product is]

The device looks and works like real headphones but is engineered to precisely deliver mild electric current to the motor cortex, an area of the brain that coordinates movement.

[margin right: change to How it works]

[margin: Who developed + sells it]

Dan Chao, cofounder and CEO of Halo Neuroscience, which developed the device and has been selling it for several months, says the company's data shows that if elite athletes wear the stimulator while they train, it can make them better at specific athletic tasks—like accelerating off the starting blocks in a sprint or hurdle race.

*[margin right: *the benefits for athletes (company claim)]*

[margin: e.g. of specific athletes trying it]

The company has been working with five athletes prepping for Rio: Hafsatu Kamara, a sprinter from Sierra Leone; Michael Tinsley, a hurdler from the US who won a silver medal in 2012; Mike Rodgers, a relay sprinter from the US; Mikel Thomas, a hurdler from Trinidad and Tobago; and Natasha Hastings, a relay sprinter from the US who won Olympic gold in 2008.

[margin: • scientific name of technique • how it can be used ↓ BUT not enough data to conclude if it works]

The stimulation technique, called transcranial direct current stimulation, is a very popular subject of neuroscience research at the moment. Scientists have shown that delivering a small amount of electrical current can make neurons more or less likely to fire. And in the past 15 years a flurry of studies have suggested that the approach can be used for many things, from improving cognition to helping stroke patients regain movement.

[margin right: Popular research subject now]
[margin right: What the technique does in the brain. • 15 years of studies done]

[margin: Arguments against current applications]

Most of the studies have been small, though, and for many potential applications there is not yet enough data to tell if the stimulation actually works. Halo chose to target the *motor cortex because it's the area where there's the most evidence that the technique does improve learning, says Chao. Since it is not intended for a medical purpose, the device, called the Halo Sport, is not regulated by the US Food and Drug Administration. And athletes who use it are not violating any existing Olympic rules.

*[margin right: *area with most positive evidence]*
[margin right: Not regulated = legal for athlete use]

[margin: Argument against selling the H.S.]

But some researchers argue that marketing the technology directly to consumers is not appropriate because we don't yet know enough about what it does to the brain. Though ample evidence suggests that transcranial direct current stimulation is safe as long as established protocols are followed, there could be downsides that aren't clear yet, says Charlotte Stagg, head of the physiological neuroimaging group in the Department of Clinical Neurosciences at the University of Oxford.

[margin: Specialist researcher doubtful about H.S.]

As for the claim that the technology can enhance athletic performance: "I think it's unlikely that we understand enough to be able to successfully use it for that kind of thing at the moment," says Stagg. That's because scientists understand its effects on the motor cortex only in the context of lab studies involving relatively simple tasks. Athletic training is more complex, involving more muscles and many brain regions, she says.

[margin: Company refutation]

Chao says the results from Halo's work with elite athletes suggests otherwise. "For us, our results are proof enough," he says, adding that the company does plan to submit some of this data for scientific peer review in the near future.

Orcutt, Mike. "Olympians Look for an Edge with Brain Stimulation." *MIT Technology Review*, 26 July 2016, https://www.technologyreview.com/s/601950/olympians-look-for-an-edge-with-brain-stimulation/. Accessed 30 Oct. 2017.

Summarizing

A summary restates the main ideas of a work. It gives the reader a clear, objective outline or synopsis of the original piece (text, video, or audio clip) in a condensed form. It identifies the author's key message, purpose, and essential supporting ideas. It does not include any of the examples, quotes, or statistics from the original text.

An **informative summary** restates the main idea of an original work and the key supporting ideas in a condensed version, leaving out minor details. An informative summary for an article should be between one-quarter to one-third the length of the original text.

A **descriptive summary** states the main idea and describes what the author or speaker does in the original work (i.e., it states the subtopics that the author examines, explains, compares, defines, lists, suggests, etc.). It does not restate all of the key supporting ideas in the original work the way that an informative summary does.

The marginal notes beside each of the summaries below will help you better understand the similarities and differences between these two types of summaries.

Informative summary example

Introduces the source
States the main idea
Describes the headphones and explains how they work
Explains how the technology works and states the benefits
Lists the arguments why the technology should not be marketed yet
States the company's refutation and explains their claim

In his article titled "Olympians Look for an Edge with Brain Stimulation" from MIT Technology Review, Mike Orcutt expresses doubts about the effectiveness of the new "brain-zapping headphones" being sold to athletes for the purpose of helping them improve their training and performance. These stylish new headphones, called "Halo Sport," are made by Halo Neuroscience. They play music while simultaneously delivering mild electric currents to the part of the brain responsible for coordinating movement. The technology is based on scientific research that suggests such stimulation can affect neuron function, which may help people perform certain tasks, and possibly even improve cognition. However, Orcutt notes that most studies have been small and that Halo Neuroscience's research has not been peer reviewed. He notes that other researchers argue the technology should not be marketed yet; not enough is known about its effectiveness beyond simple lab tasks or about the potential negative effects. The article concludes with Halo Neuroscience's affirmation that results the company has seen from its work with athletes are proof enough that its product works.

Descriptive summary example

States the source and topic of the article. States only that the following subtopics are covered in the article (the product, the science behind them, the positive effects for athletes) but does not provide a description of the product nor any explanation or details about those subtopics.
Concludes that he is skeptical about the technology, but does not list the reasons. States the company's claims that their technology works, but doesn't give the company's reason for its claim (i.e., the company's confidence in its own research).

In his article titled "Olympians Look for an Edge with Brain Stimulation" from MIT Technology Review, Mike Orcutt discusses "Halo Sport," a new technological product being sold to athletes. He describes the science behind these brain-stimulating headphones and how they are supposed to benefit athletic training and performance (according to Halo Neuroscience, the company that invented and sells them). Orcutt concludes by explaining why he and other researchers are skeptical about the company's claims that this technology improves athletic achievement.

Checklist for Summary Writing

Check to make sure that you have addressed each of the following elements in your summary. If not, revise your summary accordingly.

❑ State the source of the original work. Mention the type of work (e.g., book, film, scholarly journal article, newspaper article, online video, etc.), the author and/or publisher, and the title of the work.

❑ State the main idea of the work.

> **EXAMPLES**
>
> In an article from *MIT Technology Review* titled "Olympians Look for an Edge with Brain Stimulation," Mike Orcutt expresses doubt about "Halo Sport," a new technological product being sold to athletes.
>
> In the article "Olympians Look for an Edge with Brain Stimulation" published in *MIT Technology Review*, Mike Orcutt discusses . . .
>
> "Olympians Look for an Edge with Brain Stimulation," an article by Mike Orcutt published in *MIT Technology Review*, suggests that . . .

❑ Include only the essential supporting ideas (in an informative summary) OR note the main subtopics (in a descriptive summary). Stick to the appropriate length—maximum of one-third the length of the original text for an informative summary.

❑ Do not include any information that was not in the original work or any personal opinions or references to yourself.

❑ Present information in the order it appeared in the original work. (Occasionally it may be necessary to reorganize some information to maintain cohesion in the summary.)

❑ Refer to the author at least once in the body of the summary to remind the reader that the ideas expressed are not yours. Use phrases such as

> According to [author], . . .;
> The author claims that . . .;
> [Author] describes . . .;
> [Author] concludes that . . .

❑ Conclude the summary by restating the author's conclusion from the original work. Do not add your own conclusion.

❑ Put ideas in your own words—do not plagiarize. Do not use direct quotations.

❑ Use complete sentences throughout (no point form or list of points).

In exceptional cases, one direct quotation may be acceptable, for example, in the case of a well-known quotation or idea that just cannot be rephrased. Check your teacher's rules regarding the use of quotations in a summary.

Creating Visual Summaries Using Graphic Organizers

The essential ideas of a text (or audio or video) can also be summarized using a graphic organizer, which outlines the essential ideas of a source material in a visual way. It shows the key points (most often in point form) and illustrates how these ideas are organized and connected through the use of headings, subheadings, boxes, circles, numbers, letters, bullets, dashes, squiggly lines, arrows, images, and so on.

Visual summary example

"Olympians Look for an Edge with Brain Stimulation"

from *MIT Technology Review*, by Mike Orcutt

Topic: Halo Sport—a tech product being sold to athletes

People doubtful about the product:

1. Orcutt (author of text)
   Why?
   - lack of peer-reviewed evidence
   - most studies have been small
   - not enough data to show if technique works

2. Other researchers
   Why?
   - possible negative effects on the brain not yet known
   - scientists understand its effects only on simple tasks in a lab (not complex tasks like athletic training)

Claims about Halo Sport by manufacturer (Halo Neuroscience) based on its own research with Olympic athletes:

1. helps athletes get more out of their training
2. makes athletes better at specific athletic tasks
3. use doesn't violate any Olympic rules

Description of the product:

- headphones that work as a brain stimulator
- stylish
- look and work like regular headphones

How they work:

- deliver mild electric currents to area of the brain that coordinates movement

Other studies suggest the technique can:

- make neurons more or less likely to fire
- improve cognition
- help stroke victims regain movement

Graphic organizer examples

Graphic organizers can take many different forms. Choose the style that best suits your objective and task. Try experimenting with outline, hierarchical, bubble, or mixed style graphic organizers.

Outline style

Main idea: xxx

1. Supporting idea

    1.1 detail

    1.2 detail

2. Supporting idea

    2.1 detail

    2.2 detail

3. Supporting idea

    3.1 detail

    3.2 detail

Conclusion: xxx

Hierarchical style

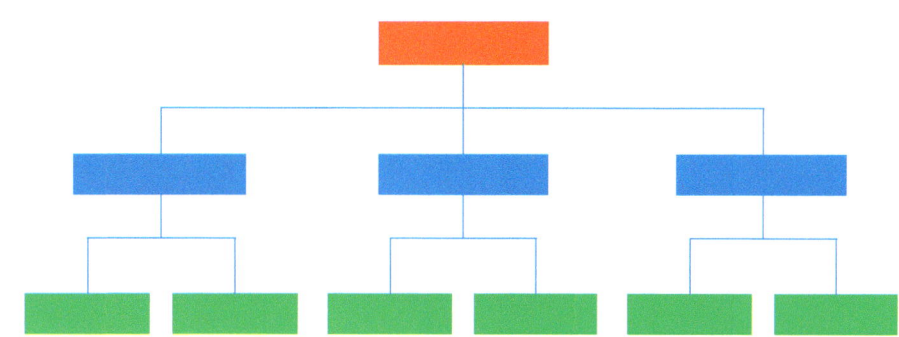

Bubble style

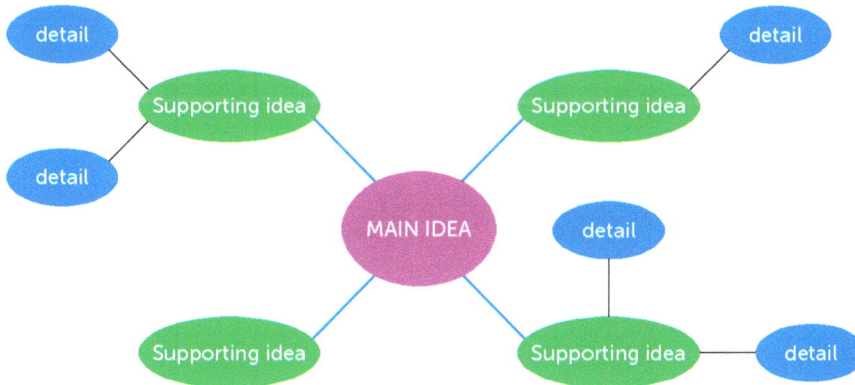

Mixed style

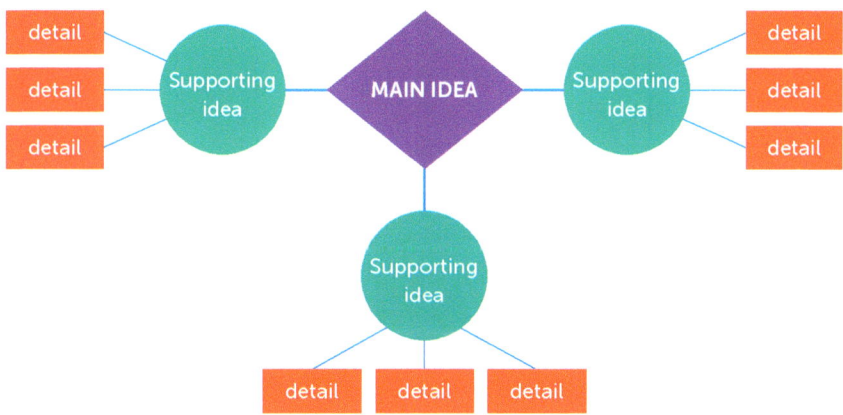

Listening Strategies

In academic and professional environments, you will need to listen to and understand information in English in various situations, such as classroom discussions, meetings, lectures, and presentations (in person or as video or audio recordings).

Listening for Essential Ideas

The essential ideas you listen for in any given situation will be determined by your purpose for listening and what you will need to do with the information.

The following strategies will help you understand and extract the essential ideas as you listen.

Before you listen, ask yourself . . .

- Why am I listening? What will I have to do with the information? What kind of information do I need to listen for?
- Do I have to listen only for the general ideas or do I have to listen for specific details, facts, or statistics?
- What do I already know about the subject and what information do I think will be discussed?

While you listen . . .

For a list of good note-taking strategies, see below.

- Take notes using good note-taking strategies.
- Listen carefully to the introductory remarks to determine the main idea and key points that will be discussed in the audio or video clip.
- Listen for transitional words, phrases, sentences, and questions that indicate a new supporting point or subtopic is being introduced.
- Listen for key words and concepts that are emphasized or repeated.
- Listen carefully to the conclusion, in which the main idea and key points are often summed up.

For a list of transitional words and expressions, see Writing Strategies, page 134.

After you listen . . .

- Listen carefully to any follow-up discussion or comments.
- Compare your notes (or answers to questions) and discuss the topic with another person when possible.
- Review, add to, edit, and reorganize your notes as necessary.
- Look up unfamiliar vocabulary.
- Do further research on the topic if necessary.

Note-Taking

Taking notes helps you listen actively and become a more critical listener. It is important to take good notes in order to understand and recall the key points you will need to complete future tasks (e.g., to complete an exam, write a report, or give an oral presentation).

Note-taking strategies

1. Listen for the essential ideas (i.e., the necessary information related to your purpose for listening). Do not try to write down every word and detail.

2. Note only key words and short phrases—use point form. Do not write in complete sentences.

3. Make use of abbreviations and symbols.

   EXAMPLE   L. for *laughter*, ben for *benefits*, ↑ for *increases*

4. Use headings and subheadings to organize and group ideas.

> EXAMPLE   Reasons, Benefits, How to, Necessary factors

5. Organize the information on the page effectively and use numbers, letters, bullets, dashes, squiggly lines, arrows, or whatever other marks or symbols make sense to you to visually represent the organization of information and the relationships between ideas. For example, indent information or use numbers to indicate a subpoint of a general point and arrows or a dash to indicate a detail. Another way to organize information is to put main ideas on the left side and supporting details on the right.

> EXAMPLE   (from "Humour at Work," Unit 1, page 10)   You may also find it useful to create a graphic organizer like this:

Reasons to ↑ L. at work ⟶ **Even fake L. has some of the same ben. as real L.**

1. creates social bonding
   – L. is contagious
   – creates sense of team/unity

2. physically/mentally good for us
   – effects faster than alcohol/valium
   – belly laugh = 1–2 min on rowing machine re. calories burned

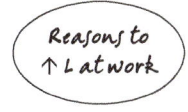 Reasons to ↑ L at work = **Benefits**

i. creates social bonding
   – L. is contagious
   – creates sense of team/unity

ii. physical/mental ben.
   – effects faster than alcohol/valium
   – belly laugh = 1–2 min on rowing machine re. calories burned

⟶ **Even fake L. has some of the same ben. as real L.**

6. Write neatly to ensure you'll be able to understand your notes when you go back to review them later.

7. Add any essential points to your notes that you missed but gathered from follow-up discussions or comments.

Exercise

Look at the two sets of notes below taken during the lecture "How to Ace an Interview."

Which set of notes (Example 1 or 2) would you find more effective if you were going to use them to study for an exam or to prepare an oral presentation? Explain why you find one set of notes more effective than the other.

Example 1

Job interviews: tips for success

- before interview do research about yourself, position, employer & industry
- prepare short stories about yourself (re. your skills)
- practise answers to common questions
- day of the interview be punctual, leave good impression
- after interview establish next steps, have closing statement (why u r interested in posit'n; why u r great match), send thank you

Example 2

Job interviews: tips for success

Before interview
1. do research about →
   i.   yourself
   ii. the position
   iii. the employer & industry
2. prepare short stories about yourself (re. your skills)
3. practise answers to common questions

Day of interview
1. be punctual
2. leave a good impression

After interview
1. establish next steps
2. have closing statement (why u r interested in posit'n; why u r great match)
3. send thank you

Writing Strategies

Before you write a text you must consider the following:

Writer   Who is writing the text? You must consider what role you are taking on as the writer. Are you being asked to write a news article? If so, you would be a journalist. Consequently, you must write from the perspective of a journalist.

Reader(s) Who will read the text? Consider who the readers will be and what they know.

Purpose   What is the purpose or objective of the text? Always keep your reason for writing in mind.

These three elements will determine the content, style, and register of the text.

The Writing Process

Any type of professional or academic writing is a process. To produce a clear, focused, well-organized, and error-free text, follow these steps:

Step 1: Prepare—brainstorm and freewrite

- Determine the purpose and topic of your text.
- Consider all aspects of your topic by brainstorming and freewriting. You can do this by jotting down any ideas that come to mind.
- Establish the main idea of your text and which supporting ideas will best strengthen it.
- Decide what other details are necessary to further develop those supporting ideas.

Step 2: Plan—create an outline using a graphic organizer

- Decide how you will organize your ideas and make a point-form graphic organizer to outline and represent your ideas.

Step 3: Write a rough draft

- Use your graphic organizer to write a rough draft of your text.

Step 4: Revise—examine the overall content of your text

- Check that ideas are clear, complete, well organized, and well connected.
- Add, delete, reorganize, or reword information where necessary.
- Make sure you have not plagiarized.
- Make sure you have used an appropriate style, tone, and register.
- Make sure that you have used the proper format and structure (i.e., essay, report, etc.).

Step 5: Edit—examine your text at the sentence level

- Check for and correct any grammar or spelling errors.

Step 6: Polish and Publish

- Make sure you have cited sources using the proper style.
- Write your final copy to be published and submitted.

Style relates to a writer's choice of language and structure of the text (including vocabulary choice, sentence length and complexity, point of view).

Register refers to the level of formality. For information about register, see page 133.

Some writers prefer to revise and edit simultaneously.

Checklists

Checklists are practical organizational tools you can use when you have an academic, professional, or other task to complete. In your academic work, use a checklist to ensure you have fulfilled all the teacher's requirements in your assignment. Sometimes teachers provide a checklist; if not, create your own.

Tips for creating checklists for academic assignments

1. Read your teacher's instructions for the assignment. Take note of any elements that you must include. For example, if you need to include examples to support your points in an essay, add this requirement to your checklist.

2. Review the teacher's evaluation grid. Add any elements of evaluation to your checklist.

3. Think carefully about what your teacher has asked you to do. For example, if required to write a research essay, you must plan for and conduct research, which may include identifying someone to interview, arranging the interview, transcribing the recorded conversation, and so on. Each task must be added to your checklist.

4. Verify the deadline date. Break up and organize your workload into steps and set deadlines for each step if necessary to ensure that you complete the assignment on time.

Register

Register is the level of formality with which you write (or speak). It is reflected in your choice of grammar and vocabulary. We use different registers—ranging from very informal (e.g., street language) to very formal (e.g., ceremonial language)—in different contexts. It is important to use the appropriate register for your reader, your purpose, and the type of text you are writing.

Informal register is casual. It is generally used in personal emails or texts between people who know each other well. Texts of an informal register often contain slang, phrasal verbs, idioms, abbreviations, and even errors in grammar and spelling.

 For more on phrasal verbs see Grammar Guide, page 190.

> **EXAMPLE**   Hey, let's hook up at about ten tonight. The party's gonna be lit.

Formal register is impersonal and composed. It is the register most commonly used in business writing (for emails and reports) and academic writing (e.g., essays and research papers).

> **EXAMPLE**   Mr. Degault, I was wondering if you would be free tonight at 6:00. It would be my pleasure to discuss details of the project together over dinner.

Using formal register

When you are using a formal register, follow these rules:

1. Write from the third-person point of view. Avoid using *I, you, we, me, us, my, your*, or *our* where possible.

   > Formal   Malaria is typically found in tropical climates.
   > Informal   You can catch malaria in tropical climates.

2. Do not use contractions (e.g., use *will not* instead of *won't*).

3. Avoid slang (non-standard language, e.g., *thirty bucks*), idioms (expressions that don't translate literally, e.g., *kick the bucket*) or clichés (overused expressions, e.g., *the tip of the iceberg*).

4. Avoid using phrasal verbs where possible.

   > **EXAMPLE**   Use *complete* rather than *fill out*, and *meet* rather than *get together*.

5. Do not use abbreviated forms of words (e.g., *flu, tbsp*).

6. Do not use acronyms that are common on social media (e.g., *BTW, FYI, LOL*).

7. If you use a standard acronym that may not be familiar to the reader, write the words in full followed by the acronym in parentheses the first time you use it. Thereafter, use only the acronym.

> **EXAMPLE** Leadership in Energy and Environmental Design (LEED) is the most recognized green building rating system in the world. It is an advantage for companies to have LEED certification.

8. Use indirect questions and more formal modals such as *could* and *would*.

> **Formal**   I wonder if you could replace me. / Would you mind replacing me?
>
> **Informal** Will you replace me? / Can you replace me?

Paragraph Structure

In academic or professional writing, you must express your ideas clearly to the reader. Good paragraph structure will help ensure that each paragraph of your text

- includes a clear main idea, supporting ideas, and details
- contains logically organized ideas
- shows a clear connection between ideas
- contains no unnecessary information

Follow these tips to ensure good paragraph structure:

- Include a **topic sentence** at or near the beginning of each paragraph that clearly states the main idea.
- Use **transitional expressions** as necessary to introduce each **supporting idea**.
- Write a **concluding sentence** at the end that completes the paragraph in a smooth and satisfying way. A concluding sentence may rephrase the main idea; offer advice, a prediction, or commentary; or suggest an action to be taken. (Within a multi-paragraph text, the concluding sentence may provide a link to the following paragraph.)

> Some paragraphs do not have a topic sentence that explicitly states the main idea; sometimes the main idea will be implicit and must be inferred from the information in the text.

Transitional words and expressions

Transitional words and expressions improve the flow and clarity of a text by making smooth connections and showing the relationships between ideas. Review the list below of transitional expressions you can use in your writing and oral presentations.

Enumeration/ Sequence	Example	Comparison	Emphasis
first of all to begin first(ly) second(ly) third(ly) finally*	for example for instance to illustrate	A, as well as B, . . . in the same way like likewise similarly	clearly indeed in fact
Addition	**Cause/ Consequence**	**Contrast**	**Conclusion**
also another furthermore in addition moreover	because (of) due to since as a result consequently hence** therefore thus	compared to however in contrast on the contrary on the other hand unlike whereas while	in conclusion in short to conclude to sum up

*Use *finally* to introduce the last item in a list; do not use it to begin a concluding sentence or concluding paragraph, unless it is introducing the last action or event in a narrative.
**The word *hence* is very formal.

Writing an Essay

An essay is a type of text often required in academia. An essay has a specific structure that includes an introduction, body paragraphs, and a conclusion.

Introduction

The purpose of the introduction is to capture the reader's attention and introduce the main idea of the essay. An introduction often begins with general information that builds toward more specific information and ends with a thesis statement that expresses the main idea of the text.

An introduction may include one or more of these elements:

- general information about a topic
- a brief history of a topic
- an interesting and relevant anecdote, example, quote, statistic, or fact

Body paragraphs

The body of the essay includes at least two paragraphs that develop and support the main idea expressed in the thesis statement. Each paragraph should maintain good paragraph structure and connect the main idea of that paragraph to the main idea of the essay (thesis statement).

Conclusion

The conclusion brings the essay to a logical close. It generally restates the main idea using different words than the thesis statement. It may also include advice, a prediction, or a call to action related to the main idea. New supporting ideas should never be introduced in the conclusion.

Essay example

Go to Explore Online for information about how to write a Critical Response Essay and to read an example essay.

For information about how to write a well-structured paragraph, see page 134.

Performance-Enhancing Drugs: Legalization

On September 24, 1988, at the Summer Olympics in Seoul, Ben Johnson won the gold medal in the 100-metre race. Three days later, he was stripped of his medal because he had been caught cheating. It was revealed that Johnson had used steroids. What he did was against the rules, but not everybody would consider it to be wrong. In fact, the use of performance-enhancing drugs (PEDs) should be legal.

First of all, legalizing PEDs would eliminate the unfair advantage that some athletes have. Today, so many athletes take PEDs that they are in the majority. Indeed, athletes must take drugs to be competitive. For example, after Lance Armstrong was stripped of his seven Tour de France titles, the athletes who inherited the medals "have all been implicated in doping scandals" (Smith). In other words, Armstrong was the one who got caught but was not the only one taking drugs. In addition, Ben Johnson's gold medal at the 1988 Olympics went to Carl Lewis, who later "acknowledged that he failed three tests during the 1988 US Olympic trials" (Mackay). As a result of these tests, Lewis should have been forced to return the medal he inherited from Johnson. Thus, if the majority of top athletes are all taking PEDs, then the only way to have fair competitions is to legalize the drugs for everyone. This way, all athletes would have the same opportunities.

In an academic essay, the first sentence of every paragraph should be indented by half an inch.

Introduction

Begins with a hook—an interesting anecdote and fact.

Thesis statement (main idea)

Body

Topic sentence: introduces the first supporting point

Note the use of external sources. Be sure to use proper citation style in your essays. For information about citing sources, see page 118.

Topic sentence: introduces the second supporting point

Paraphrase: the writer refers to idea from the source text but does not use the same words. Usually, paraphrases start with *that*. For information about paraphrasing, see page 118.

Conclusion

Here the writer restates the main idea and the main supporting points.

Transition words have been underlined throughout the essay.

Remember that your Works Cited must appear on a separate page and each line of an entry must be double spaced.

Second, legalizing PEDs would raise the level of competition. Athletes are constantly striving to improve their abilities and athletic performances to the maximum. With the use of legalized PEDs this would be possible. In a study published by the *New England Journal of Medicine*, Dr. Bhasin and his team conducted a study to find out the effects of steroids on men. What they learned was that steroids significantly build muscle mass (Bhasin). In fact, the research team reported that the group of men who took steroids but did no exercise at all increased muscle mass by seven pounds. In many sports, having additional muscle would help the athlete reach a higher level of performance. Of course, without natural skill, dedication, and practice, an athlete will not become a star simply by taking PEDs. However, PEDs would certainly help elite athletes reach their full potential and increase competition levels to the maximum.

In conclusion, if there is a desire to have a fair and level playing field for all athletes and to raise the level of competition, it would only make sense to allow performance-enhancing drugs to be used in competitions. Instead of constantly trying to regulate PEDs and unfairly punishing only those users who get caught, athletic associations should allow athletes to make their own choices about whether or not to use PEDs and let us see what humans can really accomplish in the world of sports.

Works Cited

Bhasin, Shalender, et al. "The Effects of Supraphysiologic Doses of Testosterone on Muscle Size and Strength in Normal Men." *New England Journal of Medicine*, vol. 335, 1996, pp. 1–7, doi:10.1056/NEJM199607043350101.

Mackay, Duncan. "Lewis: 'Who Cares I Failed Drug Test?' " *The Guardian*, 24 Apr. 2003, www.theguardian.com/sport/2003/apr/24/athletics.duncanmackay. Accessed 22 Feb. 2019.

Smith, Chris. "Why It's Time to Legalize Steroids in Professional Sports." *Forbes*, 24 Aug. 2012, www.forbes.com/sites/chrissmith/2012/08/24/why-its-time-to-legalize-steroids-in-professional-sports/#7e6e69c365d2. Accessed 25 Feb. 2019.

Professional Writing

In the workplace, you will need to read and write different types of documents, such as emails, business letters, and reports. All professional writing should be clear, concise, and follow the appropriate format and structure according to the type of document.

Writing an Email

Email is a common form of business communication. Emails should be clear, concise, and polite. They can be formal or informal. Although an email is generally less formal than a business letter, the level of formality depends on who the recipient is and the purpose of the message. Below are general rules to follow when writing a professional email.

Go to Explore Online for information about writing a business memorandum, another common form of business communication. An example memo is provided.

There are no definite rules regarding the length of an email, but write your message as concisely as possible.

1. Write a clear and precise subject line as it is often used for classifying and searching for emails. Thus, "Minutes of the March 25, 2018 Meeting" is a better subject line than "Minutes."

2. Always address the recipient in an appropriate manner. If you are not on a first name basis, you should address the person with either Mr., Ms., or an appropriate courtesy title such as Dr. followed by the person's last name (e.g., Dear Mr./Ms./Dr. [Last name]) and a comma (or colon in more formal messages). If you do not know the appropriate courtesy title to use, it is best to address the recipient by first and last name (e.g., Dear Kim Smith).

3. Explain who you are (if necessary), why you are writing, and then state your message clearly and concisely.

4. Respect rules of grammar and punctuation. Your written communication reflects your professionalism. Do not overuse exclamation marks to convey tone or all caps (which is considered aggressive).

5. Structure your text appropriately, with complete sentences and paragraphs. Use lists and point form only where appropriate.

6. Do not use emojis or symbols.

7. Mention any attachments that may be included.

8. End with a polite wish or thank you when necessary (e.g., Have a nice day. / Thank you in advance for your help.).

9. Close with a standard phrase followed by a comma (e.g., Sincerely, Regards, Best wishes) and your name. Include your contact information if necessary.

10. Always proofread your message before you send it.

Email example

Subject: Diversity Project—New Schedule as of 1 Jan. 2020

Dear Ms. Thompson and Mr. Williams:

I supervise the EPS development team at PPB Canada. I am writing to you about the newly revised schedule for the diversity project. There have been delays in the original schedule, and I wanted to explain these delays and provide a new schedule, effective 1 January 2020.

> Use acronyms and short forms only when you are sure that the recipient will understand the reference.

Thank you for your patience during the redrafting of the schedule. I apologize for any inconvenience caused by the delay in setting the final schedule.

As I'm sure you can understand, completion dates need to be set to maximize benefits. Resources and schedules must be planned carefully. For the diversity project, it was difficult for me to determine the final completion date because I was missing necessary materials from related projects. I deferred setting the final schedule until those materials were available. Reflecting on the delay, I realize that I should have been in more frequent contact with you regarding the challenges our development team was facing. For this lapse in communication, I apologize. Should we encounter any further delays, I will provide timely, substantive updates to you.

I have included the new schedule (attached as an MS Word document). I do appreciate that this revamped schedule puts pressure on you in terms of deadlines, but the project absolutely must be completed according to the new timeline. Although this schedule is tight, we are confident we can all work together toward meeting the project goal.

> Note the use of the word *do* here for emphasis.

Please feel free to contact me at any time with comments or questions.

Sincerely,
Ian McWhirter
PPB Canada Ltd.
88 Salmon Avenue
Brampton, ON L6W 3C5
T: 905.555.0987 x 2018
F: 905.555.0345
mcwhirter_i@ppb.ca

> In this context, "x" means *extension*.

Writing a Cover Letter

You may want to have students write a cover letter as part of the Job Project (page 110).

Go to Explore Online for an example of a cover letter written by a college student applying for a field placement.

A cover letter is a letter of introduction sent with a resumé to convince a potential employer that you are the ideal candidate for the job. The letter highlights who you are, why you want the job, and what you can bring to the company. It also highlights your hard skills and soft skills, and explains how these skills match the position's requirements and the company's culture.

Be sure to research the company to which you are applying: understanding its mission, philosophy, and culture will help you tailor your cover letter and resumé to the job. Always include a cover letter with your resumé unless the job posting specifically says not to.

Most cover letters and resumés are submitted online. Follow the submission instructions carefully: send both documents as email attachments unless otherwise specified and be sure to use the requested file type (e.g., Word or PDF).

Cover letter dos and don'ts	
Your cover letter should . . .	Your cover letter should not . . .
<ul><li>be a maximum of one page</li><li>include the job posting reference number if given</li><li>be addressed to a specific individual</li><li>be tailored to the specific job you are applying for (i.e., include key skills mentioned in the job ad)</li><li>highlight your hard and soft skills and explain how they match the position's requirements</li><li>contain action verbs to highlight your skills and accomplishments</li><li>demonstrate knowledge of the company's mission or philosophy and demonstrate how you fit in with the company's culture</li></ul>	<ul><li>simply repeat information contained in your resumé</li><li>contain false information</li><li>convey a negative attitude</li><li>contain informal language or contractions</li><li>contain any grammatical or spelling errors or typos</li></ul>

Hard skills are technical skills or knowledge that enable you to perform specific tasks. These skills can be defined, taught, and measured. Hard skills are often specific to industries or professions.

EXAMPLE proficiency in a foreign language, ability to use a specific software or database, ability to operate a particular type of machine or use certain tools

Soft skills are less tangible, interpersonal skills. Soft skills relate more to personality than knowledge or professional training. People with strong soft skills are highly valued by employers for their contribution to the work environment and productivity.

EXAMPLE teamwork; communication skills; organizational skills; decision making, creative thinking, conflict resolution, and problem-solving skills; work ethic; positivity; flexibility

Action verbs help highlight past responsibilities and accomplishments.

Action verbs to use in your resumé and cover letter				
accomplished	collaborated	enhanced	introduced	provided
applied	communicated	facilitated	managed	spearheaded
assisted	contributed	focused	obtained	strengthened
attained	coordinated	identified	participated	structured
authored	corresponded	improved	performed	surpassed
built	demonstrated	initiated	persuaded	upgraded

Adjectives help highlight personal and professional qualities and skills.

Adjectives to use in your resumé and cover letter				
attentive	diligent	enthusiastic	motivated	resilient
conscientious	dynamic	flexible	organized	skillful
consistent	energetic	hard-working	professional	trustworthy
determined	enterprising	industrious	reliable	

Job posting/advertisement for the example cover letter

Registered Nurse, Emergency

Northern General Hospital, Government of Nunavut–Iqaluit, NU

Please submit your application to Helen Arlooktoo with a cover letter and resumé quoting reference number: ABC12345.

The Emergency Registered Nurse is part of the nursing team, providing acute care to emergency department patients, responding to health issues with a culturally sensitive, holistic approach. The incumbent must work 12-hour rotating shifts and reports to the Nurse Manager of Emergency. The ER nurse is responsible for the safe, proficient provision of nursing services in collaboration with other health care team members and support groups responsible for providing care.

To succeed in this position, the incumbent requires a working knowledge of the following areas: emergency care, maternal and newborn, pediatric, psychiatry, gerontology, palliative, medicine, infectious disease control, and employee health and wellness.

The knowledge, skills, and abilities required for this job require a Bachelor of Science in Nursing from a recognized university and a minimum of one year recent experience in the emergency department. Candidates must be eligible to register with the Registered Nurses Association of the Northwest Territories and Nunavut. Current ACLS and CPR required.

Assets include: one-year ICU experience, ability to function in a cross-cultural setting, CTAS, TNCC, ENPC, Neonatal Resuscitation, EKG Interpretation, PALS, Non-Violent Crisis Intervention, Certification Nursing Practice Specialties, and basic computer skills.

Knowledge of Inuit language, communities, culture, land, and Inuit Qaujimajatuqangit is an asset.

Only those candidates selected for an interview will be contacted.

This sample job posting was adapted from a posting on indeed.com.

Cover letter example

Applicant's name, address, and contact information.

There is no comma between the number and the street.

Company/Institution's name

Include the reference number when requested.

Always try to address to a specific person using the appropriate courtesy title or first and last name. If not, use *Dear Sir or Madam* or *Dear Hiring Team*.

The first paragraph should explain why you are writing. Refer to the position, job ad, and where you found it. Include a sentence that shows your enthusiasm or states why you are the ideal candidate.

The second paragraph should focus on your skills (hard and soft), job-related accomplishments, and what makes you the best candidate for the job. It should make specific links to requirements mentioned in the job ad.

The concluding paragraph should establish a positive impression in the employer's mind. It should note your desire for a job interview and reiterate why the employer should hire you. You can also add *Thank you for your time and consideration*.

Other options: *Sincerely yours,* or *Regards,*

Thea Sands
333 Aspen Avenue
London, ON N5V 2H2
519-555-5555
tsands@gmail.com

1 January 2020

Northern General Hospital
1 Ring Road
Iqaluit, NU X0A 0H0

Subject: Application for Position of Emergency Registered Nurse (Reference # N123)

Dear Ms. Arlooktoo:

I am very interested in applying for the position of Emergency Registered Nurse, which I saw posted on indeed.com. I believe I am the ideal candidate for this position as I have been working in the emergency room of Victoria Hospital in London, Ontario since 2016 and am now ready to take on a new challenge.

I obtained my Bachelor of Science in Nursing and I am a licensed member of the College of Nurses of Ontario. I have knowledge and experience in a number of areas, including pediatrics and gerontology, as well as in the ER. I take a holistic approach to nursing and I subscribe to the *Journal of Holistic Nursing*. My education and professional experience have taught me to collaborate well with colleagues and patients from diverse cultural backgrounds. I have learned to adapt my care plan according to each patient's unique needs. I am a good team player and perform well in crisis situations, which is why management transferred me to the ER team at Victoria Hospital soon after I was hired. Finally, I am familiar with Inuit Qaujimajatuqangit and am very interested in deepening my understanding of Inuit language and culture.

I am excited to learn more about the opportunity to work in Northern Canada. I look forward to meeting you in person to discuss how my capabilities and devotion to my patients would make me a great addition to your community and health care team.

Sincerely,

Thea Sands

Writing a Resumé

Employers receive many resumés for each open position. To make an impression, your resumé must be clear, easy to read, and professional.

Resumé dos and don'ts	
Your resumé should . . .	Your resumé should not . . .
<ul><li>be a maximum of two pages</li><li>be tailored to the job you are applying for</li><li>make contact information visible</li><li>use key words listed in the job ad (Electronic scanners will look for them.)</li><li>include a summary of your strengths</li><li>highlight your hard skills and soft skills</li><li>contain action verbs</li></ul>	<ul><li>contain false information</li><li>simply repeat information contained in your cover letter</li><li>contain informal language or contractions</li><li>contain any grammatical or spelling errors or typos</li><li>include a list of references, unless the job posting specifically requests one</li></ul>

Resumé example

There are numerous resumé templates online. Choose one that best suits your needs. In addition, you should look at examples of resumés related to the specific job for which you are applying.

333 Aspen Avenue, London, ON N5V 2H2
519-555-555 • tsands@email.com

Thea Sands

OBJECTIVE

To obtain a position as a registered emergency nurse

EXPERIENCE

2016–present   **Victoria Hospital**   **London, ON**

Emergency Room Nurse

- Prioritize care based on severity of patient condition
- Take vital signs and administer medication
- Monitor patient health conditions
- Provide treatment

2014–2015   **Toronto Medical Centre**   **Toronto, ON**

Nurse

- Took vital signs
- Observed and monitored patient condition
- Maintained records
- Communicated with doctors

EDUCATION

2017   Ryerson University   Toronto, ON
Certificate in Aging and Gerontology

2016   Resuscitation Canada   Toronto, ON
Certificate in Advanced Cardiovascular Life Support (ALCS) and CPR

2012–2016   University of Toronto   Toronto, ON
Bachelor of Science in Nursing

PROFESSIONAL QUALIFICATION

Member of College of Nurses of Ontario

SKILLS

- EKG interpretation
- Crisis intervention skills
- Advanced computer skills
- Communication
- Leadership
- Attention to detail

Languages
English and French (fluent); Inuit (basic)

References
References are available upon request.

Applicant's address

For Experience and Education, list items in reverse chronological order.

Use present tense verbs for current jobs and past tense for past jobs.

Link skills to those listed in the job ad.

Do not give references until you are asked for them by the potential employer. Always make sure you have permission before including someone on your reference list.

Preparing for a Job Interview

Once a potential employer has read your cover letter and resumé, you may be contacted for a job interview. It is essential to be well prepared. In addition to researching the potential employer and preparing for specific questions they may ask, you may want to review (and practise answering) the 10 most common interview questions (regardless of industry).

Top 10 common job interview questions

1. What can you tell us about yourself?

2. Why did you apply for this position?

3. Why should we hire you?

4. What are your strengths?

5. What are your weaknesses?

6. Describe a time that you handled a difficult situation involving people.

7. Tell us about a mistake you made and how you handled it.

8. What are your career objectives for the next five years?

9. What are your salary expectations?

10. Do you have any questions for us?

Types of job interviews

There are several different types of job interviews. Research what kinds of interviews are commonly used in your field of study or future career. You may be interviewed using one—or a combination—of these techniques:

- **One-to-one interview**: the applicant is interviewed in person by one person.
- **Panel interview**: the applicant is interviewed in person by more than one person at the same time.
- **Remote video (or telephone) interview**: the applicant is interviewed using video conferencing technology like Skype, Google Hangouts, or FaceTime.
- **Group interview**: the applicant is interviewed in a group, along with other applicants.
- **Chat or lunch interview**: the interview is conducted in an informal setting, like a conversation over coffee or lunch.
- **Impromptu career fair interview**: the applicant has a 10- to 15-minute on-the-spot interview in which he or she must convince the recruiter to grant a full interview.
- **Technical interview**: the applicant is asked to perform workplace tasks to demonstrate competence.
- **Behavioural interview**: the applicant is asked to describe examples to demonstrate their skills and show how they behave in various situations (especially difficult or challenging situations). Typical prompts include "Tell me about a time when . . ." or "Describe an experience in which you . . ."

Writing a Report

A report presents research findings, analyses, and recommendations. Like an essay, a report has a thesis statement or central idea, but unlike an essay, it is organized with headings and subheadings. In addition, it will often include graphs, tables, or other visuals to present the results or other data.

Survey report example

Social Engagement among the College Student Population

Abstract

The goal of this study was to investigate college students' beliefs and behaviours concerning community engagement. Community engagement is here defined as getting involved and working collaboratively with people to improve conditions and solve problems that negatively affect the common good. A survey was conducted on students' attitudes and behaviours in relation to their engagement at various levels of society. The results showed that students claim that being involved in society is important to them; however, their actual level of involvement is surprisingly low. Moreover, the survey results suggest that many students are unsure about what actions they can take to effect positive social change. This report concludes that more research is required to determine the reason for college students' low level of social engagement and that appropriate measures should to be taken to increase students' self-motivation to engage more at all levels of society.

Introduction

One of the main goals of college is to help students develop into responsible citizens who will improve society. To this end, colleges create a social environment similar to a state in which students can participate in various social activities such as playing on a sports team, participating in social justice activities, discussing and taking political actions, and more. This study examined college students' attitudes and behaviours regarding their engagement in their college environment and at the community, national, and international level. It was hypothesized that college students believe social engagement to be important and that students are more involved in their school communities than other levels of society. Both hypotheses proved true. However, despite students' claims that social engagement was important to them, their actual level of engagement suggests otherwise.

Method

Research was conducted over a two-week period using an online questionnaire posted on SurveyMonkey. Eighty-two college students, 40 women and 42 men, answered 10 questions about their attitudes and behaviours regarding social engagement. The survey used multiple choice questions, rating and ranking scales, and open-ended questions.

Results

The results showed that almost all students rate being involved in society as *important* or *very important*; however, when asked to rate their current level of engagement in their school environment, only 30% of respondents reported a high level of engagement. Moreover, only 26% reported engagement at the municipal or national level. The actions most taken by respondents who supported a cause in the six months prior to the survey were volunteer work (50%) and financial donations (28%). The actions least taken were organizing an event (7%) and participating in a protest (7%). When asked what they could do to effect positive change in their school environment, some students gave answers such as "petition for the addition of a sign language course" and "participate in more school activities." To improve citizens' lives at the municipal level, they mentioned "fight to improve public transportation" and "help decrease pollution." At the

---

Title

The **abstract** summarizes the key points, findings, and conclusion of the report. It gives the reader a preview of the complete document and defines essential terms when necessary.

The **introduction** provides background information and context for the subject.

It explains the purpose/reason(s) for the study. The introduction ends with a clear thesis statement that is the basis of the complete report.

Thesis statement

The **body** is subdivided into sections consisting of method/process; results/findings; and discussion/analysis and interpretation of the results.

national and international levels, students mentioned "fight for equality for all" and "participate in elections." However, the percentage of respondents who chose N/A (not applicable) when asked how they could effect positive change was 50% at the school level, 61% at the municipal level, and 33% at the national and international level.

Discussion

Students' level of actual engagement is surprisingly low considering that all students claim that social engagement is important or very important. Another significant finding is the high percentage of students who have no opinions to offer (in relation to all levels of society) as to how they can effect positive change. These findings indicate that students do in fact have a positive attitude toward social engagement and thus, most likely, a willingness to engage. However, this positive attitude and willingness to engage do not seem enough to motivate the great majority of students to take action and actually get involved in activities that aim to effect positive social change.

Limitations of the study

One limitation of the study was the choice of some of the survey questions, which rendered some of the survey results ineffective. For example, the question "Which of the following do you believe is the worst problem in society?" offered answer choices such as texting while driving, gaming addiction, and driving under the influence. Neither the question nor the answer choices provided insight into students' beliefs or behaviours regarding community engagement. Another limitation was the number of respondents. The goal was to have a minimum of 300 respondents, but only 82 students completed the survey. More respondents would have meant more statistically significant results.

Conclusion

> The **conclusion** reiterates the topic and purpose of the report. It sums up the main ideas, evaluates the results, and makes recommendations.

It is recommended that additional research be done to determine the reason for college students' low level of engagement and to find out what can be done to motivate them to more fully engage at various levels of society. Creating more opportunities for college students to participate in society is good, but the key is to create in them a self-desire to seek out and create their own opportunities for effecting positive social change.

Writing a Blog

You might want to have students research and review blogs related to their fields of study or future careers.

A blog is a regularly updated text (or series of texts) on a web page. It is generally written by an individual—but can be a group effort—in an informal or casual style.

Before starting a blog, read the following advice.

1. Your blog should have a well-defined focus. Choose what you want to write about (e.g., food, fashion, music, or work).

2. Keep the tone conversational and casual, like talking to a friend. A blog should be easy to read and relatable; it can be written how you speak.

3. Write short paragraphs.

4. Invite readers to be part of the experience. Ask questions and encourage responses from your public.

5. A blog can be a creative piece of work. Have fun with your writing and don't be afraid to take risks.

Speaking Strategies

Giving an Effective Oral Presentation

You will need to give oral presentations in college, at university, and possibly at work. The more you prepare and practise, the better you will become at oral presentations.

Preparing your presentation

Review the presentation requirements carefully before preparing any content. Choose your subject, brainstorm ideas, then narrow down your topic and begin your research. Once you're ready to begin developing content, structure your presentation into an Introduction, Body, and Conclusion.

Introduction

- Use an effective opening to capture the audience's attention and get them interested in your subject. Consider beginning your presentation by
  - referring to the familiar—making the topic relevant to your listeners
  - involving the audience (e.g., by asking a question)
  - starting with an interesting, unusual, or funny anecdote, quotation, or statistic

- When you have the attention and interest of your audience, give a clear outline of your talk.

  EXAMPLE I am going to define dystonia and talk about the symptoms, causes, and treatments of this rather mysterious, but not-so-uncommon, disease. I will conclude with my personal analysis of which direction future research of dystonia should take.

Go to Explore Online for examples of each attention-getting technique.

You may act out the example introductions for your students and have them guess which technique you are using for each one. Or have students work in teams to complete the worksheet.

Body

- Organize your ideas into three to five main points or sections.

  EXAMPLE 1. definition, 2. symptoms, 3. causes, 4. treatments, 5. future research

- Make clear transitions between your ideas. Provide internal summaries of each main point or section before you move on.

  EXAMPLE So those were the main symptoms of dystonia. Now let's examine some possible causes.

Conclusion

Deliver an effective closing with transition words like "In conclusion" or "To sum up." Do not end abruptly—your audience should not be left asking, "Oh, is the presentation finished? Should I clap now?"

Your conclusion may do one or more of the following:

- briefly summarize the main points
- end with a prediction, a recommendation, some advice, or a call to action
- refer to the interesting, unusual, or funny anecdote, quotation, or statistic that you used in your introduction

Delivering your presentation

For more information about acceptable and unacceptable cue cards, see below.

- Be sure to practise and time yourself before the day of your presentation. Deliver your presentation in front of others and ask for feedback.
- Glance at cue cards or your slides (with key words only) to guide you through your talk—but do not read from or constantly refer to your cards or slides as you speak.
- Speak clearly and at an appropriate pace—not too fast nor too slow.
- Monitor the understanding and interest of your audience and adjust your speech accordingly by stressing some words, speaking more loudly or slowly to emphasize key points, gesturing, repeating, or moving around when necessary.
- Make eye contact with members of the audience. Do not focus entirely on one person or one spot. If you wish to avoid direct eye contact, look between audience members.
- Maintain positive body language: stand straight, act confident, look interested and happy to be there. Look as though you're saying, "Listen to me—I have something interesting and important to share."

Using visual aids

Using visual aids, such as a slide presentation, can help ensure that your ideas are communicated clearly to the audience in an engaging manner. Another type of visual aid—one that serves you, the speaker, rather than the audience—is the cue card. Both types of visual aids are discussed below.

Cue cards

Presentations should be carefully prepared but not memorized. Know the content but keep the delivery fresh. Prepare cue cards with key words, statistics, dates, or names to help you remember essential points and how you've organized them. Do not write out your entire presentation and do not read from your cue cards; glance at them only as necessary.

Acceptable cue card	Unacceptable cue card

Topic: Dystonia
 	
1. Definition
  • neurological
  • main types a & b
  • + define affected parts
 	
2. Symptoms
  • loss of a + b + c + d
  • aching in . . .
	Topic: Dystonia
	
	1. Definition
	  • Dystonia is a neurological disorder.
	  • There are two types: focal and generalized. Focal dystonia is localized. Generalized is over a large area of the body. It may affect your neck, back, tongue, limbs.
	
	2. Symptoms
	  • It causes loss of control of affected body part(s).
	  • Can cause a loss of feeling in affected area
	  • Or a loss of strength and flexibility
	  • Can also cause aching of joints & muscles

Slide presentations

Unlike cue cards, slide presentations are prepared for the audience. Using slides (or other visuals) effectively can leave a lasting impression on your audience, so plan your slides (and other visual support) carefully to ensure they make your presentation better, not worse.

Go to Explore Online to see a PowerPoint presentation on creating effective visual aids using various software (e.g., PowerPoint or Prezi).

Slide presentation dos and don'ts	
Your slides should . . .	Your slides should not . . .
• use key words only (maximum five points per slide) • include pictures, charts, or other visuals • be proofread carefully for correct grammar, vocabulary, and spelling • be written in a large, clear, simple font (18 to 48 pts) • have a consistent background with a neutral background colour that's easy on the eyes • make use of high-contrast colours (e.g., light background/dark text or dark background/light text—white on black is best)	• contain long, complete sentences • include the complete text of what you plan to say • have mistakes or typos • overuse bullets • use distracting graphics or too much animation • be written in small, difficult-to-read font • have different backgrounds for every slide or complex patterned backgrounds or images that render the text difficult to read • have a low-contrast colour scheme (hard to read)

English stress patterns

During your oral presentations, it is essential that you pronounce key words correctly. Part of correct pronunciation means putting word stress in the correct place. A stressed syllable is emphasized more and longer than unstressed syllables in multisyllable words. In English, stress is placed on individual syllables of single words. Primary stress indicates the loudest and longest syllable(s) in a word; secondary stress indicates syllables that are slightly stressed, but not as much as those with primary stress. Primary stress within a word is determined by the structure of the word and its parts (the root, prefixes, and suffixes).

Common stress patterns in English

Only primary stress is shown in the following examples (not secondary stress). The syllable with primary stress is indicated with capital letters.

1. With **two-syllable words**, the stress most often falls on the first syllable (e.g., **le**gal, **pri**son). However, there are a significant number of exceptions (especially verbs).

2. With **compound nouns**, the stress always falls on the first syllable (e.g., **foot**print, **scape**goat).

3. With **two-syllable words that can function as a noun or a verb**, the stress changes depending on the part of speech.
   a) When the word is a *noun*, the first syllable is stressed (e.g., an **in**crease, a **re**cord).
   b) When the word is a *verb*, the second syllable is stressed (e.g., to in**crease**, to re**cord**).

4. Adding certain **suffixes** can result in a stress shift.
   a) **Certain suffixes receive stress themselves.** These are often suffixes that have come from French, such as *-aire, -ee, -eer, -ese, -esque, -ette, -eur/-euse, -ique, -oon*, and *-et/-ey*.

      EXAMPLES   employ**ee**, pio**neer**, tech**nique**

To practise pronouncing words and stressing the appropriate syllables, see Unit 4, Pronunciation, page 83.

In dictionaries, primary stress is often indicated by a short vertical line at the top left of the stressed syllable and secondary stress is indicated with a short vertical line at the bottom left of the syllable. (Sometimes the syllables with primary stress are capitalized.)

EXAMPLES

ˌpre-ˌsen-ˈta-tion

co-ˈm(m)e-mo-ˌrate

b) **Some suffixes cause the stress to shift to the syllable just before the suffix.**
These include *-eous*, *-graphy*, *-logy*, *-meter* and the following suffixes that start with *-i* or *-u*: *-ial*, *-ian*, *-ic*, *-ical*, *-ious*, *-ity*, *-ion*, *-ual*. (Exceptions that do not affect word stress: *-ist*, *-ism*, *-ize*, and *-ing*)

> **EXAMPLES** ad**van**tage → advan**tag**eous
>
> **pho**to → pho**to**graphy/photo**graph**ic
>
> tech**nique** → **tech**nical/techni**cal**ity
>
> al**lege** → alle**ga**tion
>
> **cri**minal → crimina**lis**tic/crimi**no**logy
> but **cri**minal*ist*/**cri**minal*ize* (no change)

c) With the suffix *-ate*, the stress depends on how many syllables there are in the word.

With most two-syllable *-ate* verbs, the stress is on the second syllable (do**nate**, cre**ate**, se**date**).

With three-syllable *-ate* verbs, the stress is on the first syllable (**sit**uate, **gra**duate, **el**evate).

With four-syllable *-ate* verbs, the stress is on the second syllable (com**mu**nicate, dis**se**minate, ac**cum**mulate).

With five-syllable *-ate* verbs, the stress is on the third syllable (differ**en**tiate, reha**bil**itate, rein**vig**orate).

These rules are helpful, but the best way to learn the correct stress of English words is through practice and repetition.

Vocabulary Strategies

Building your vocabulary is an essential step in the process of learning a language. One of the best ways to build your vocabulary is by reading. To read effectively, you should not stop and look up every new word in a dictionary. Doing so is not only slow but often unnecessary. Practise using the following strategies to deduce the meaning of unknown words without having to check them in a dictionary.

Finding the Meaning of Unknown Words

Word clues

Sometimes clues within the word itself can help you guess the meaning of an unknown word. Here are three ways to get a clue to meaning from the word itself.

1. Determine if the word is a **cognate**. If so, check if the meaning of that word in your first language fits. The majority of English/French cognates have the same meaning in both languages.
2. Identify the **part of speech**: is the word is a noun, verb, adjective, adverb, or other?
3. Check if there is a **prefix** (e.g., *dis-*, *ir-*), **word root** (e.g., *carcin*, *pedo*), **suffix** (*-pathy*, *-phile*) or **word within a word** (e.g., *white-collar*) that gives a clue to meaning.

Context clues

Use context to guess the meaning of unknown words. Check to see if any information given within the sentence (or in preceding or following sentences) provides a clue to a word's meaning.

Here are a few ways to find clues within the context of the sentence.

1. Look for **definitions**. Authors sometimes provide definitions within the text to help explain difficult words. The word *or* can sometimes introduce a definition.

   > **EXAMPLE**   Psychosomatic disorders (or illnesses caused by psychological factors) should not be confused with imagined disorders.

2. Look for **synonyms** (words with similar meanings) or **antonyms** (words with opposite meanings) near the unknown word. Writers often give a synonym to explain key terms, or an antonym to define a word by what it is not.
3. Look for **examples** or **any other information** that may help you deduce the meaning of the unknown word. Authors sometimes provide examples to help explain key terms and concepts.

Dictionaries

Occasionally, there are no helpful word or context clues and using a dictionary is the only way to discover the meaning of an unknown word. Many words have more than one meaning, however, so check the context in which it is used to ensure you've found the correct definition.

Dictionaries provide more than just the definition of a word. A dictionary entry can also give you the following information about a word:

- pronunciation, including syllables and word stress (Printed dictionaries use the phonetic alphabet to show pronunciation and many online dictionaries provide an option to hear the pronunciation.)
- part of speech (e.g., n for "noun" or adj for "adjective")
- whether a verb is transitive or intransitive (transitive verbs require an object, e.g., *send* + something, while intransitive verbs do not need an object, e.g., *talk*)
- whether a noun is countable or uncountable (e.g., research—uncountable; study—countable)
- synonyms and antonyms
- collocations (words that are often used together with the given word, e.g., collocations with the verb *break* include *break the law, break the news, break a promise, break a leg*)

Cognates are words from two languages that share a common origin, look the same, and have similar meanings.

Examples of English/French cognates are *attention* and *intelligent*. Sometimes the spelling can vary slightly (e.g., *pourcent/percent*, *adress/address*).

Be careful of false cognates—words that look similar but have different meanings in the two languages.

GG For more information about cognates and false cognates, see Grammar Guide, page 218.

GG For more information about prefixes, word roots, and suffixes, see Grammar Guide, page 213.

Building Your Vocabulary

The key to building your vocabulary is to immerse yourself in the target language as much as possible and make effective use of practice and repetition. The following tools can help you do just that.

Word lists and quizzes

All the word lists mentioned here are available free but you must properly cite the source site.

Making use of word lists can help you build your vocabulary.

The New General Service List (NGSL) is a list of the most commonly used words in English. Studies show that if learners are familiar with these words and their word families, they can understand 92 percent of most general English language texts.

Other useful word lists are the *New Academic Word List (NAWL)*, the *TOEIC Service List (TSL)*, the *Business Service List (BSL)*, and the *New General Service List Spoken (NGSL-S)*.

Most of the word list sites above also provide quizzes. To find out whether you know the most frequently used words in English, search online using the key words *vocabulary size online quizzes* or *lextutor*.

Word form charts

Learning the various forms of a word will help you learn many words at once. To keep track of word forms, create a chart like the one below. Dictionaries often list word forms to help you fill out your chart.

Word and meaning	Verb	Noun	Adjective	Adverb
innovate—to introduce change and new ideas	innovate	innovator innovation	innovative	innovatively

Vocabulary graphic organizer

For more information about graphic organizers, see page 128.

You can ask students to create graphic organizers related to their fields of study and have them define the words and explain the relationships between the words to their classmates in a small group.

A vocabulary graphic organizer is a visual way to build vocabulary on a topic. They are effective for building field-specific vocabulary. When you create a graphic organizer, you make links, or associations, between new words and words you already know. The more you think about and use these words, the stronger these links become and the more you will expand your vocabulary.

To make a vocabulary graphic organizer, think of a word (e.g., *linguistics*) and put it in a box at the centre of your page. Now think of a related word and connect it to the first word with a line. Keep adding new words to the page, along with connecting lines that show the relationships between the terms in a logical way. Stop when you have reached your targeted number of words or can no longer think of new words.

Graphic organizer created by a student in linguistics

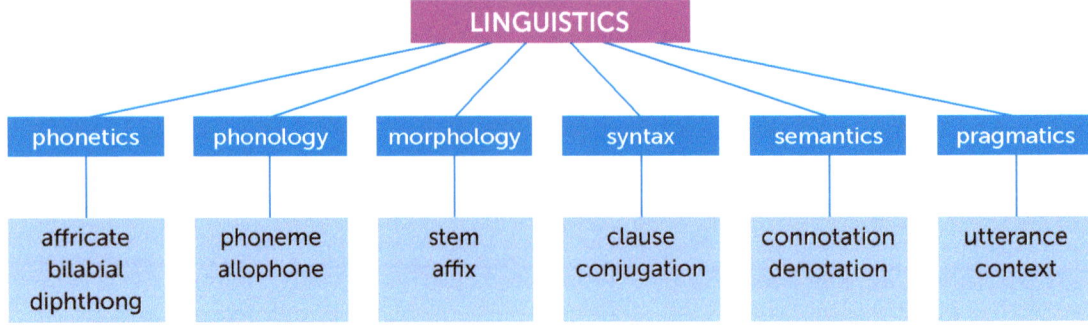

Grammar Guide

CHAPTER 1
Sentence Structure

You might try walking into the classroom and making these statements one by one to see the students' reactions to each.

Consider how you would react to the following statements and what you would say in response:

Your teacher walks into the room at the beginning of class and says, "While I was on my way to school this morning."

Your teacher walks into the room at the beginning of class and says, "I had a car accident."

In response to the second statement, you would probably say something like "Are you okay?" or "What happened?"

However, your reaction to the first statement might be something like "Yeah, okay . . . What about it?"

You would be understandably confused because the first statement is an incomplete thought that doesn't make sense on its own—it is not a complete sentence.

A sentence expresses a complete thought. A sentence must have a subject and a complete verb. The subject is generally what the sentence is about; it is the doer of the action (or agent of the verb). The verb indicates what the subject does or is (i.e., the subject's action or state).

Independent and Dependent Clauses

To understand different types of sentences, you need to understand clauses. A **clause** is a group of words that contains a subject and a complete verb. There are two types of clauses: independent and dependent.

An **independent clause** expresses a complete thought and can stand on its own as a sentence.

EXAMPLE   He got a promotion.

A **dependent** (or **subordinate**) **clause** does not express a complete thought—it depends on another (independent) clause to make its meaning clear. The dependent clause starts with a subordinating conjunction and can come before the independent clause or after it.

EXAMPLE   **Because** he works very hard, . . .
                      subordinating
                      conjunction

                . . . **because** he works very hard.

You may want to point out that dependent clauses can also be verbless, in which a verb is not stated but implied.

Coordinating conjunctions

A coordinating conjunction is used to connect two independent clauses into one sentence. There are seven coordinating conjunctions (listed here in order of most frequent usage): *and, but, so, or, nor, for, yet*. Put a comma at the end of the first independent clause before the coordinating conjunction.

EXAMPLE   She wants to go to university, **but** she is not sure which program to study.

For more information about punctuation used with coordinating conjunctions, see Grammar Appendix 4, page 227.

To remember the coordinating conjunctions, think of the acronym FANBOYS: *for, and, nor, but, or, yet, so.*

Coordinating conjunction	Use	Example
and	adds an idea	Students must pay half, **and** the school will pay the rest.
but	shows a contrast	I worked last summer, **but** I won't work this summer.
so	shows a consequence	The course is compulsory, **so** it is always full.
or	introduces an alternative	You can bring a lunch, **or** you can buy a meal in the cafeteria.
nor	adds another negative statement	The candidate doesn't have the education, **nor** does he have enough work experience.
for	gives a reason	She quit her job, **for** the working conditions were awful.
yet	introduces a contrast or contradiction	That coffee shop is so expensive, **yet** it is always full.

Note the special construction used with *nor* (auxiliary + subject + verb). Use the verb *do* as an auxiliary when the clause contains a one-word verb.

Exercise 1

Use one of the coordinating conjunctions to add an independent clause to the following sentences. Use a different conjunction each time. Use proper punctuation in the new sentence.

1. You should study for the next exam. _____

2. He was not dressed appropriately. _____

3. You seem to be having a bad day. _____

Subordinating conjunctions

A subordinating conjunction is used to introduce a dependent clause. It indicates the relationship between the idea expressed in the dependent clause and that expressed in the independent clause (cause, effect, time, etc.). Put a comma after a dependent clause when it precedes the independent clause.

EXAMPLE   **Because** he works very hard, he got a promotion.

In most cases, there is no comma before the subordinating conjunction when it follows the independent clause (except when the writer wishes to indicate an intentional pause at that point in the sentence).

EXAMPLE   He got a promotion **because** he works very hard.

For more information about punctuation used with subordinating conjunctions, see Grammar Appendix 4, page 228.

Subordinating conjunction	Use	Example
as	shows a reason	I must take the day off work **as** I am feeling sick.
because		I must take the day off work **because** I am feeling sick.
since		I must take the day off work **since** I am feeling sick.
although	shows a concession or contrast; makes main idea seem surprising or unlikely	She did not get the job **although** she was qualified.
even though		She did not get the job **even though** she was qualified.
though		She did not get the job **though** she was qualified.
even if		She may not get the job **even if** she was qualified.
as long as	indicates a condition	**As long as** you apply on time, you will be considered.
if		**If** you apply on time, you will be considered.
provided that		**Provided that** you apply on time, you will be considered.
unless*		**Unless** you apply late, you will be considered.
whereas	shows a contrast	My brothers are very tall **whereas** I am short.
while		**While** I am short, my brothers are very tall.
once	indicates sequence/time	You will start to work full time **once** your training is done.
until		You cannot work full time **until** your training is done.
whenever		I get a headache **whenever** I don't get enough sleep.
while		You had two calls **while** you were out.

Note how *unless* is used differently than the other subordinating conjunctions indicating condition.

There are conflicting views on whether to use a comma before *while* and *whereas* when they begin a dependent clause that follows an independent clause. Use a comma if it helps to clarify your statement.

Exercise 2

Fill in the blanks with an appropriate subordinating conjunction from the chart. More than one answer may be possible.

1. The company had to lay me off <u>even though/although/though</u> my superiors were pleased with my performance.

2. <u>Whereas/While</u> economics deals with the consumption of goods and services, ergonomics is related to people's work environments.

3. The job is yours <u>as long as/provided that</u> you pass the criminal record check.

4. I didn't get accepted into the program <u>because/since/as</u> the university received my application after the deadline.

5. <u>Even if/Unless</u> I pull an all-nighter, I won't be able to finish the assignment on time.

When reviewing the answers, it is helpful to mention all possible correct answers.

Both *even if* and *unless* work in Question 5, but be sure to point out the difference in meaning between the two sentences.

Exercise 3

Choose a dependent clause from Column B to follow each independent clause in Column A. Write the appropriate punctuation required between the two clauses in the punctuation box. If no punctuation is required, put an X in the box.

Column A Independent clause	Answer (a−e)	Punctuation required	Column B Dependent clause
1. The store gets busier during the Christmas season	e	,	a) since my own computer crashed.
2. I enjoyed my previous job	d	X	b) yet she prefers to take the subway to work.
3. I had to complete my research at the library	a	X	c) whereas others would rather live in residence.
4. My roommate has a car	b	,	d) until it was no longer challenging.
5. Some university students prefer to share an apartment	c	X or ,	e) so we hire extra employees during that period.

Sentence Types

There are four types of sentences: simple, compound, complex, and compound-complex.

Sentence type	Contains	Example
simple	one independent clause	I have a master's degree.
compound	two or more independent clauses	IC IC I completed my bachelor's degree in Ontario, but I did my master's degree in Quebec.
complex	one independent clause and at least one dependent clause	DC IC After I received my bachelor's degree, I moved to Quebec.
compound-complex	two or more independent clauses and at least one dependent clause	IC IC I completed my bachelor's degree in Ontario, but then I moved to Quebec because I wanted to do a master's degree at DC Concordia University.

Exercise 4

Underline the independent clause(s) in each sentence and put a wavy line under any dependent clauses. Then indicate the sentence type: S = simple, C = compound, CX = complex, CC = compound-complex.

1. You should take a night course if you want to improve your skills, and you would have a better chance of a promotion   CC

2. Students in the master's program can register for the thesis option, or they can register for the course-based option.   C

3. Most of us don't start off with our ideal job.   S

4. You didn't receive my email because I sent it to the wrong address.   CX

Sentence Structure Errors

In fiction, an author may use an unusual or grammatically incorrect sentence structure for literary effect.

Sentence structure errors make your ideas difficult to understand and your writing appear less professional. To avoid these errors, make sure a clause always contains both a subject and verb and be careful with punctuation when writing compound and complex sentences. The major sentence structure errors to avoid are incomplete sentences (including sentence fragments), run-ons, and comma splices.

Incomplete sentences (including sentence fragments)

A sentence fragment occurs when a dependent clause is mistakenly treated as an independent clause (i.e., it's punctuated as a complete sentence but it is not connected to an independent clause). To fix a sentence fragment, connect the dependent clause to an independent clause (and add appropriate punctuation if necessary). Sometimes, you can simply drop the subordinating conjunction to create a complete sentence.

Incorrect   ~~Since your resumé is out of date.~~

Correct   Since your resumé is out of date, you need to revise it.

Correct   Your resumé is out of date.

An incomplete sentence (but not a fragment) can also occur when a clause is missing either a subject or a verb.

Incorrect   ~~The job no longer available.~~

Correct   The job *is* no longer available.

Run-on sentences

A run-on sentence occurs when two independent clauses are incorrectly joined without any punctuation. To fix a run-on sentence, put a period or semicolon between the two independent clauses, or add a conjunction (with appropriate punctuation) to connect the two independent clauses.

Incorrect   ~~The job interview was stressful they asked many difficult questions.~~

Correct   The job interview was stressful. They asked many difficult questions.

             The job interview was stressful; they asked many difficult questions.

             The job interview was stressful because they asked many difficult questions.

Comma splices

Do not overuse the semicolon. Connect two independent clauses with a semicolon only if the idea in the second independent clause is closely related to and somehow completes the information given in the first.

A comma splice occurs when two independent clauses are incorrectly joined together by a comma. To fix a comma splice, change the comma between the two independent clauses to a period or semicolon.

Incorrect   ~~You've done a lot of volunteer work, you should put it on your resumé.~~

Correct   You've done a lot of volunteer work. You should put it on your resumé.

             You've done a lot of volunteer work; you should put it on your resumé.

Exercise 5

Indicate the type of sentence structure error in each sentence below. Then rewrite each sentence to correct the error. Add words where necessary. Write C (Correct) if the sentence contains no error.

INC = incomplete sentence
INC/SF = sentence fragment
RO = run-on
CS = comma splice

1. The position is only part time, there are no full-time positions available.   **CS**

   The position is only part time. There are no full-time positions available.

   There are other possible answers in addition to those given.

2. To complete a doctorate degree usually two to four years.   **INC**

   *To complete a doctorate degree usually **takes** two to four years.*

3. My husband had to go on workers' compensation because he hurt his back at work.   **C**

4. My father retired early he was only 50 years old when he took his retirement.   **RO**

   *My father retired early. **He** was only 50 years old when he took his retirement.*

5. Even though purchasing a membership card costs about $100 per year.   **INC/SF**

   *Even though purchasing a membership card costs about $100 per year, **the benefits are worth it**.*

Conjunctive adverbs

A conjunctive adverb is used to connect two independent clauses. Its function is to show the relationship between the ideas and provide a smooth transition to help the reader move logically from one idea to the next.

Conjunctive adverbs are sometimes referred to as **transition words** or **transitional expressions**.

A semicolon (or period) is placed before the conjunctive adverb and a comma usually follows it.

> **EXAMPLE** I enjoy playing tennis; however, I prefer swimming.
>   independent   conjunctive   independent
>   clause   adverb   clause

Conjunctive adverb	Use	Example
furthermore	adds an idea	The apartment is furnished; **furthermore**, it is close to the subway.
moreover		The apartment is furnished; **moreover**, it is close to the subway.
in addition		The apartment is furnished; **in addition**, it is close to the subway.
however	shows a concession or contrast	He apologized for his behaviour; **however**, she still felt angry.
nevertheless		He apologized for his behaviour; **nevertheless**, she still felt angry.
nonetheless		He apologized for his behaviour; **nonetheless**, she still felt angry.
on the other hand		The job was boring; **on the other hand**, it paid well.
indeed	shows emphasis	You did a great job; **indeed**, you surpassed all expectations.
in fact		She is a great student; **in fact**, she received a scholarship.
for example	introduces an example	Many animals make good pets; **for example**, a ferret is fun.
for instance		Many animals make good pets; **for instance**, a ferret is fun.
consequently	indicates a consequence	The storm is bad; **consequently**, many flights have been cancelled.
hence		The storm is bad; **hence**, many flights have been cancelled.
therefore		The storm is bad; **therefore**, many flights have been cancelled.
thus		The storm is bad; **thus**, many flights have been cancelled.
otherwise		I must work during the summers; **otherwise**, I can't afford tuition.
meanwhile	indicates a time sequence	You set the table; **meanwhile**, I'll prepare the salad.
subsequently		I saved money all year; **subsequently**, I was able to go on a trip.
then		We'll finish the meeting; **then**, we can go out for lunch.

Hence is more formal than some of the other options.

Otherwise indicates the consequence if the condition is *not* met.

In this example, it is not essential to use a comma after *then*. For ease of readability, this comma could be considered superfluous and removed.

Conjunctive adverbs are sometimes used in the middle of a clause. In such cases, the adverb should be placed between commas—except in the case of a short clause or where no pause is desired within the sentence.

EXAMPLE   The company went bankrupt. The news of its bankruptcy, however, was not a total surprise.

Exercise 6

Fill in the blanks with an appropriate conjunctive adverb from the chart. More than one answer may be possible.

1. The new employee was lazy; _consequently/hence/therefore/thus_, she got fired.

2. It is an excellent job offer; _however/nevertheless/nonetheless_, I am not going to accept the job.

3. You misunderstood. _____ _In fact_ _____, I am majoring in languages, not literature.

4. This project is going to require strict adherence to deadlines; _____ _otherwise_ _____, we won't be able to complete it on time.

5. Our supervisor said to take our time finishing the report; _____ _subsequently/then_ _____, he changed his mind and said it was urgent.

Review Exercises

1. Fill in the blanks with the correct word from the box below. If more than one word is appropriate, write all correct answers. Check sentence punctuation for a clue to the answers.

although	even though	since	thus
because	for	so	whereas
but	however	therefore	while
consequently			

a) The two brothers are so different! _Whereas/While/Although_ Bob is quite hard-working, John is extremely lazy.

b) I failed the final exam, _____ _so_ _____ I had to retake the course.

c) I got called in for a job interview. _____ _However,_ _____ I didn't get the job.

d) I have to work a lot of overtime, _____ _for_ _____ I need money.

e) _____ _Although/Even though_ _____ my boss wouldn't give me a raise, I'm not mad at her.

2. Correct any sentence fragments, run-ons, and comma splices in the following paragraph. Also, add any missing punctuation.

> Humour is very important in my life, indeed I believe that humour attracts and creates positivity. For example, at work I'm always laughing, it improves my co-workers' moods. Moreover I sometimes volunteer at a seniors' residence I think it's good to joke with the patients it helps to reduce their stress. Even though it's difficult in certain situations. I always try to maintain a sense of humour. Because humour helps me get through painful or stressful situations.

Communicative Activity

With a partner, choose a mix of eight to ten conjunctions (coordinating or subordinating) and conjunctive adverbs from this unit and make a quiz for your classmates. You may include any type of question, including fill-in-the-blank, multiple choice, find the errors, match words and meanings, and so on. Choose conjunctions and adverbs that are new to you or that you seldom use. Provide an answer key.

CHAPTER 2

Commas, Semicolons, and Colons

Comma (,)

1. Use a comma to separate three or more words or phrases in a list.

    EXAMPLE   Amelie has applied to McDonald's, Wendy's, and Burger King.

2. Use a comma after an introductory word or phrase.

    EXAMPLE   Last night, I rewrote my resumé.

3. Use a comma between the day and the year when writing a date.

    EXAMPLE   The Dominion of Canada was created on July 1, 1867.

4. Use a comma following the closing in formal business letters.

    EXAMPLE   Sincerely,

5. Use a comma before and after non-essential words, phrases, or clauses in a sentence to set these non-essential elements off from the rest of the sentence.

    EXAMPLE   Work, no matter what field it is in, should be stimulating.

6. Use a comma after a dependent clause that comes at the beginning of a sentence.

	dependent clause independent clause
EXAMPLE	When I wait until the last minute to study, I don't often do well on exams.

    NOTE If the clauses are reversed—if the dependent clause follows the independent clause—a comma is not needed.

    EXAMPLE   I don't often do well on exams when I wait until the last minute to study.

    Never use a comma to combine two independent clauses. Doing so creates an error called a comma splice, which can create confusion for the reader.

    Incorrect   ~~Maryse wants to get a job, she likes manual labour.~~

    Correct   Maryse wants to get a job. She likes manual labour.

7. Use a comma to set off a direct quotation from the speaker's tag.

    EXAMPLE   Mariah said, "I don't know what to do."

A clause is a group of words that contains a subject and a verb. A dependent clause does not express a complete idea and cannot stand on its own as a sentence; it must always be connected to an independent clause to complete its meaning. An independent clause expresses a complete thought and can stand on its own. For more information about dependent and independent clauses, see Grammar Guide, page 152.

Semicolon (;)

Use a semicolon to connect two independent clauses when the idea in the second clause is closely related to that in the first clause.

> **EXAMPLE**   I must choose a university to go to next year; the choice is not going to be easy.

When connecting two independent clauses with a conjunctive adverb, use a semicolon before the adverb and a comma after it. Do not capitalize the first letter of the word that follows the semicolon.

> **EXAMPLE**   I applied to many companies; however, I haven't had any calls for an interview.

GG For a list of conjunctive adverbs, see Grammar Guide, page 157.

OCAD University, Toronto, ON

Colon (:)

1. Use a colon to introduce an item, list of items, or explanation preceded by an independent clause.

   > **EXAMPLE**   When Leonard was young, he wanted to be many things: an electrician, a doctor, and a firefighter.

   > **EXAMPLE**   I quit the job for one reason: I had to work too much overtime.

2. Use a colon after a complete sentence when introducing a bulleted or numbered list.

   > **EXAMPLE**   You must bring these items to your medical exam:
   > - your provincial health card,
   > - a list of your current medications.

3. Use a colon following the salutation in formal business letters.

   > **EXAMPLE**   Dear Mr. Jones:

The punctuation applied to items in a list depends on the style guide that you follow. The bulleted list in example 2 could also be presented with no punctuation.

> You must bring these items to your medical exam:
> - your provincial health card
> - a list of your current medications

Ask your teacher which style you are required to use in your work. Then apply that style consistently throughout your text.

Exercise 1

Fill in the blanks with the correct punctuation. If no punctuation is required, put an X in the blank.

1. Pierre decided to apply to university at McGill ____,____ Concordia ____,____ and Bishop's.

2. Because of the lack of work ____,____ many people are returning to school.

3. I love school ____;____ however, I don't enjoy doing all the homework.

4. Yesterday ____,____ my boss said ____,____ "Get off your butt and get to work." He was not happy.

5. A good employee needs three things ____:____ patience ____,____ initiative ____,____ and perseverance.

6. Though Maxime has been working hard ____,____ he will have to work even harder to get into medical school.

7. Jerry studied all night long ____;____ therefore ____,____ he should do well on the exam.

8. We need to change one thing in the classroom ____:____ the colour of the walls.

9. Last week ____,____ Diane slept in twice and missed two classes.

10. When my friend called ____,____ I didn't hear the phone because I was wearing earbuds.

Exercise 2

This message is missing several commas, semicolons, and colons. Add the correct punctuation.

Dear Ms. Stanford:

I am writing to you concerning your email sent June 30, 2019, in which you identify serious problems in our company.

First, I would like to summarize the issues you mentioned. In your email, you note the following:

- lack of communication between departments,

- staff's lack of familiarity with accounting software,

- lack of leadership from supervisors.

After meeting with my department heads, I would like to propose the following changes.

In order to improve communication between departments, our IT team is going to build a network platform that will allow all employees to follow changes in the various files, portfolios, and projects they are working on. With this change, we hope that different departments will be more aware of what the others are doing.

In addition, we have planned a series of workshops and seminars to train employees on the most recent accounting software. We believe we can have all employees up to date by mid-February; however, this is a tight deadline and any unforeseen delays will extend the mid-February date.

this → This

Finally, lack of leadership is a more complex problem. However, we believe it is essential to remedy this problem as soon as possible. Therefore, an immediate evaluation of all supervisors has been ordered. this evaluation will focus on three elements: efficiency in resolving problems, subordinate satisfaction, and productivity.

To conclude, we have taken the necessary steps to correct the issues that you brought to our attention and hope that we have responded to your concerns adequately.

Sincerely,

Lyne Statton

 **Field-specific activity**

Exercise 3

Working on your own, think of a field- or career-related situation and write a short email message (approximately 10 sentences) in which you make a complaint. Include at least six punctuation errors (missing or misused commas, semicolons, or colons). Exchange messages with your partner and try to find all the errors in each other's email.

CHAPTER 3

Verb Tense Review

Simple Tenses

Simple tenses describe actions at a point in time.

Simple past

Use the simple past for actions (or a series of actions) completed at a specific time in the past.

> **EXAMPLES** Last summer, Peter completed an apprenticeship.
>
> After school yesterday, I walked home, ate, studied, and went to bed.

Sentences in the simple past do not always contain a specific time word.

> **EXAMPLE**
>
> Peter completed an apprenticeship.

Forming the simple past

	Affirmative	Negative	Question
regular verbs	**verb + -ed** I **liked** the movie.	*did* + *not* + **verb** (base form) I **did not (didn't) like** the movie.	*did* + **subject** + **verb** (base form) **Did** you **like** the movie? How much **did** you **like** the movie?
irregular verb	eat → ate I **ate** popcorn.	*did* + *not* + **verb** (base form) I **did not (didn't) eat** popcorn.	*did* + **subject** + **verb** (base form) **Did** you **eat** popcorn? How much popcorn **did** you **eat**?

NOTE The simple past tense is formed in the same way for all subjects (I/You/She/He/It/We/They).

Simple present

1. Use the simple present for facts.

    > **EXAMPLE** Earth **is** the third planet from the sun.
    >
    > Our department **has** three meetings per semester.

2. Use the simple present for habits or routines.

    > **EXAMPLE** Every day, Janice **gets** up at 6:00 to go to work.

3. Use the simple present for generalizations.

    > **EXAMPLE** A good job **starts** with a good education.

In the affirmative, add *-es* to the verb in the third-person singular when the verb ends in *-o*, *-s*, *-z*, *-ch*, *-sh*, or *-x*.

> **EXAMPLES** does, teaches, washes

In both the negative and the question form, the verb takes the base form for all subjects. No *-s* or *-es* is added to the third-person singular.

Forming the simple present

Affirmative	Negative	Question
Use the verb in base form; add *-s* or *-es* to third-person singular subjects.	*do/does* + *not* + **verb**	*Do/Does* + **subject** + **verb**
I **like** work. You **like** work. She/He/It **likes** work. We **like** work. You **like** work. They **like** work.	I **do not (don't) like** work. You **do not like** work. She/He/It **does not (doesn't) like** work. We **do not like** work. You **do not like** work. They **do not like** work.	**Do** you **like** work? **Does** he **like** work? Why **do** you **like** work? Why **does** he **like** work?

Simple future

1. Use the simple future with *will* or *be going to* to make a prediction.

    EXAMPLES   The Montreal Canadiens **will win** the Stanley Cup.

    The Montreal Canadiens **are going to win** the Stanley Cup.

2. Use *be going to* + verb to express a definite plan.

    EXAMPLE   Leo **is going to** study at McGill next year.

3. Use *will* + verb to express a promise or a spontaneous voluntary action.

    EXAMPLES   I **will help** you study for the final exam.

    You look tired. I **will go** to the meeting for you.

In the simple future, the verb always takes the base form. No *-s* or *-es* is added to the third-person singular.

Forming the simple future

Simple future using *will*		
Affirmative	**Negative**	**Question**
will + **verb**	*will* + *not* + **verb**	*Will* + **subject** + **verb**
I/You/She/He/It **will work**.	I/You/She/He/It **will not (won't) work**.	**Will** you **work**? Where **will** you **work**?
We/You/They **will work**.	We **will not (won't) work**.	**Will** they **work**? Where **will** they **work**?

Simple future using *be going to*		
Affirmative	**Negative**	**Question**
be going to + **verb**	*be* + *not* + *going to* + **verb**	*be* + **subject** + *going to* + **verb**
I **am going to work**.	I **am not going to work**.	**Am** I **going to work**?
You **are going to work**.	You **are not going to work**.	**Are** you **going to work**?
He/She/It **is going to work**.	She **is not going to work**.	**Is** she **going to work**?
We/You/They **are going to work**.	They **are not going to work**.	**Are** they **going to work**?

*Conjugate *be* in the simple present.

Progressive Tenses

Progressive tenses describe actions that are ongoing or in progress at some point in time.

Stative verbs (verbs that describe states or opinions rather than actions) are not normally used in the progressive tense. Some examples of stative verbs are *be*, *seem*, *taste*, *agree*, and *believe*.

Past progressive

1. Use the past progressive when an action in the past was interrupted by another action.

    EXAMPLE   I **was working** when my boss entered the office.

2. Use the past progressive when an action was in progress at a specific time in the past.

    EXAMPLE   Last night at 10:00, I **was working** on a report for my boss.

Forming the past progressive

Affirmative	Negative	Question
be* + verb + **-ing**	**be*** + **not** + verb + **-ing**	**be***+ subject + verb + **-ing**
I **was working**.	I **was not working**.	**Was** I **working**?
You **were working**.	You **were not working**.	**Were** you **working**?
He/She/It **was working**.	He **was not working**.	**Was** he **working**?
We/You/They **were working**.	We **were not working**.	**Were** we **working**?

*Conjugate *be* in the simple past.

Present progressive

1. Use the present progressive for an action in progress at the moment.

    EXAMPLE   Do you hear that? Somebody **is screaming**.

2. Use the present progressive for temporary longer term actions that are in progress but not necessarily at the specific moment.

    EXAMPLE   This semester, the students **are learning** to code.

3. Use the present progressive for a planned future action or event.

    EXAMPLE   This summer, I **am flying** to Morocco. I bought my plane ticket.

Forming the present progressive

Affirmative	Negative	Question
be + verb + **-ing**	**be** + **not** + verb + **-ing**	**Be** + subject + verb + **-ing**
I **am working**.	I **am not working**.	**Am** I **working**?
You **are working**.	You **are not working**.	**Are** you **working**?
He/She/It **is working**.	She **is not working**.	**Is** she **working**?
We/You/They **are working**.	They **are not working**.	**Are** they **working**?

*Conjugate *be* in the simple present.

Future progressive

1. Use the future progressive for a future action that will be interrupted by another action.

    EXAMPLE   When Jose arrives tonight, Peter **will be studying**.

2. Use the future progressive for a future action that will be in progress at a specific time.

    EXAMPLE   Maggie **will be working** on the financial statement at 12:00 tomorrow.

The *-ing* form of the verb is called the present participle.

The *-ing* form of the verb is called the present participle.

Forming the future progressive

Future progressive using *will*		
Affirmative	**Negative**	**Question**
will + *be* + verb + *-ing*	*will* + *not* + *be* + verb + *-ing*	*will* + subject + *be* + verb + *-ing*
I/You **will be working**.	I **will not be working**.	**Will** I **be working**?
He/She/It **will be working**.	He **will not be working**.	**Will** he **be working**?
We/You/They **will be working**.	They **will not be working**.	**Will** they **be working**?

Future progressive using *be going to**		
Affirmative	**Negative**	**Question**
be going to + *be* + verb + *-ing*	*be* + *not* + *going to be* + verb + *-ing*	*Be* + subject + *going to be* + verb + *-ing*
I **am going to be working**.	I **am not going to be working**.	**Am** I **going to be working**?
You **are going to be working**.	You **are not going to be working**.	**Are** you **going to be working**?
He/She/It **is going to be working**.	He **is not going to be working**.	**Is** he **going to be working**?
We/You/They **are going to be working**.	They **are not going to be working**.	**Are** they **going to be working**?

*Conjugate *be* in the simple present.

Perfect Tenses

Perfect tenses describe actions or events completed before another action, event, or point in time.

Past perfect

Use the past perfect for an action in the past that occurs before another past action.

> **EXAMPLE**   Joshua **had finished** recording before Clive arrived.

Forming the past perfect

The past participle form of regular verbs is **verb + -ed** (e.g., *started*, *learned*). For a list of the past participles of irregular verbs, see Appendix 2, page 224.

Affirmative	**Negative**	**Question**
had + past participle	*had* + *not* + past participle	*Had* + subject + past participle
I/You **had worked** . . .	You **had not worked** . . .	**Had** you **worked** . . .?
He/She/It **had worked** . . .	She **had not worked** . . .	**Had** she **worked** . . .?
We/You/They **had worked** . . .	They **had not worked** . . .	**Had** they **worked** . . .?

Present perfect

1. Use the present perfect to talk about actions or situations that occurred in the past but when you do not have a specific past incident in mind.

   EXAMPLE   The company **has been** through some rough times in the past, but it is doing well at the moment.

2. Use the present perfect to talk about actions or situations that have happened more than once up to the present time. Key words often used with this meaning are *so far, recently, already, up to now,* and *lately.*

   EXAMPLE   You **have been** late twice already.

3. Use the present perfect with *for* or *since* to talk about actions or situations that started in the past and continue in the present. Use *for* with a duration of time. Use *since* with a specific time marker (day, month, or year).

   EXAMPLE   He **has worked** here for over 20 years.

   She **has worked** here since 2018.

4. Use the present perfect to talk about a finished action with a connection to or result in the present. (The simple past is also commonly used for this meaning.)

   EXAMPLE   Okay, you **have finished** the first exercise, so you can go on to the second one.

> The present perfect progressive (*have/has* + *been* + verb + *-ing*) can also be used for this meaning. It is used to stress the ongoing nature of the action.
>
> EXAMPLE
>
> Wow, he **has been working** here for over 20 years!

Forming the present perfect

Affirmative	Negative	Question
have/has + **past participle**	*have/has* + *not* + **past participle**	*Have/Has* + **subject** + **past participle**
I/You **have worked** . . .	You **have not worked** . . .	**Have** you **worked** . . .?
He/She/It **has worked** . . .	She **has not worked** . . .	**Has** she **worked** . . .?
We/You/They **have worked** . . .	They **have not worked** . . .	**Have** they **worked** . . .?

Future perfect

1. Use the future perfect for a future action that will be completed before another future action or date.

   EXAMPLE   Marcus **will have graduated** by December next year.

2. Use the future perfect to show the duration of a future action that will have been completed before another future action or time.

   EXAMPLE   Jazz **will have worked** for 16 hours straight by the time the project is completed.

   Anthony **is going to have studied** for six hours by the time he goes to bed tonight.

Forming the future perfect

Future perfect using *will*		
Affirmative	**Negative**	**Question**
will + *have* + past participle	*will* + *not* + *have* + past participle	*Will* + subject + *have* + past participle
I/You **will have worked** . . .	I **will not have worked** . . .	**Will** I **have worked** . . .?
He/She/It **will have worked** . . .	She **will not have worked** . . .	**Will** she **have worked** . . .?
We/You/They **will have worked** . . .	They **will not have worked** . . .	**Will** they **have worked** . . .?
Future perfect using *be going to**		
Affirmative	**Negative**	**Question**
be going to + *have* + past participle	*be* + *not* + *going to* + *have* + past participle	*Be* + subject + *going to* + *have* + past participle
I **am going to have worked** . . .	I **am not going to have worked** . . .	**Am** I **going to have worked** . . .?
You **are going to have worked** . . .	You **are not going to have worked** . . .	**Are** you **going to have worked** . . .?
He/She/It **is going to have worked** . . .	She **is not going to have worked** . . .	**Is** she **going to have worked** . . .?
We/You/They **are going to have worked**	They **are not going to have worked** . . .	**Are** they **going to have worked** . . .?

*Conjugate *be* in the simple present.

Perfect Progressive Tenses

Perfect progressive tenses describe actions or events that are ongoing but expected to be completed at a later time.

The perfect progressive tenses often express how long an activity has been in progress.

> **EXAMPLE**   Q: How long **have you been working** on that project?
>
> A: I **have been working** on it for three months.

Past perfect progressive

Use the past perfect progressive to show how long a past action had been in progress before another past action happened.

> **EXAMPLE**   April **had been waiting** for the financial statements for three hours when they finally arrived.

Forming the past perfect progressive

Affirmative	**Negative**	**Question**
had been + verb + *-ing*	*had* + *not* + *been* + verb + *-ing*	*Had* + subject + *been* + verb + *-ing*
I/You He/She/It **had been working** . . .	I **had not been working** . . .	**Had** I **been working** . . .?
We/You/They **had been working** . . .	We **had not been working** . . .	**Had** we **been working** . . .?

Present perfect progressive

1. Use the present perfect progressive to indicate how long a current action has been in progress.

    EXAMPLE   James **has been looking** for the file for two whole days.

    Lawrence **has been studying** since Wednesday for the science exam.

2. Use the present perfect progressive for recent ongoing actions.

    EXAMPLE   Miley **has been exercising** a lot recently.

Forming the present perfect progressive

Affirmative	Negative	Question
has/have been + verb + *-ing*	*has/have* + *not* + *been* + verb + *-ing*	*has/have* + subject + *been* + verb + *-ing*
I/You **have been working**.	I **have not been working**.	**Have** I **been working**?
He/She/It **has been working**.	He **has not been working**.	**Has** he **been working**?
We/You/They **have been working**.	We **have not been working**.	**Have** they **been working**?

Future perfect progressive

Use the future perfect progressive to indicate how long a future action will have been in progress before another future action or time.

    EXAMPLE   Reginald **will have been training** for 20 minutes by the time Harrison arrives.

Forming the future perfect progressive

Future perfect progressive using *will*		
Affirmative	Negative	Question
will + *have been* + verb + *-ing*	*will* + *not* + *have been* + verb + *-ing*	*Will* + subject + *have been* + verb + *-ing*
I/You/He/She/It **will have been working** . . .	I **will not have been working** . . .	**Will** I **have been working** . . .?
We/You/They **will have been working** . . .	We **will not have been working** . . .	**Will** we **have been working** . . .?
Future perfect progressive using *be going to**		
Affirmative	Negative	Question
be + *going to* + *have been* + verb + *-ing*	*be* + *not* + *going to* + *have been* + verb + *-ing*	*Be* + subject + *going to* + *have been* + verb + *-ing*
I **am going to have been working** . . .	I **am not going to have been working** . . .	**Am** I **going to have been working** . . .?
You **are going to have been working** . . .	You **are not going to have been working** . . .	**Are** you **going to have been working** . . .?
He/She/It **is going to have been working** . . .	He **is not going to have been working** . . .	**Is** he **going to have been working** . . .?
We/You/They **are going to have been working** . . .	We **are not going to have been working** . . .	**Are** we **going to have been working** . . .?

*Conjugate *be* in the simple present tense.

Exercise 1 Simple present tenses

Write the correct form of the verb. You may use the simple past, simple present, or simple future.

1. Steen usually _____arrives_____ (arrive) early for work, but today he _____arrived_____ (arrive) late.

2. Leena _____hates_____ (hate) working overtime, but she _____doesn't have_____ (have, *neg*.) a choice today.

3. When Luke was young, he _____wanted_____ (want) to become a firefighter. However, when he got older, he _____changed_____ (change) his mind and _____became_____ (become) a police officer instead.

4. Harry ___will start / is going to start___ (start) the new project soon.

5. I predict that London ___will be / is going to be___ (be) the location of the new division.

Exercise 2 Progressive tenses

Write the correct form of the verb. You may use the past progressive, present progressive, or future progressive tenses.

1. Right now, Paul _____is working_____ (work) on a plan that will change the future of online entertainment.

2. When Vincent's supervisor arrived yesterday, James _____was_____ still _____testing_____ (test) the video game.

3. Tomorrow at precisely noon, the client _____will be waiting_____ (wait) at the entrance to the warehouse. We must make sure that someone is there to meet her.

4. While Stan and Lee _____were working_____ (work) on the project last week, they made a huge mistake. Right now, they _____are trying_____ (try) to fix it before their boss notices.

5. I bought a lottery ticket. I hope that next week at this time, I _____will be collecting_____ (collect) my winnings.

Exercise 3 Perfect tenses

Write the correct form of the verb. You may use the past perfect, present perfect, or future perfect.

1. Montreal ___will have celebrated___ (celebrate) its 400th anniversary by the end of 2042.

2. Jose _____had contemplated_____ (contemplate) moving to New York last year before he moved to Montreal.

3. Sly _____has lived_____ (live) in Quebec for one year now. He really likes living there.

4. My roommate _____had left_____ (leave) by the time I got out of bed.

5. Devin _____has travelled_____ (travel) to China several times. His next trip will be his fifth time.

Exercise 4 Perfect progressive tenses

Write the correct form of the verb in the space provided. You may use the past perfect progressive, present perfect progressive, or future perfect progressive.

1. Adam _____has been looking_____ (look) for a new job for the past six months.

2. Dr. Zerbo _____will have been operating_____ (operate) for six hours by the time the procedure is complete.

3. Larry _____had been installing_____ (install) the lab equipment for only a couple of minutes before his boss decided to make changes.

4. Sheila _____has not been exercising_____ (exercise, *neg*.) recently and therefore, she has been more stressed.

5. He _____had been waiting_____ for weeks before the parcel finally arrived in the mail.

Exercise 5

Write the correct form of the verb. You may use any of the tenses you've practised in this chapter.

1. In 2016, the youth unemployment rate _____was_____ (be) approximately 12.6 percent. This rate _____remained_____ (remain) relatively stable throughout the year and into 2017. Youth employment _____is_____ (be) an important issue in our society. Often a student _____needs_____ (need) a job to be able to pursue his or her education. When students _____are_____ (be) unable to pay for their own education, many of them _____drop_____ (drop) out of school, which _____is_____ (be) terrible for both the students and society as a whole.

2. For how long _____are_____ you _____going to study_____ (study)? How long _____will_____ you _____have been studying_____ (study) by the time you finish your education? These _____are_____ (be) questions that many of us _____ask_____ (ask) ourselves every day. I _____have_____ (have) a friend who _____will be / is going to be_____ (be) 35 years old next October. He _____has been going / has gone_____ (go) to school since he _____was_____ (be) six years old. That _____is / has been_____ (be) almost 30 years. He _____has_____ (have) another two years to go before he _____finishes / will be finished_____ (finish) his latest degree. He _____will have gone / will have been going_____ (go) to school for a total of 31 years by the time he is done. Hopefully, he _____will get / is going to get_____ (get) a job when he _____finishes_____ (finish) instead of starting another university degree.

3. For the past two years, Rachid _____has planned / has been planning_____ (plan) to take part in a student work exchange program in Australia. He _____has had_____ (have) to save a lot of money to pay for the ticket and buy a new computer. He _____has worked / has been working_____ (work) very hard for the past six months to make sure that he _____has_____ (have) the money, as well as the marks, for the program. The program _____accepts_____ (accept) only a limited number of students and they only _____take_____ (take) students with excellent marks. Right now, Rachid _____has_____ (have) a 3.75 GPA and he _____hopes_____ (hope) that will be good enough.

4. Last night while I ___was studying___ (study) for a big physics exam, a weird thing ___happened___ (happen). There ___was___ (be) a thunderstorm raging outside while I ___was trying___ (try) to work. Around 11:00 PM, I ___heard___ (hear) a loud crack. I ___looked___ (look) outside and ___saw___ (see) a large maple tree lying on the ground, smoking. It had been hit by lightning and ___broke___ (break) in two. The really weird thing ___is___ (be) that I ___had been studying___ (study) electricity for my physics exam. Isn't that a coincidence?

Exercise 6

Find the verb errors in the texts below and correct them.

Dear Mr. Macllelan:

I write in response to the job posting for a teaching assistant that I have seen on Monster.com on June 19. I am dynamic and passionate about education. For these reasons, I am believing I am the best candidate for this job.

For the past two years, I have been work with children at a day camp in the Laurentians. I worked at this camp for three years and I continue to work there next year. Presently, I am being a camp counsellor, responsible for supervising and planning the activities that the students did each day. These activities will include swimming, hiking, and horseback riding. I am also responsible for the registration of new campers. Next year, I plan and monitor the activities for the junior counsellors as well as supervise them. My employers will be confident in my abilities and have often comment on the quality of my work and how happy they are with me. They allowed me to grow and develop my skills at the camp. I will have appreciated the confidence that they will have had in me. I am embracing new challenges and I looked forward to the new responsibilities I will be having. In the future, I hoping to go to university to become a teacher.

I will thank you for considering my application and I am hoping to hear from you in the near future. Please feel free to contact me at your earliest convenience.

Sincerely,
Peter Jackson

am writing   saw

believe

have been working

have worked   will continue /
                am going to continue

am
do
include
will plan
are
have commented
have allowed
appreciate   have / have had
embrace   look / am looking
will have / am going to have   hope

thank   hope

CHAPTER 4

Review of Contrasting Tenses and Question Forms

Exercise 1 Simple past or present perfect

Write the correct form of the verb. Use only the simple past or the present perfect.

1. Last year, Phil ____designed____ (design) his first building.

2. George ____has been____ (be) sick a lot lately.

3. Trisha ____has spoken____ (speak) at many conferences since starting work at her new job.

4. Pat ____walked____ (walk) to school every day when he ____was____ (be) young.

5. Charles-Antoine ____has competed____ (compete) in many competitions so far this year. In his last competition, he ____won____ (win) a gold medal.

Exercise 2 Simple past or past progressive

Write the correct form of the verb. Use only the simple past or the past progressive.

1. While I ____was typing____ (type) my assignment, my computer ____crashed____. (crash).

2. As a young man, I often ____worked____ (work) late into the night to complete school projects.

3. When my boss came into the office, I ____was surfing____ (surf) online.

4. Last year, I ____was____ (be) so busy at school that I ____forgot____ (forget) to visit my family.

5. While William ____was working____ (work) on his resumé, the phone ____rang____ (ring) and he ____was____ (be) offered a job.

Exercise 3 Simple present or present progressive

Write the correct form of the verb. Use only the simple present or the present progressive.

1. At the moment, I _____am looking_____ (look) for new job opportunities. My current job _____lacks_____ (lacks) variety.

2. James _____is meeting_____ (meet) with the manager. He _____expects_____ (expect) to get a promotion. I _____hope_____ (hope) he gets it.

3. Dr. Nicolay _____is trying_____ (try) to find a cure for AIDS. She _____believes_____ (believe) that she is close to a cure.

4. Lyne _____is doing_____ (do) her homework, but _____does not understand_____ (understand, neg.) the question she is working on. She _____wants_____ (want) to get a tutor as soon as possible.

5. The students _____are_____ working (work) on a school project. Ariane _____is not participating_____ (participate, neg.) enough, so the other students _____are complaining_____. (complain)

Exercise 4 All tenses

Read the text below and write the correct form of the verb.

Dear Mr. Clay:

I _____received/have received_____ (receive) your email requesting information about our upcoming seminar. I _____appreciate_____ (appreciate) your interest in the Innovation Today seminar, which will be held on November 9.

In response to your first question, you _____are / will be_____ (is) required to pay the complete fee in full before the seminar. Ironically, I _____was_____ just _____updating_____ (update) our website with this information at the exact moment that I _____received_____ (receive) your email.

Second, the organizing committee _____has arranged / will arrange_____ (arrange) valet parking for participants. However, there _____is_____ (be) limited space and thus, it _____is_____ (be) imperative that participants arrive early if they _____wish_____ (wish) to take advantage of this service.

Finally, hotel accommodations _____have been_____ (be) booked for those who _____made / have made_____ (make) the request for rooms. The hotel _____has asked_____ (ask) that we _____inform_____ (inform) all participants to register at the hotel upon their arrival. This _____reduces_____ (reduce) confusion and long lines. Please make sure you have all your registration information ready in order to expedite the process.

We _____look_____ (look) forward to seeing you at the conference. If you _____have_____ (have) any other questions, please do not hesitate to ask.

Sincerely,
Martin Jones

Exercise 5 Question forms

Correct the errors in the following questions. To review the rules for question formation, see Appendix 3, page 225.

1. Why so many people are anxious?

   Why are so many people anxious?

2. From where job satisfaction come from?

   Where does job satisfaction come from?

3. Why does the use of drugs has increased?

   Why has the use of drugs increased?

4. What does multiple sclerosis is?

   What is multiple sclerosis?

5. What the benefits are of adopting your proposal?

   What are the benefits of adopting your proposal?

6. How we can explain the increase in obesity rates?

   How can we explain the increase in obesity rates?

7. What impact has culture on our health?

   What impact does culture have on our health?

8. Will the legalization of cannabis has an effect on the crime rate?

   Will the legalization of cannabis have an effect on the crime rate?

9. What the solutions are the issue of biodiversity loss?

   What are the solutions to the issue of biodiversity loss?

10. How long you have worked as a photojournalist?

    How long have you worked as a photojournalist?

Exercise 6

 Field-specific activity

Write a short dialogue related to your field of study or future career. Include at least six questions and a variety of verb tenses. For example, if you are studying social work, you could write a dialogue between a social worker and a troubled teen; if you are studying agriculture, you could write a dialogue between a sales person and farmer interested in purchasing a new tractor.

You could have students work in teams and perform their dialogues for the class. Observers could guess what the situation is and who the people in the dialogue are. Students could also make a short video.

Communicative Activities

With a partner, answer the following questions.

1. Explain the difference in meaning between the following pairs of sentences:

   a) I work at a convenience store.
   b) I am working at a convenience store.

   a) Mr. Shepherd accomplished much in his lifetime.
   b) Mr. Shepherd has accomplished much in his lifetime.

Scenario 1

c) is the worst—they definitely saw his pants split.

a) is second—there is a chance they didn't see his pants split.

b) is the best—they didn't see his pants split.

Scenario 2

c) is the worst—he definitely missed the bus.

a) is second—there is a chance he caught the bus.

b) is the best—he definitely caught the bus.

2. For each situation, rank the sentences in order of worst to best scenario for Jean-Pierre (Write 1, 2 or 3 beside each sentence, with 1 being the worst possible scenario.) Explain your ranking.

_2_ a) When the ladies were leaving the room, Jean-Pierre's tight pants split open.

_3_ b) When the ladies had left the room, Jean-Pierre's tight pants split open.

_1_ c) When the ladies entered the room, Jean-Pierre's tight pants split open.

_2_ a) When Jean-Pierre arrives at the station, the bus will be leaving.

_3_ b) When Jean-Pierre arrives at the station, the bus will leave.

_1_ c) When Jean-Pierre arrives at the station, the bus will have left.

3. Write dialogue in the speech bubbles for each photo. Use a variety of verb tenses. Each photo must contain at least one question in the bubbles.

CHAPTER 5

Modals

A modal is an auxiliary used with a verb that adds meaning to the main verb.

Do not conjugate modal auxiliaries (except *have to* and *be able to*).

Correct	He can work for hours and hours without a break.
Incorrect	~~He cans work for hours and hours without a break.~~

The only modals that are conjugated are *have to* and *be able to*. They can be conjugated in the past, present, and future.

EXAMPLES You **have to** go to work.

He **had to** go to work.

I **will have to** go to work.

You **are able to** complete the homework by yourself.

He **was able to** complete the homework by himself.

I **will be able to** complete the homework by myself.

In a question that contains a modal, there is no need to add *do*, *does*, or *did* to the question because the modal functions as the auxiliary.

Correct	Where must I hand in the form?
Incorrect	~~Where do I must hand in the form?~~

EXCEPTION Only add an auxiliary *do/does/did* with the modal auxiliary *have to/ has to*.

Where do I have to hand in the form?

Where does he have to hand in the form?

Common Modal Auxiliaries

Modals	Used to express	Example sentence
can (cannot/can't)	permission	**Can** I go to the bathroom? (informal)
	possibility	We **can** go to a restaurant for lunch.
	ability	Eva **can** speak Japanese.
	request	**Can** I borrow some money? (informal)
	deduction— certainty*	Bob **can't** be sick; he never misses work. *Can is rarely used in the affirmative form for this meaning.
could (could not/couldn't)	permission	**Could** I go to the bathroom? (more formal)
	possibility	We **could** go to a restaurant for lunch.
	past ability	Eva **could** speak Japanese when she was younger.
	polite request	**Could** I borrow some money? (more formal)
	deduction	Bob **could** be sick; he rarely misses work.

Modals	Used to express	Example sentence
may **(may not)**	permission	**May** I go to the bathroom? (most formal)
	possibility	We **may** go to a restaurant for lunch.
	polite request	**May** I borrow some money?
	deduction	Bob **may** be sick; he rarely misses work.
might **(might not)**	permission	**May** I go to the bathroom? (most formal)
	possibility	Damien **might** get the job because he is a good candidate.
	deduction	Bob **might** be sick; he rarely misses work.
should **(should not/shouldn't)**	advice	You **should** always do your best.
must	obligation	You **must** pass the final exam to pass the course.
	deduction—certainty	Bob **must** be sick; he never misses work.
must not/mustn't	prohibition	Students **must not** use their phones in class.
	deduction—certainty	Bob **must** not be feeling well because he rarely misses work.
have/has to **(do not have to—** **means it is not** **necessary to)**	obligation	You **have to** pass the final exam to pass the course. Students do **not have to** leave their phones in their lockers.
be able to (be not able to)	ability	She **was able to** finish the race.
would **(would not/wouldn't)**	request	**Would** you be able to help me with my work? (formal)
will **(will not/won't)**	promise or willingness	I **will** help you with your homework.

Past Form Modal Auxiliaries

Modals	Used to express	Example sentence
could **(could not)**	ability	When he was young, he **could** read for hours on end.
would **(would not)**	past habit/behaviour	In her youth, she **would not** listen to anyone.
had to **(did not have to)**	obligation	Yesterday, he **had to** go to the hospital.
could have	possibility	Nicola **could have worked** at Facebook, but she chose Google instead.
could have **may have** **might have** **must have** **had to have*** **(could not have** **may not have** **might not have** **must not have** **can't have)**	deduction	Stuey **could have had** an accident; he didn't show up for the meeting. Melissa **may have wanted** the big promotion, but we are not sure. He **must have finished** the project yesterday because he went home early. Adham **can't have skipped** class because he is a very serious student.
should have **(should not have)**	advice not taken	You **should have studied** harder for the final exam.

had to have cannot be made negative.

The past modals *could have, may have, might have, must have, had to have,* and *should have* (and their negatives) are followed by the past participle of the verb (e.g., *may have wanted*). This is different from all other modals, which are followed by the verb in its base form (e.g., *would want*).

Could, may, and *might* express 50 percent certainty, while *must, had to,* and *can't* express the most certainty (99 percent).

Exercise 1

Write the correct modal.

A person ___should / must___ not assume that success will be easy. If you wish to start a company, you ___must___ work hard. It ___may / might / could___ be the hardest thing you will ever do. However, if you work hard, you ___can / should___ succeed. There are many examples of successful business people who ___would___ work all day and night, with minimal sleep. Obviously, this is extreme and you ___should___ never compromise your health while striving to achieve your goals.

Exercise 2

In a small group, invent a situation for each modal in column 2 that will bring out a response that includes the targeted modal in column 1. Write each situation in the appropriate box. Then survey a classmate who is not part of your group. Write his or her response to each situation in column 4. Each response must contain one of the targeted modals from column 1. Each person in your group should survey a different person.

When you have completed the chart, rejoin your original group and share the responses that each of you received for each situation. Add the new responses to your chart. Then decide as a group what the best response was for each situation.

Examples have been provided for two of the modals, along with a sample response for each.

1. Modal	2. Use	3. Situation	4. Response
can could	possibility	My company has to expand. I need to find more capital. What are the possibilities?	You could ask your parents to invest.
could may might	deduction	Our English teacher is going to quit his job. What are the possible reasons?	He could be tired of correcting homework.
can	ability		
can could would	request		
should	advice		
must have to	obligation		

Exercise 3

Change the following text into the past. Revise as necessary but try to keep as many of the ideas from the original text as possible. Use as many past form modals as possible. The first sentence has been done for you.

> Megan must create a company for a school project. She must work hard to finish the project on time. She should not leave her work until the last minute. Her mother will have to help her if she isn't able to finish on time. That can be avoided by good time management.

Megan had to create a company for a school project. _____

_____

_____

_____

_____

You can have students create their own short scenarios that include a variety of modals and have students rewrite one another's texts in the past form.

CHAPTER 6

Conditionals

Conditional sentences are used when the speaker wishes to express what the result of a condition is, will be, would be, or would have been, or when the speaker wants to present the condition that is necessary for a particular result.

Conditional sentences contain two parts: an *if* clause that describes a condition and a *result* clause that describes the result.

Forms of the Conditional

In English, there are three forms of the conditional.

Conditional	Use	*If* clause + result clause
First conditional (real in the present)	1. to express a general truth, rule, or habit (i.e., If X happens, Y happens.)	If my boss **asks** me to, I **work** overtime. Use simple present in the *if* clause. Use simple present in the result clause if the result always happens.
	2. to express a truth with a future result (i.e., If X happens, Y will happen.)	If my boss **asks** me to (today), I **will work** overtime (this evening). Use simple present in the *if* clause. Use simple future in the result clause if the result will happen in the future.
Second conditional (unreal in the present)	to speak about a hypothetical situation (one that does not exist but can be imagined—often, the situation is unlikely to happen.)	If I **stole** from the company, my boss **would fire** me. Use simple past in the *if* clause (here, past tense does not signify past time). Use *would* + verb in the result clause.
		If I **were** rich, I **would quit** my job. When the *if* clause contains the verb *to be*, it is conjugated as *were* (not *was*). Use *would* + verb in the result clause.
Third conditional (unreal in the past)	to refer to a hypothetical situation in the past (i.e., imagining that past events had happened differently than they actually did)	If you **had come** to the meeting, you **would have received** the document. (But you did not come to the meeting, so you did not receive the document.) Use the past perfect form in the *if* clause. Use *would* + *have* + past participle in the result clause.

For the first conditional, you can use other modals (e.g., *may, can, should*) in the result clause.

In the second conditional, *was* is often used instead of *were* for the first- and third-person singular in informal contexts.

EXAMPLE

If I was you, I would not take that job.

Mixed conditionals

In mixed conditionals, the times in the *if* clause and the result clause are different.

EXAMPLES   If I **were** not so shy, I **would have** spoken more at the meeting yesterday.
            present   past

Ifyou **hadn't drunk** so much last night, you wouldn't **feel** so awful today.
            past   present

In any form of the conditional, *would* is never used in the *if* clause.

INCORRECT

If you **would have been** nicer yesterday, I **wouldn't** be mad at you now.

Punctuation with conditionals

The *if* clause can come before or after the result clause.

When the *if* clause comes first, put a comma between the two clauses.

EXAMPLE   **If Miranda misses any more classes**, she will fail the course.

When the *if* clause comes after the result clause, do not put a comma between the two clauses.

EXAMPLE   Miranda will fail the course **if she misses any more classes**.

Wish

Use the word *wish* to indicate a desire for something to be different from reality. *Wish* can be used for the past, present, or future. Note the special verb forms used following *wish*.

	Reality	Wish
Past wish	Alex did not come to the meeting last night.	I wish Alex **had come** to the meeting last night. (past perfect)
Present wish	Dan doesn't get along with his boss.	I wish Dan **got** along with his boss. (simple past)
Future wish	Dave will not attend the graduation ceremony tomorrow. Dave is not going to attend the graduation ceremony tomorrow.	I wish Dave **would attend** the graduation ceremony. (*would* rather than *will*) I wish Dave **were** going to attend the ceremony. (*were going to* rather than *is/are going to*)

Using *hope* and *wish*

Hope and *wish* have similar meanings. Use *wish* to refer to how events are or could have been different from the actual reality—in the past, present, or future. Use *hope* for possible events in the future.

EXAMPLES   Sylvie worked really hard this year. She **hopes** she gets the promotion.
            Nobody has gotten the promotion yet, so there is a possibility Sylvie will get it.

            Johnathan got the promotion because he worked harder than everybody else. Lou **wishes** he had gotten it.
            Lou did not get the promotion. He wanted the situation to turn out differently from the way it did.

Exercise 1

Fill in the blanks with the correct form of the conditional.

First conditional

1. If my boyfriend _____gets_____ (get) next weekend off work, we _go / are going to go_ (go) skiing.

2. She always _____turns_____ (turn) off her cellphone if she _____needs_____ (need) to focus on homework.

3. If the vending machine _____is_____ (be) still not working tomorrow, I _____will call_____ (call) the repair company.

Second conditional

4. If you _____found_____ (find) a wallet full of money, what _____would_____ you _____do_____ (do)?

5. If I _____had_____ (have) the opportunity to live in another country, I _____would live_____ (live) in Australia.

6. She _____would not be_____ (be, *neg.*) late all the time if she _____were_____ (be) more organized.

Third conditional

7. I didn't apply for a job. However, if I _____had known_____ (know) the company was hiring, I _____would have applied_____ (apply) for a job there.

8. You missed your bus. You _____would not have missed_____ (miss, *neg.*) your bus if you _____had woken up_____ (wake up) earlier.

9. She didn't get a good mark. She _____would have received_____ (receive) a better mark on her oral presentation if she _____had been_____ (be) better prepared.

Exercise 2

Change the following statements into wishes.

Statement of reality	Wish
1. My boss scrapped the project.	**I wish my boss had not scrapped the project.**
2. Jim did not get the job.	I wish Jim had gotten the job.
3. Becky is always late.	I wish Becky were not always late.
4. Jessie will not answer my calls.	I wish Jessie would answer my calls.
5. Stuart is not going to represent the company at the next conference.	I wish Stuart were going to represent the company at the next conference.

As with the second conditional, *were* is used instead of *was* when the verb *to be* is used in an expression of a wish.

Exercise 3

Complete the following using either *wish* or *hope*.

1. I worked all night on the project. I **hope I get a good mark.**

2. Diane got sick last week and missed her plane to Cuba. She _____

3. Lyne's company was very successful last year. She _____

4. Walid failed the exam yesterday. He _____

Answers will vary.

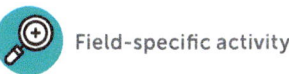
Communicative Activities

1. Discuss your answers to the following questions with your classmates. An example answer is provided.

    EXAMPLE   Question   If you were a millionaire, what would you do?

    Answer   If I were a millionaire, I would buy my own jet because I love to travel.

    a) If you could have any job you wanted, what would it be?
    b) If you could have dinner with anyone, living or dead, who would it be?
    c) If you could live in another country, where would you live?
    d) If you could change something you have done in your life, what would it be?

2. Think of three situations related to your field of study or future career and give hindsight advice. For each situation, write two sentences. Use *should have* + past participle in the first sentence and use the *third conditional* in the second sentence.

    EXAMPLE

    Situation   The technician didn't do regular maintenance. The machine broke down.

    Advice   The technician *should have done* regular maintenance.

    If the technician *had done* regular maintenance, the machine *wouldn't have broken* down.

    a) Situation _____

    _____

    Advice _____

    _____

    _____

    b) Situation _____

    _____

    Advice _____

    _____

    _____

    c) Situation _____

    _____

    Advice _____

    _____

    _____

 GG For more information about modals and their past forms, see Grammar Guide, Chapter 5, page 178.

CHAPTER 7

Passive Voice

The passive voice is used in English to place the focus on the action or result instead of the person or thing doing the action (the agent). In passive voice sentences, the agent may not be known. The subject of a passive voice sentence is not the person or thing doing the action. The subject of a sentence in the passive voice is the object (preceded by the word *by*) of the corresponding active sentence.

In the **active voice**, the subject of the sentence performs the action.

EXAMPLE   Markus **completed** the project on time.

| agent (performing the action) | past tense verb | object |

> The *by phrase* in the passive voice is optional.

By contrast, the **passive voice** is used when the focus is on the action or result instead of on the agent.

EXAMPLE   The project **was completed** [by Markus] on time.

| The object of the active sentence has become the subject of the passive sentence | The auxiliary verb *be* has been added to the main verb | The subject of the active voice sentence follows *by* in the passive voice sentence. The *by* phrase may be omitted. |

The passive voice may be used in a number of situations:

- to focus on the action rather than on who performed the action

    EXAMPLE   The project was cancelled.

- when the agent is unknown

    EXAMPLE   A new project **might be proposed**.

- the agent is obvious, or the agent's identity is not important

    EXAMPLE   Markus **was penalized** when the project failed.

- when the agent is not specific, but rather people in general

    EXAMPLE   Not many projects **are completed** on time and on budget.

- when the speaker wants to be polite or avoid blaming someone

    EXAMPLE   The project **was completed** below the expected standard.

- to introduce known information before new information

    EXAMPLE   The project proposal that we were discussing yesterday **has been accepted**.

Forming the passive voice

The passive voice is formed by conjugating the auxiliary *be* (for person and tense) + the past participle of the main verb. Only transitive verbs (verbs that are followed by an object) can be used in the passive voice.

Tense	Active voice	Passive voice
Simple present	James mistreats his employees.	The employees **are mistreated**.
Simple past	Markus did not send his application on time.	Markus's application **was not sent** on time.
Simple future	The company will fire some employees.	Some employees **will be fired**.
Present progressive	The committee is considering the proposal.	The proposal **is being considered**.
Past progressive	Floyd was analyzing the software.	The software **was being analyzed** by Floyd.
Present perfect	We have interviewed many candidates.	Many candidates **have been interviewed**.
Past perfect	Jill had completed the project before she quit.	The project **had been completed** before Jill quit.
Future perfect	Bob will have completed the project before November.	The project **will have been completed** by Bob before November.
Modal (present form)	We **should print** fifty copies.	Fifty copies **should be printed**.
Modal (past form)	The pollster **should have surveyed** more people.	More people **should have been surveyed**.

Note that the passive voice is never used with the future progressive, present perfect progressive, past perfect progressive, and future perfect progressive.

Exercise 1

Rewrite the sentences below. If the sentence is in the passive voice, put it in the active voice. If the sentence is in the active voice, put it in the passive voice. Do not change the verb tense.

1. Management refused your proposal.

   Your proposal was refused by management.

2. François manages the office.

   The office is managed by François.

3. You should have submitted your proposal before the deadline.

   Your proposal should have been submitted before the deadline.

4. The administrative assistant was fired by Mr. Cash yesterday.

   Mr. Cash fired the administrative assistant yesterday.

5. Lyne will finish the account statements by tomorrow.

   The account statements will be finished by tomorrow.

6. The school will have given out 20 awards by the end of the evening.

   Twenty awards will have been given out by the end of the evening.

7. Someone is monitoring the construction site.

   The construction site is being monitored.

8. Freddie has been assigned to the account by the CFO.

   The CFO has assigned the account to Freddie.

9. The tax form is being completed by Yngwie.

   Yngwie is completing the tax form.

Exercise 2

Read the text and correct the errors in the use of the passive voice.

was finished

was completed   was given

was made

The project was finish yesterday. However, there were many problems with the project before it was complete. When the project was give to Loretta's team, her boss told her that the deadline for the project was in three months. It was make clear that this deadline was not flexible. Unfortunately, there were many problems and delays.

had been assigned

were expected

One problem was team members' absences. A total of six employees had been assign to the team. Three of them were absent a week after the project started. Of those three, two of them are still off work. Thus, from the beginning, three employees was expect to do the work of six.

have been created   will be required

are expected

As a result, new rules have been create. Now the project leader will be require to assign alternate project members to step in if necessary. The alternates are expect to attend all project meetings so that they are up to date and ready to take the place of any member who leaves the team.

was delayed

This new approach will address a key reason why the project was delay.

Exercise 3

Work with a partner. Each of you will write five sentences and then exchange sentences. Convert your partner's sentences from passive to active or from active to passive. This is a race, so see if you can write the new sentences faster than your partner. Once one of you has rewritten all five sentences, you must both stop writing. The person with the most sentences written correctly at that time is the winner. Follow these steps:

1. In the table below, write five sentences in the first column. Make sure that some of your sentences are active and some passive and that you use a variety of verb tenses. Remember that an active sentence must contain an object in order to be transformed into the passive voice.

2. When you are ready, exchange your book with your partner and begin the race.

My sentences	My sentences—converted by my partner
1.	1.
2.	2.
3.	3.
4.	4.
5.	5.

CHAPTER 8

Prepositional Verbs, Phrasal Verbs, and Adjective-Preposition Combinations

Prepositional Verbs

A prepositional verb is a two-word verb that includes a preposition. The combination of the verb and preposition does not change the original meaning of the verb. A prepositional verb is always followed by an object.

For a definition of parts of speech (adjective, adverb, etc.), see Grammar Guide, Chapter 13, page 212.

EXAMPLE   The organizers hope that at least 100 people will **participate in** the fundraiser.

Common prepositional verbs

adapt to	consist of	laugh at	respond to
agree on (something); agree with (somebody)	contribute to	lead to	result from (to be a result of); result in (to cause something)
allow for	correlate with	lecture on	search for
apologize for (something); apologize to (somebody)	decide against	listen to	speak to/with
approve of	depend on	look at (to direct your eyes); look for (to search)	specialize in
arrive at (a time or place); arrive in (city, country)	derive from	participate in	subscribe to
associate with	deviate from	pay for	suffer from
attribute to	differ from	prepare for	sympathize with
believe in	disagree with	profit from	talk to/with
belong to	disappear from	recover from	think about/of
benefit from	excel at/in	refer to	
commit to	hear about/of	rely on	
complain about	insist on	reply to	

Phrasal Verbs

A phrasal verb is a multi-word verb that includes a preposition or an adverb (or both). The combination of the words in a phrasal verb usually creates a new meaning, different from the definition of the separate words.

For example, consider the denotative definitions of the words *look* and *up*: *look* means to focus one's eyes on something, and *up* is the opposite of down. However, when these two words are used together, it can form the phrasal verb look up, which can mean two things:

- to do research to find a piece of information

    EXAMPLE   I need to **look up** that word in a dictionary.

- to improve

    EXAMPLE   Things are **looking up**!

In formal writing, if there is a one-word verb that expresses the same meaning as a phrasal verb, use the single-word verb.

Informal   We should **put off** the meeting until we **sort out** our problems.

Formal   We should **postpone** the meeting until we **resolve** our problems.

Types of phrasal verbs

There are three types of phrasal verbs.

Type 1: **Intransitive** phrasal verbs—like all intransitive verbs, these are not followed by a direct object.

EXAMPLE   **dress up**

Guests have to **dress up** because it's a formal affair.

Type 2: **Inseparable transitive** phrasal verbs—the verb and the direct object cannot be separated. Most phrasal verbs with more than two words are inseparable.

EXAMPLE   **take after (somebody)**

He really **takes after** his father.

Incorrect   ~~He really *takes* his father *after*.~~

Type 3: **Separable transitive** phrasal verbs—the verb and the direct object can be separated.

EXAMPLE   **fill out**

Please **fill out** this form.

Please **fill** this form **out**.

When the direct object is a pronoun, the pronoun must immediately follow the verb.

EXAMPLE   Please **fill** it **out**.

Incorrect ~~Please *fill out* it.~~

A transitive verb must be followed by a direct object. Some transitive verbs require both a direct object and an indirect object.

EXAMPLES

I bought a book.

I gave a present to my mother.

Common phrasal verbs

Type 1: Intransitive phrasal verbs

Phrasal verb	Meaning	Example sentence
blow over	to be forgotten in time with no serious consequences	I hope this embarrassing situation **blows over** soon.
break down	to stop functioning physically or emotionally	The car **broke down** along the highway. She **broke down** upon hearing the bad news.
catch on	to understand what is meant or how to do something	It might take a while to **catch on** to the new procedure.
catch up	to reach a previous level or the same standard as somebody; to talk about and exchange news	I need to **catch up** on my sleep. The runner **caught up** with the rest of the pack. We need to meet for coffee and **catch up** soon!
come about	to happen or occur	The layoffs **came about** due to automation.
come up	to be mentioned or discussed; to occur unexpectedly; to be about to happen in the near future	The subject of layoffs **came up** at the meeting. Sorry, I can't go—something unexpected **came up**. My birthday is **coming up**.
dress up	to dress formally	You need to **dress up** for the party.
eat out	to eat at a restaurant	The team **eats out** together about once a month.
fall through	to stop, fail, or be left incomplete	Unfortunately, the deal **fell through**.
get along	to have a good relationship with	My office mate and I really **get along**.
get around	to become known or heard about by a lot of people	Word **got around** that you had a fight with the boss.
get together	to meet to talk or do something	We need to **get together** to talk about our plan.
go ahead/on	to continue	Sorry, **go on/ahead** with what you were saying.
grow up	to go from being a child to an adult (in age or behaviour)	I **grew up** in Toronto. You need to **grow up**! (i.e., act like an adult)
hold on	to wait for an amount of time (usually a short time period)	**Hold on**; I'll be right back.
pitch in	to join a group of people to help with a task or activity; to donate money	Would you mind **pitching in** to clean up? We're asking everyone to **pitch in** for a gift.
show off	to make a deliberate display of your abilities/accomplishments	Leaving all your trophies on your desk might seem like **showing off**.
show up	to arrive at and attend an event	How many people **showed up** for the party?
take off	to become successful quickly	Our new business is really **taking off**.
take place	to happen or occur	The meeting will **take place** next Friday.
turn around	to get better or improve	The economy seems to be **turning around**.
turn out	to prove to be the case or result	Things **turned out** better than expected.
turn up	to be found after being lost; to arrive at and attend an event	That missing file has got to **turn up** somewhere! Many employees **turned up** for the meeting.

Type 2: Inseparable transitive phrasal verbs

Phrasal verb	Meaning	Example sentence
arrive at	to reach an agreement	Has the administration **arrived at** a decision?
ask for	to behave in a way that makes something likely to happen	You are **asking for** trouble by ignoring her messages.
believe in	to have trust or confidence in something or somebody	I **believe in** the power of hard work.
brush up on	to refresh one's memory of knowledge or skills already learned but partly forgotten	I have to **brush up on** my Spanish before I go to Spain.
check in with (somebody)	to contact somebody quickly to let them know or find out if everything is okay	During the training period, the supervisor will **check in with** you several times a day.
come across	to meet somebody or find something by chance; to give somebody a particular impression	I **came across** the book you were looking for while I was cleaning out the drawer. During a job interview, you should try to **come across** as positive and cheerful.
come up with	to think of and suggest	He is always **coming up with** innovative ideas.
count on	to have trust in and rely on	You can **count on** me to be there if you need help.
cut back on	to reduce	We must **cut back on** our monthly expenses.
deal with	to face or find a solution to	They need to **deal with** the problem quickly.
do away with	to eliminate	The company **did away with** employee bonuses.
fall for	to believe that a joke or trick is true	I always **fall for** your April Fool's jokes.
fill in for	to replace somebody temporarily	Could somebody **fill in for** Sarah today? She is sick.
find out about	to discover a piece of information	She **found out about** the surprise party.
follow up on	to investigate	We need to **follow up on** the customer's complaint.
get back to	to communicate with somebody at a later date about something; to return to doing something	I will **get back to** you about the matter as soon as possible. I will **get back to** playing tennis regularly as soon as my knee heals.
get into	to start to enjoy or get very involved in something	Look at him swaying. He's really **getting into** the music. She has **gotten into** judo, volunteering for every event.
get over	to start to feel well again after a bad experience	He still hasn't **gotten over** his divorce.
get rid of	to throw or give away something; to eliminate something unwanted	Let's **get rid of** all the unused stuff in this room. Do you know a good way to **get rid of** weeds naturally?
get through get through to (somebody)	to manage to deal with a difficult situation; to get somebody to understand something	I **got through** my oral presentation! Yahoo! Please try to **get through to** her that she must not quit school!
give in to	to submit or surrender	Do not **give in to** his demand to lower the price.
go over	to examine or check something carefully	Please **go over** the problems outlined in the report and come up with some solutions by next week.
look forward to	to be excited and happy about a future event	They are really **looking forward to** their holidays.

Phrasal verb	Meaning	Example sentence
look into	to try to discover the facts about something	The university is **looking into** how it can improve its student services.
look up to	to admire and respect	I really **look up to** you for all your achievements.
make up for	to compensate for	Nothing can **make up for** the damage it caused.
put up with	to accept a disagreeable situation or behaviour	I don't know how you **put up with** your grumpy boss.
run into	to meet somebody by chance; to start to have difficulties or problems	I **ran into** an old friend on the subway yesterday. We are going to **run into** problems if we don't have enough volunteers at the event.
run out	to use all of something so none is left	The printer has **run out of** paper.

Type 3: Separable transitive phrasal verbs

Phrasal verb	Meaning	Example sentence
back up	to offer facts as proof to support somebody's words as truth	You need to **back** your opinion **up** with facts. Will you **back** me **up** when I say I didn't do it?
call off	to cancel	They are going to **call** the wedding **off**.
cut off	to interrupt a person while she or he is talking	You **cut** me **off** in the middle of my sentence.
drop off	to drive somebody to a designated spot	The bus will **drop** you **off** in front of the building.
fill in	to explain something to somebody	You will have to **fill** me **in** on what happened.
keep up	to continue doing something	**Keep up** the good work. / Good job! **Keep** it **up**.
lay off	to end a person's employment because there is not enough work	The company had to **lay** 50 employees **off**.
leave out	to not include something or someone	You **left** some people **out** in your speech.
let down	to disappoint somebody	He **let** his team **down** by not giving his best effort.
look over	to examine something	Please **look** the report **over** before the meeting.
look up	to do research to find information	I will have to **look** the address **up** online.
make up	to invent something	Is that the real reason or did you **make** it **up**?
pick up (somebody or something)	to fetch something or go get a person by some means of transport	I'll **pick** you **up** after work with my new car.
point out	to tell somebody something	We haven't met. **Point** her **out** when she arrives.
put off	to postpone something to a later time	Don't **put** your work **off** for too long.
set up	to arrange or plan something	We will have to **set** a meeting time **up** soon.
sort out	to solve or make arrangements for something	If a problem arises, we will **sort** it **out**.
take back	to retract a statement	I **take** my comment **back**. It was unfair.
turn down	to refuse something	You shouldn't **turn** the job offer **down**.
turn off/on	to stop something from working by pushing a button or moving a switch	Please **turn** the lights **off** before you leave the room.
work out	to deal with and try to solve something	We need to **work** our problems **out** together.

Adjective-Preposition Combinations

Adjectives are often combined with prepositions. There are no rules governing which prepositions to use with each adjective; you must learn the combinations through practice and use.

Common adjective-preposition combinations

Concerned about means worried about something, whereas to be *concerned with* means involved with something.

accustomed to	dedicated to	interested in	scared of
acquainted with	concerned about/ with	in charge of	satisfied with
afraid of	different from	involved in (something); involved with (somebody)	similar to
angry at . . . about (something); angry at . . . with (somebody)	discouraged about/at; discouraged by/ over (a situation); discouraged from (doing something)	jealous of	skilled in/at
ashamed of	enthusiastic about	known for	sorry for
aware of	familiar with	opposed to	suitable for
bored with/by/of	fed up with	pleased with	sure about/of
capable of	fond of	proud of	tired of
certain of/about	glad about	relevant to	upset about (something); upset with (somebody)
committed to	happy about (something) happy with (somebody)	responsible for	worried about

If you are not sure which preposition to use with a certain verb, adjective, or noun, look up the word in a dictionary or online and check example sentences in which the word is used to find out which preposition should follow.

Exercise 1

Complete the prepositional verbs with the correct preposition.

1. When you **arrive** _____in_____ Toronto, somebody will be waiting for you at the airport.

2. Are you going to **participate** _____in_____ any extracurricular activities?

3. The salary will **depend** _____on_____ the employee's past job experience and training.

4. New hires can **benefit** a lot _____from_____ the advice of experienced employees.

5. A digital camera **consists** _____of_____ an optical system with a CCD detector.

Exercise 2

Fill in each blank with the correct Type 1 phrasal verb. Conjugate the verb for tense and person if necessary.

1. Negotiations _____broke down_____ after one party failed to budge on one of the conditions.

2. Everybody in the office already knows that! You know how word ___gets around___.

3. We are collecting money for Kathy's gift. Do you want to ___pitch in___?

4. How did your first date ___turn out___?

5. Don't worry! I'm sure your girlfriend won't be mad for long! Things will ___blow over___.

6. The applicant was born and ___grew up___ in BC, but he is now living in Quebec.

7. The client accepted the fee and said we can ___go ahead___ and start the renovations.

8. Sorry, could you please ___hold on___ for a second while I check the information?

Exercise 3

Complete each of the phrasal verbs with the correct preposition to form Type 2 and 3 phrasal verbs.

1. The offer was so fantastic that I couldn't **turn** it ___down___.

2. Due to the lack of participation, the Writing Centre has decided to **do away** ___with___ the extra workshops it used to offer during exam time.

3. Can anybody **fill in** ___for___ John today? He can't work his overtime shift.

4. I wonder if she is telling the truth or if she just **made it** ___up___.

5. Please order more ink in case we **run** ___out___.

6. I must remember to **point** ___out___ the rules about break times to the new trainees.

7. You didn't **fall** ___for___ his sob story and offer to do the work for him, did you?

8. What evidence is there to **back** ___up___ that theory?

9. The police are going to **look** ___into___ the incident to find the culprit.

10. He didn't live up to our expectations. He really **let** us ___down___.

Exercise 4

Fill in each blank with a phrasal verb that matches the meaning in parentheses. Conjugate the verb where necessary.

Hi Bob,

I'm so glad I ___ran into___ (accidently met) you yesterday in Montreal and we got a chance to ___catch up___ (exchange news about ourselves). I was happy to hear that the business you started is really ___taking off___ (becoming successful).

I was wondering if you'd like to ___get together___ (meet) again sometime soon. Maybe we could go to dinner. It's been a while since I ___ate out___ (eat at a restaurant) I could stop by and ___pick___ you ___up___ (fetch) if you like. Let me know.

I ___look forward to___ (eagerly await) seeing you again!

Meryl

Exercise 5

Replace the underlined phrasal verbs with a more formal one-word verb.

EXAMPLE   The accused <u>left out</u> a number of important details in his account of the story. _____**omitted**_____

1. You need to <u>make up</u> for the days you took off work by working some overtime. _____compensate_____

2. The government has <u>turned down</u> all the union's proposals. _____rejected_____

3. They lied and <u>made up</u> the entire story. _____invented_____

4. We need to <u>set up</u> a meeting as soon as possible. _____arrange/organize_____

5. My son's behaviour and grades have really <u>turned around</u>. _____improved_____

Exercise 6

Fill in the blanks with the correct preposition to follow the bolded adjective.

1. This document will help you become **acquainted** _____with_____ our workplace regulations.

2. The student was expelled for being **involved** _____in_____ illegal activities on campus.

3. The person **in charge** _____of_____ marketing will be responsible _____for_____ the promotion of all the company's products.

4. She is **interested** _____in_____ pursuing her education and obtaining a PhD.

5. If you follow these recommendations, you will surely be **satisfied** _____with_____ the results.

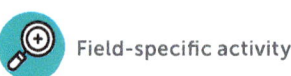

Field-specific activity

You could have students perform their dialogues in front of the class. Students could write down the phrasal verbs they hear their classmates use. Students could also vote for their favourite dialogue or you could award a prize for the group that used the most phrasal verbs correctly.

Communicative Activities

1. In a small group, create a short dialogue (3–4 minutes) in which you use as many phrasal verbs as possible. Your dialogue must be coherent and you must fit the phrases into the dialogue in the most logical, natural way possible.

2. Find an Internet site (or other publication) that posts information related to your field of study. If necessary, you may refer to more than one site or source. Write down six to eight examples from the site (or publication) in which prepositions are used as part of a prepositional verb, phrasal verb, or adjective-preposition combination. Include the sentence from which each preposition was taken and note the source(s) of your information. Be ready to share your findings with your classmates and tell them whether the preposition is part of a prepositional verb, phrasal verb, or adjective-preposition combination.

CHAPTER 9

Gerunds and Infinitives

A **gerund** is the *-ing* form of a verb, which functions as a noun: **verb + -ing**.

> **EXAMPLE**   The job involves **travelling** to Europe once a month.
> gerund

An **infinitive** is a verb form that acts as a noun and is preceded by the word *to*: ***to* + verb**. Infinitives are not conjugated for tense or person. Never add a third-person *-s* or use a past tense form with an infinitive.

> **EXAMPLE**   He threatened **to quit** his job if he didn't get a wage increase.
> infinitive

Gerunds and infinitives can function as subjects of a sentence.

> **EXAMPLES**   **Volunteering** is a good way to get work experience.
> gerund
>
> **To volunteer** at a seniors' residence would be a good idea.
> infinitive

Gerunds and infinitives can also come after verbs and function as objects or complements of verbs.

> **EXAMPLES**
>
> Students really enjoy **going** outside for gym class.
> gerund
>
> The students' favourite gym activities are **playing** soccer and **kayaking**.
> gerund   gerund

When gerunds function as objects or complements after a verb, it is the verb that determines whether a gerund or infinitive will follow. Some verbs are always followed by a gerund, while others are always followed by an infinitive. A small group of verbs can be followed by either a gerund or infinitive with no change in meaning. Finally, there are a few verbs that can be followed by either a gerund or an infinitive but with a difference in meaning.

When unsure whether to use the gerund or infinitive form after a verb, the following guidelines can help you to choose the correct form most of the time.

Guidelines for when to use the gerund or infinitive form

Use a gerund (verb + *-ing*)	Use an infinitive (*to* + verb)
1. after verbs from List 1 below	1. after verbs from List 2 on page 201
2. when the information that follows the verb answers the question "What?" **EXAMPLE** I remember (what?) **putting** the file on your desk.	2. when the information that follows the verb answers the question "To do what?" or "For what purpose?" or "In order to do what?" **EXAMPLES** He promised (to do what?) **to finish** the report by Monday. I agreed with the decision (in order to do what?) **to keep** everybody happy.
3. after the verb *go* when it is followed by a recreational sport or activity **EXAMPLE** We should go **hiking** next weekend.	3. after verb + object constructions (see List 5 on page 201) **EXAMPLE** object The teacher urged her student **to become** a tutor.
4. after any preposition (including prepositions that are part of a phrasal verb)* **EXAMPLES** preposition Are you afraid of **flying**? preposition preposition I look forward to **meeting** you in person.	4. after most adjectives **EXAMPLES** adjective He is unwilling **to work** overtime. adjective We were happy **to come** to your party.
5. after a noun in certain expressions: have difficulties/trouble have a hard/good time have fun spend/waste one's time **EXAMPLES** I have difficulty **learning** names. Don't waste your time **trying** to fix it.	5. after most nouns when the information that follows answers the question "to do what?" **EXAMPLES** noun You need permission **to do** that. noun Travelling gives you the opportunity **to make** business contacts.

You might want to point out that the *to* in "I look forward to meeting you" is part of the phrasal verb *look forward to* and not part of an infinitive form.

*****EXCEPTION** The verb *used to* is used only in the past tense and is followed by an infinitive.

    EXAMPLE   He used to smoke.
                    He smoked habitually in the past but doesn't smoke anymore.

The expression *to be used to* is followed by a gerund.

    EXAMPLE   She is used to getting her own way.
                    She is in the habit of getting her own way.

List 1: Common verbs always followed by a gerund (verb + *-ing*)

    EXAMPLE   Would you mind **helping** me with this?

acknowledge	delay	imagine	miss	recommend
admit	deny	include	postpone	resent
advise	detest	involve	practise	risk
anticipate	discuss	justify	quit	suggest
appreciate	dislike	keep	recall	tolerate
avoid	enjoy	mention		
consider	finish	mind		

List 2: Common verbs always followed by an infinitive (*to* + verb)

EXAMPLE   She threatened **to quit** her job if the work conditions did not improve.

afford	claim	get	manage	promise
agree	decide	happen	need	refuse
appear	demand	hesitate	neglect	tend
arrange	deserve	hope	offer	threaten
ask	expect	intend	plan	volunteer
choose	fail	learn	pretend	wait

List 3: Common verbs that can be followed by a gerund or infinitive with no change of meaning

EXAMPLE   He began **to work** at the age of 15.

He began **working** at the age of 15.

Both example sentences have the same meaning.

begin	hate	prefer
continue	like/love	start

When *like* or *love* is used in the simple past or present perfect tense to mean *enjoy the experience of,* use the gerund form after the verb rather than the infinitive.

Correct	I liked dancing with you last night.
Incorrect	~~I liked to dance with you last night.~~
Correct	I have liked working with you.
Incorrect	~~I have liked to work with you.~~

List 4: Common verbs that can be followed by a gerund or infinitive but with a change in meaning

forget	regret	stop
need	remember	try

With these verbs, following the guidelines in the chart on page 200 can help you choose the correct form most of the time. See Guideline 2 for an example.

EXAMPLE   John needs (what?) **training**.

John needs (to do what?) **to train** Pierre.

NOTE The verb *regret* is almost always followed by a gerund; however, it can be used with the infinitive *to inform* to introduce bad news.

EXAMPLES   She regrets **quitting** her job.

We regret **to inform** you that your flight has been delayed.

List 5: Verbs commonly used with verb + object (+ infinitive) constructions

advise	expect	permit	urge
ask	invite	persuade	want
convince	order	tell	warn
encourage			

                                                                                          object
EXAMPLES   Our top salesperson has convinced <u>many clients</u> **to buy** the new model.

                                                              object
The psychologist advised <u>her</u> **to take** some time off work.

Exercise 1

Read the short job posting below. Underline all the gerunds and infinitives. Refer to chart on page 200 and note which guideline applies to each verb. Write the number of the guideline above each gerund and infinitive.

Are you having difficulty **finding** [5] a flexible, part-time job that will look great on your resumé? We have the perfect job for you! The English Department is looking for high-performing, dependable students from advanced-level English courses **to tutor** [2] students that want extra help with their English studies. The position requires you **to meet** [2] 50 minutes a week with two students **to give** [3] them practice with **learning** [4] English. If you are interested in **applying** [4], fill out the job application form on the college website. We look forward to **receiving** [4/2] your application!

Exercise 2

Underline the correct word (gerund or infinitive) that follows the verb.

EXAMPLE   The university has been considering **to offer / offering** that course for a long time.

1.   The job involves **selling / to sell** products door to door.

2.   Many students would probably enjoy **taking / to take** a yoga class between classes.

3.   His friend often tries to persuade him **skipping / to skip** class.

4.   I should stop **buying / to buy** lunch from the food truck every day; it's expensive.

5.   The technician must postpone **training / to train** the new staff until his injury is healed.

Exercise 3

Write the correct form of the verb in parenthesis (gerund or infinitive) to complete each sentence.

EXAMPLE   The bank agreed __to finance__ (finance) our project.

1.   The entire staff is going to go __rafting__ (raft) together this summer.

2.   You won't regret __buying__ (buy) stocks in the company.

3.   Don't you remember __meeting__ (meet) him last year?

4.   You must not forget __to register__ (register) before the deadline.

5.   The students really liked __watching__ (watch) the film in class yesterday.

Field-specific activity

You can ask students to send their messages electronically and have the recipients respond.

Communicative Activities

1.   Find a job posting related to your field of study. Underline the gerunds and infinitives used in the ad.

2.   Write five to seven sentences that describe a job related to your field of study but do not actually state what the job is. Try to give information that is informative but doesn't give the answer away too easily. Each sentence must include a gerund or infinitive. Exchange sentences with a partner. Your partner must underline the gerunds and infinitives in your sentences and guess what job you are describing.

EXAMPLE

You need **to have** a doctorate degree. **Having** good communication skills is an asset. Your clients expect you **to have** a clean working environment. You cannot mind **seeing** blood. The job requires **working** with animals. Answer: Veterinarian

CHAPTER 10

Noun Clauses That Begin with a Question Word (*wh-* Noun Clauses)

A noun clause is a dependent clause that functions as a noun. It can act as a subject, object, or complement in a sentence. Noun clauses that begin with a question word are referred to as *wh-* noun clauses because most question words begin with *wh-*.

 For more information about clauses, see Grammar Guide Chapter 1, page 152.

EXAMPLES
subject
What he told you is not true.

object
I don't know **whose keys these are**.

complement
This is **where the main office will be**.

Indirect questions with *wh-* noun clauses

Sometimes to be polite, we use an indirect question rather than asking directly.

Indirect questions start with phrases such as

Do you know . . .	Do you have any idea . . .	Please tell me . . .
Would you know . . .	Do you mind if I ask . . .	Please explain . . .
Could you tell me . . .	Would you mind telling me . . .	

These phrases are followed by a noun clause that begins with a question word (*who, what, where, when, why, which, whose, whom,* or *how*).

The rules for question formation do not apply to *wh-* noun clauses. The question word in the noun clause is followed directly by the subject and verb. No form of the auxiliary *do* is ever added to the question.

EXAMPLE   Would you mind telling me who is coming to the meeting?
question   verb
word

When a *Yes/No* question is turned into an indirect question, the words *if* or *whether* or *whether or not* are used to introduce the noun clause. The use of *whether* (or *whether or not*) is more formal than the use of *if*.

EXAMPLE   Could you tell me whether or not Johnathan is coming to the meeting?

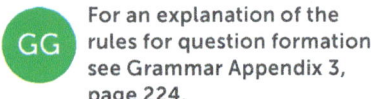 **GG** For an explanation of the rules for question formation, see Grammar Appendix 3, page 224.

With indirect questions, an answer is expected from the person(s) being addressed, but they don't always end in a question mark. An indirect question ends with a question mark when the main clause it is attached to is a question (e.g., Do you know . . .?), but ends in a period when the main clause is a statement (e.g., Please tell me . . ..)

Direct question	Indirect question
verb subject What **is** his email address?	subject verb Do you know what his email address **is**?
subject verb Where **is** the meeting **going to be**?	subject verb Would you know where the meeting **is going to be**?
subject verb Why **did** you **miss** class?	subject verb Please tell me why you **missed** class.
subject verb **Are** classes **cancelled** today?	subject verb Could you tell me if classes **are cancelled**? subject verb Do you know whether (or not) classes **are cancelled**?

When the noun clause of an indirect question begins with *who, what,* or *which/whose* + object and the question word is the subject of the verb, then the verb comes directly after the question word (*who, what, which* + object).

Direct question	Indirect question
subject verb Who **won** the prize?	subject verb Do you know who **won** the prize?
subject verb What **happened**?	subject verb Do you mind if I ask what **happened**?
subject verb Which dealer **offered** the best price?	subject verb Could you tell me which dealer **offered** the best price?

Exercise 1

Turn each of the following direct questions into an indirect question. Begin each indirect question with a different phrase from page 201.

1. Where are the restrooms?

   _____

2. Is there a special fare for students?

   _____

3. Why didn't you finish the report?

   _____

4. Where was the conference held last year?

   _____

5. Who is spreading the rumours about me?

   _____

Wh- noun clauses that are not indirect questions

Wh- noun clauses do not always indicate that there is an embedded question for which a response is required. In some cases, the *wh*- noun clause is simply functioning as a subject, object, or complement in a sentence; it is not meant as a question to the person being addressed.

EXAMPLES **What the director said at the meeting** surprised everybody.

I can't remember **how old he is**.

Her proudest moment was **when she received her doctorate degree**.

Note that all the rules explained above for indirect questions with *wh*- noun clauses also apply to *wh*- noun clauses that are not questions.

Exercise 2

Complete the sentence that follows each question with a *wh*- noun clause (related to the question). The first sentence has been done for you.

1. How does a car engine work?

   The teacher will explain _____**how a car engine works.**_____

2. When is our assignment due?

   Let's ask the teacher __when our assignment is due.__

3. Which kind of computer should I buy?

   I wonder _which kind of computer I should buy.__

4. What effect can the colour red have on a person?

   The study examined __what effect the colour red can have on a person.__

5. Why did he quit his job?

   _Why he quit his job_____ is a mystery.

6. Who is responsible for ordering office supplies?

   We need to find out _who is responsible for ordering office supplies.__

Wh- noun clauses with an infinitive

Most *wh*- noun clauses that begin with a question word (except *why* and *if*) can include an infinitive (*to* + verb) structure after the *wh*- word. In such cases, the infinitive expresses the meaning *should* (advice) or *can/could* (possibility). The subject and verb are omitted in these cases.

In each pair of sentences below, the meaning is the same.

EXAMPLES

Could you please explain how **I can get** to your office?
Could you please explain how **to get** to your office?

I didn't know if **I should call** at such an early hour.
I didn't know whether* **to call** at such an early hour.

*The word *whether* replaces the word *if* because *if* cannot be followed by an infinitive.

Incorrect   I didn't know if to call at such an early hour.

Exercise 3

Write a second sentence that means the same as the first. If the first sentence contains an infinitive in the *wh-* noun clause, rewrite it without the infinitive. If the first sentence does not contain an infinitive, rewrite it using an infinitive in the *wh-* noun clause.

1. The architect suggested which materials we should use.

    The architect suggested which materials to use.

2. We need to check how we should install the lights.

    We need to check how to install the lights.

3. The video editor will suggest which segments of the footage you should cut.

    The video editor will suggest which segments of the footage to cut.

4. The teacher explained how to get a good mark on the assignment.

    The teacher explained how students could get a good mark on the assignment.

 **Field-specific activity**

Communicative Activity

In a small group, state your field of study or future career. The other group members will ask you five indirect questions (that include *wh-* noun clauses) related to your field of study or future career using phrases from the list on page 201 of this unit. The questioners must include information questions and *Yes/No* questions. (If necessary, explain to your group what topics your field of study covers or what a professional in your field does.)

In your response to each indirect question, include a *wh-* noun clause. Begin each response with a different phrase such as *I don't know, I can't remember, Why do you want to know, Do you really care, You wouldn't believe, It is unbelievable,* and so on.

EXAMPLES

For a student who wants to study medicine

Question: Do you know how many patients a doctor sees in a day?

Response: I am not sure how many patients a doctor sees in a day.

For a student who studies social science

Question: Could you tell me what kind of experiments social scientists conduct?

Response: What kind of experiments social scientists conduct is a mystery to me.

CHAPTER 11

Quoted and Reported Speech

When writing or speaking, we sometimes want to report what somebody else has said. Sometimes this is required to add support to our arguments. One way to do this is to use quoted speech—or direct speech—to convey the speaker's exact words.

When quoting directly,

- Use a reporting verb followed by a comma. (blue)
- Put the quoted words inside quotation marks. (green)
- Put end-of-sentence punctuation inside the final quotation marks. (purple)

> **Direct quote**   Johnathan said, "I am extremely tired."

Another option is to use reported speech—or indirect speech—to describe what someone else wrote or said.

When reporting someone's speech,

- Add the word *that*. (blue)
- Use the appropriate pronoun. (green)
- Change the verb tense if necessary. (purple)

> **Reported speech**   Johnathan said that he was extremely tired.

Reporting verbs include *advise, announce, claim, comment, conclude, confess, declare, exclaim, explain, insist, remark, reply, report, reveal, say, state, tell* (someone), *vow.*

Verb tenses used in direct quotes and reported speech

Note that most tenses change when direct speech becomes reported speech.

Direct quote	Reported speech
Simple past	**Past perfect**
My mother said, "Julie finished her PhD."	My mother said that Julie had finished her PhD.
Simple present	**Simple past**
Peter stated, "Leo studies at McGill."	Peter stated that Leo studied at McGill.
Simple future	***would* + verb**
She said, "I will work on it tomorrow."	She said that she would work on it tomorrow.
Past progressive	**Past perfect progressive**
The doctor said, "I was waiting to perform surgery at 4:00 yesterday."	The doctor said that she had been waiting to perform surgery at 4:00 yesterday.
Present progressive	**Past progressive**
Lyne declared, "I am waiting for the financial report."	Lyne declared that she was waiting for the financial report.
Future progressive	***would* + *be* + present participle**
Mason confessed, "Maggie will be working late."	Mason confessed that Maggie would be working late.

Direct quote	Reported speech
Past perfect	**Past perfect**
Ms. Carver announced, "Since the work had not been completed, everyone had to work over the weekend."	Ms. Carver announced that since the work had not been completed, everyone had to work over the weekend.
Present perfect	**Past perfect**
The students said, "We have already studied for the test."	The students said that they had already studied for the test.
Future perfect	**Future perfect**
The teacher declared, "The students will have finished the book by the end of the semester."	The teacher declared that the students will have finished the book by the end of the semester.
Past perfect progressive	**Past perfect progressive**
My boss said, "Bill had been anticipating a profit for the third quarter."	My boss said that Bill had been anticipating a profit for the third quarter.
Present perfect progressive	**Past perfect progressive**
The salesperson said, "I have been preparing the proposals since last week."	The salesperson said that she had been preparing the proposals since last week.
Future perfect progressive	*would + have + be* + **present participle**
School officials stated, "Students will have been waiting for two weeks by the time the marks are entered."	School officials stated that students would have been waiting for two weeks by the time the marks are entered.

Modals used in direct quotes and reported speech

Note that present modals become past modals.

Direct quote	Reported speech
Buddy insisted, "I **will** take care of the books."	Buddy insisted that he **would** take care of the books.
Julie said, "Bill **can** do the job."	Julie said that Bill **could** do the job.
Stacy said, "Lenny **has to** work overtime."	Stacy said that Lenny **had to** work overtime.
Loretta insisted, "Adam **must** cover my shift."	Loretta insisted that Adam **had to** cover her shift.

When a direct quote contains a general truth or fact, the verb tense in the reported speech may remain the same.

EXAMPLE   Direct quote   Jacques said, "I love my job."

Reported speech   Jacques said that he loves his job.

Use an ellipsis (a series of three dots: . . .) to replace words that you omit from a quote. An omission must not change the original meaning of a text.

EXAMPLE   The doctor explained, "The tumour is benign . . . but it must be removed."

Exercise 1

Read the following text and rephrase the sentences by changing the direct quotes by the Elders into reported speech. Change the verb tenses as appropriate for all the quotes.

In September 2017, 5000 leaders and Elders of Indigenous communities got together for Canada's first National Gathering of Elders. The gathering was an opportunity to honour those individuals who work with Indigenous youth, sharing their wisdom and insight with the next generation. Some of the attending Elders spoke with CBC News about culture and reconciliation, offering advice to their youth:

Chief Ronnie Alec from Lake Babine First Nation stated, "All of us have to think about the young generation . . . coming . . . behind us."

Doreen Bergum, of the Métis Nation of Alberta said, "Be proud of who you are because it's worth it."

Tuktoyaktuk's Jean Gruben noted "we go whaling for the Elders to make sure they have enough food for the winter."

Lillian Elias of Inuvik insists "respect is the most important thing."

Reith, Terry. "'Be Proud of Who You Are': Indigenous Elders Offer Advice to the Young about Self-Respect and Reconciliation." *CBC News*, https://www.cbc.ca/news/canada/edmonton/voices-elders-indigenous-1.4302299. Accessed 15 Dec. 2018.

1. Chief Ronnie Alec stated that all First Nations people had to think about the younger generation coming behind them.

2. Doreen Bergum said youth need to be proud of who they were because it was worth it.

3. Jean Gruben noted that they went whaling for the Elders to make sure that they had enough food for the winter.

4. Lillian Elias insisted that respect was the most important thing.

Communicative Activity

Interview two classmates to complete the chart below. Ask your classmates to state an opinion on each of the different subjects. Write Classmate 1's answer as a direct quote. Write Classmate 2's answer as reported speech. Add your own subject to the last two rows. of the chart.

Subject	Classmate 1 (direct quote)	Classmate 2 (reported speech)
Education		
Money		
Social media		
_____		
_____		

CHAPTER 12

Adjective Clauses (or Relative Clauses)

Remember

A clause is a group of words that contains a subject and a verb.

An independent clause is a complete thought and can stand on its own as a sentence.

A dependent clause does not make sense on its own and must be connected to an independent clause.

An adjective clause is a dependent clause.

 For more information about clauses, see Grammar Guide Chapter 1, page 152.

An adjective clause is a dependent clause that gives additional information about a noun. Use an adjective clause in a sentence to express information more concisely.

> **EXAMPLE** Sam Smith is the lucky employee. Sam Smith is going to get the promotion.
>
> Sam Smith is the lucky employee **who is going to get the promotion**.

Relative Pronouns

An adjective clause may begin with the words *who*, *which*, *that*, *whom*, or *whose*. When these words are used to introduce an adjective clause, they are called relative pronouns.

- Use *who* to refer to people (not things).

  > **EXAMPLE** Mary Anderson is the woman **who invented windshield wipers in 1903**.

- Use *which* to refer to things.

  > **EXAMPLE** The pancreas is an organ, **which is a part of the human body**.

- Use *that* to refer to people or things.

  > **EXAMPLES** Mary Anderson is the woman **that invented windshield wipers in 1903**.
  >
  > The pancreas is an organ **that plays an important role in digestion**.

- Use *whom* to refer to a person who is the object of the verb in the adjective clause.

  > object   v
  > **EXAMPLE** <u>Ms. Sands</u> is the person **whom the company is going to hire**.
  > The company is going to hire Ms. Sands.

  Whom sounds very formal, especially in speech; therefore, the word *who* is generally used in informal contexts.

  In cases where the verb requires a preposition (e.g., *speak to*), the preposition may come before the adjective clause (in formal usage) or at the end of it (in more informal usage).

  > **EXAMPLE** Mr. Gagnon is the person **to whom you need to speak**.
  >
  > Mr. Gagnon is the person **who you need to speak to**.

- Use *which* or *that* in the same way as *whom* to introduce the object of the verb in an adjective clause.

  > **Formal** Ms. Sands is the person **that the company is going to hire**.
  >
  > **Informal** There is a font called Calibri, **which I use often**.

- Use *whose* to introduce something that belongs to a person.

  > **EXAMPLE** Johann Fichte was a German philosopher **whose ideas are quite difficult to grasp**.

Exercise 1

Combine the following pairs of sentences into one sentence using an adjective clause.

1. A starfish is an organism. A starfish can regenerate its entire body.

   A starfish is an organism that can regenerate its entire body.

2. The client came by the office this morning. You took the client's keys by mistake.

   You took the keys of the client who came by the office this morning.

3. Yesterday I went to lunch with a friend. I hadn't seen my friend in years.

   Yesterday, I went to lunch with a friend whom I hadn't seen in years.

4. The building is very fancy. You work in the building.

   The building that you work in is very fancy. / The building in which you work is very fancy.

5. The employee was excited. The employee won a sales award.

   The employee who won a sales award was excited.

Essential and Non-Essential Adjective Clauses

There are two types of adjective clauses: essential and non-essential. The punctuation and relative pronoun differs with each type.

An essential adjective clause adds information that is necessary in order to identify the noun being described. No commas are used with an essential adjective clause.

> **EXAMPLE** The office **that is at the end of the hall** will be for the new employee.
> The information in this adjective clause is necessary to identify which office is being referred to.

A non-essential adjective clause adds information that is not necessary to identify the noun being described. A non-essential adjective clause is set off with commas.

> **EXAMPLE** This office**, which was recently renovated,** will be for the new employee.
> The information in this adjective clause is not necessary to identify which office is being referred to. It simply adds extra information about the office.

The word *that* cannot be used as a relative pronoun in a non-essential adjective clause. *That* is used as a relative pronoun only in essential adjective clauses.

| Incorrect | ~~My office, that I don't like, is very small.~~ |
| Correct | My office, which I don't like, is very small. |

Exercise 2

Underline the adjective clause in each of the sentences below and identify it as an essential or non-essential adjective clause by writing E or NE in the space after the sentence. Add commas to sentences where necessary.

1. A snake milker, which is a job that actually exists, extracts venom from snakes. __NE__

2. The company needs to hire someone who is fluent in both French and Spanish. __E__

3. The children who hadn't eaten lunch were very hungry. __E or NE__

4. The customer that you yelled at yesterday made a formal complaint. __E__

5. Henri Matisse, whose paintings I love, was a great colourist. __NE__

Identifying clauses are used in formal definitions. For information on using formal definitions to define field-specific terms, go to Explore Online.

Students should answer that as an essential clause (with no commas) the adjective clause indicates that only those children who hadn't eaten lunch were hungry (but presumably some other children were not hungry). As a non-essential clause (with commas), it indicates that none of the children had eaten lunch and all the children were hungry.

Note that the adjective clause in question 3 could be essential or nonessential. What is the difference in meaning when this sentence is punctuated as an essential versus a non-essential clause?

Reduced Adjective Clauses

Both essential and non-essential adjective clauses may be reduced in certain cases.

1. When the relative pronoun is the object of the verb in the adjective clause, the relative pronoun may be omitted with no change in meaning.

   EXAMPLES   The book <u>that</u> we are reading in our English class is *Barney's Version*.

   The book we are reading in our English class is *Barney's Version*.

   The customer <u>whom</u> you were just speaking to seemed really angry.

   The customer you were just speaking to seemed really angry.

2. By contrast, when the relative pronoun is the subject of the verb in the adjective clause, the relative pronoun may not be omitted.

   Correct   The book **that** has the ripped cover is yours.

   Incorrect   ~~The book has the ripped cover is yours.~~

   In reduced adjective clauses, a preposition must come at the end of the clause.

   Correct   The customer you were just speaking **to** seemed really angry.

   Incorrect   ~~The customer to you were just speaking seemed really angry.~~

3. When the adjective clause contains a form of the verb *be* (as the main verb or as an auxiliary), both the relative subject pronoun and the form of the verb *be* may be omitted.

   EXAMPLE   The computer **that is** on the teacher's desk will have to be replaced.
   The computer on the teacher's desk will have to be replaced.

   The teacher **who is** replacing you has a lot of experience.
   The teacher replacing you has a lot of experience.

   NOTE 1 This rule does not apply when the verb *be* is the auxiliary verb in the future tense (*be going to*).

   Correct   The teacher who **is going to** replace you has a lot of experience.

   Incorrect   ~~The teacher going to replace you has a lot of experience.~~

   NOTE 2 When the omission of the relative pronoun and the form of the verb *be* leaves just an adjective ending in *-ing* or *-en/-ed* (which answers "what kind of?" or "which one(s)?"), you must move the adjective before the noun being described.

   EXAMPLES   The computer that is **broken** will have to be replaced.

   The **broken** computer will have to be replaced.

   When Mark Twain died, he left many works that were **unpublished**.

   When Mark Twain died, he left many **unpublished** works.

Exercise 3

Cross out the unnecessary words in any sentence where reduction of the adjective clause is possible.

   EXAMPLE   Einstein's theory of relativity is one ~~that~~ many people don't fully understand.

1. Canada, which has a relatively small population, is the second largest country in the world.

2. The man ~~who is~~ wearing the red tie is the guest speaker of the conference.

3. It appears that the <u>strike which is upcoming</u> is going to be a long one.

4. Athens, ~~which was~~ founded about 5000 years ago, is one of the world's oldest cities.

5. Wallpaper that has big stripes wouldn't look good in the reception area.

Sometimes the verb *be* functions as the main verb.

EXAMPLE

The computer **is** on the desk.

Sometimes the verb *be* functions as an auxiliary.

EXAMPLE

Another teacher **is replacing** me.

Point out to students that the adjective clause in sentence 3 ("the strike which is upcoming") can be reduced to "the upcoming strike."

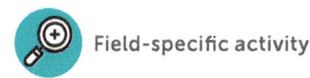
Communicative Activity

Using information and vocabulary from your field of study, write seven sentences that include an adjective clause. Include both essential and non-essential adjective clauses and a variety of relative pronouns.

Exchange sentences with a partner. Your partner must

- Underline the adjective clause in each sentence.
- Mark each adjective clause as essential (E) or non-essential (NE).
- Cross out the unnecessary words in any adjective clause where reduction is possible.

EXAMPLES

Original	Depression is a mental condition ~~that is~~ often misdiagnosed.
	<div align="center">E</div>
Reduced	Depression is an often misdiagnosed mental condition.
Original	*Romeo and Juliet*, ~~which is~~ one of Shakespeare's most popular plays, was first published in 1597.
Reduced	*Romeo and Juliet*, one of Shakespeare's most popular plays, was first published in 1597. NE

CHAPTER 13

Parts of Speech, Roots, and Affixes

Knowing the basic parts of speech, as well as common word roots and affixes, is useful in both reading and writing. This knowledge can help you guess the meaning of new words when reading, and it can help you choose the correct words when writing.

Parts of Speech

Part of speech refers to the function that a word serves within a sentence. The four main parts of speech in English are noun, verb, adjective, and adverb.

- A noun refers to a person, place, or thing (e.g., David, library, freedom).
- A verb refers an action or state of being (e.g., summarize, feel, be).
- An adjective describes a noun (e.g., complicated, gorgeous, talkative). Adjectives come before the noun they describe (e.g., **interesting** book, **tasty** meal) or follow stative verbs, such as *be, seem, appear, feel, taste,* and so on. (He appeared **nervous**. The meal tasted **great**.)
- An adverb modifies a verb, adjective, or another adverb. It answers the questions how, when, where, why, to what extent, how much, or how long (e.g., quickly, seriously, really)

Adverbs can also modify an entire sentence; however, this unit does not deal with sentence-level adverbs.

EXAMPLE

Unfortunately, my investment didn't pay off.

Exercise 1

Write the part of speech (POS) of each of the underlined words in the sentences below. Then write other words in the same word family (i.e., words that are formed from the same root but function as different parts of speech).

1. Drinking diet pop is not good for your <u>health</u>.

   POS = **noun → healthy (adj); healthily (adv)**

2. He takes his job very <u>seriously</u>.

   POS = adv → serious (adj); seriousness (noun)

3. A good nurse should always be positive and <u>optimistic</u>.

   POS = adj → optimist (noun); optimism (noun); optimistically (adv)

4. I'm sure you'll <u>succeed</u> in law school.

   POS = verb → success (noun); successful (adj); successfully (adv)

Roots and Affixes

The root is the part of a word that holds the word's basic meaning. It is the part of the word that remains after any affixes have been taken away.

EXAMPLES   *jur/jus* meaning "law," as in *jury* and *justify*

ped/pod meaning "foot," as in *centipede* and *podiatrist*

An affix is added to a word root to change the word's meaning or part of speech. There are two types of affixes: prefixes and suffixes.

A prefix is added in front of a root. Prefixes affect the meaning of the word.

> **EXAMPLES** *dis-* and *in-* which both mean "the opposite of" or "not," as in *disrespect* and *ineffective*

A suffix is added after the root. Suffixes affect the meaning of a word and its part of speech.

> **EXAMPLES** *-er* as in *designer*, which adds the meaning of "someone who" and turns the verb *design* into a noun
>
> *-ly* as in *motherly*, which adds the meaning of "having the characteristics of or done in the manner of" and turns the noun *mother* into an adjective or adverb

More than one affix can be added to a word root.

List of common prefixes

Prefix	Meaning	Example sentence
a-	not, without	His actions were **a**moral.
anti-	against	I must follow an **anti**-inflammatory diet.
auto-	self	Many famous people write an **auto**biography.
circum-	around	The earth's circumference is 40 075 kilometres.
de-	opposite	Getting fired **de**stabilized him.
dis-	not	The supervisor **dis**approves of such behaviour.
en-/em-	cause to be in a certain condition	The builders are going to **en**large the office. The pep talk **em**powered her.
epi-	on/over/outer	An **epi**taph is an inscription on a tombstone.
eu-	good/well/genuine	*Passed away* is a **eu**phemism for *died*.
in-/im-/ ir-	not	Your answer was **in**correct. It is **im**possible for us to reach our goal. The customer was being **ir**rational.
mega-	great/large	The film was a **mega**hit at the box office.
mis-	not correctly/wrong	You **mis**interpreted his reaction.
non-	not	It is a **non**-smoking room.
over-	too much/beyond the limit	I am **over**loaded with work.
pre-	prior to/before	Airlines always offer **pre**boarding services.
re-	again	You should **re**think your decision.
un-	not	She was **un**decided about what to do.

List of common roots

Root	Meaning	Example sentence
audi/audit	hear/listen/sound	The sound is in**audi**ble to human ears.
bio	life	The science program includes **bio**logy courses.
ced	go/move	A revision class will pre**ced**e the final exam.
chrono	time	The events are listed in **chrono**logical order.
derm	skin	I will see a **derm**atologist about my rash.
dic/dict	say/speak	We sometimes have **dic**tations in English class.
geo	earth	**Geo**graphy courses are mandatory in high school.
graph/gram	write/writing	*Lead* is an example of a homo**graph**.

Root	Meaning	Example sentence
jur/jus	law	We live in a **jus**t society.
ology/log	study	In university, he will major in psych**ology**.
path/pathy	feeling/disease	A naturo**path** proposes natural remedies.
phil(e)	love, lover of	He is a great **phil**anthropist who volunteers a lot.
phon	sound	**Phon**ology is a branch of linguistics.
pod/ped	foot	It is dangerous for **ped**estrians to jaywalk.
psych	mind	**Psych**osomatic illnesses can cause real symptoms.
soph	wise	Your glasses give you a very **soph**isticated look.
spect	look at	All baggage is in**spect**ed before a flight.
tele	far	Good **tele**scopes see millions of light years away.
the/theo	God/gods	**Theo**logy is the study of the divine.
therm/thermo	heat	Do not set your **thermo**stat higher than 20°C.
ver/vid/vis	true	The jury reached its **ver**dict.

List of common suffixes

Suffix	Meaning	Example sentence
-able/-ible	can be done (adj)	My teammates are very depend**able**.
-al/-ial/-ary	having the nature of (adj)	My brother is a cynic**al** person. Leonardo da Vinci was a vision**ary**.
-ed	having the condition or quality of (adj)	It's an updat**ed** file.
-en	made of/having the quality of (adj)	Use a wood**en** spoon with the pan.
-ence/-ance	action/process of/quality/state (adj/n)	Your persever**ance** will pay off. My teacher has a lot of pati**ence**.
-er/-or	a person who (n)	She works as an interpret**er**.
-er/-est	comparative/superlative (adj)	This song is long**er** than that one. That song is the long**est**.
-ful	full of (adj)	I am thank**ful** for all my blessings.
-ic/-ing	having the characteristic/quality of (adj)	Many kids are allerg**ic** to peanuts. It is an interest**ing** book.
-ing	having the quality of	That film was very amus**ing**.
-ion/-tion/-ation/-ition	action or condition (n)	Her hip opera**tion** lasted many hours.
-ism	state or condition of (n)	My perfection**ism** causes me stress.
-ist	one who does something (n)	Seeing a dent**ist** is expensive.
-ity/-ty	the state of (n)	Creativ**ity** is valued in the workplace.
-ive/-ative/-itive	doing or having a tendency to do something (adj)	The students were very talk**ative**.
-ize	the act of doing something (v)	You need to organ**ize** your files.
-less	without (adj)	I felt hope**less** after being fired.
-ly	done in the manner of (adv)	She works very efficient**ly**.
-ment	action or process (n)	There is more temporary employ**ment** today.
-ness	the state of (n)	I was absent due to sick**ness**.
-oid	like/resembling (adj)	Human**oid** robots exist.
-ous/-eous/-ious	having the quality of (adj)	Teenagers can be rebell**ious**.
-ship	the state or condition of (n)	Leader**ship** skills are an asset.
-y	having the quality of (adj)	My supervisor is very grump**y** today.

Exercise 2

Use your knowledge of roots and affixes to guess the meaning of the following words, then write a sentence using the word.

1. euphonious	Word parts: *eu* = good, *phon* = sound, *ious* = having the quality of Definition: having the quality of good sound Sentence: She has a euphonious voice.
2. apathy	Word parts: a = without, path(y) = feeling, y = having the quality of Definition: having a lack of feeling Sentence: She reacted with surprising apathy after hearing the bad news.
3. audiologist	Word parts: audi = hear, log = study, ist = one who does something Definition: someone who studies hearing and hearing disorders Sentence: I saw an audiologist about my hearing problems.
4. epidermis	Word parts: epi = outer, derm = skin Definition: the outer layer of skin Sentence: The splinter is stuck in the epidermis of my right foot.

Exercise 3

The bolded word in each sentence below is grammatically incorrect. Identify the part of speech (noun, verb, adjective, or adverb) of the word, then use a suffix or affix to change it into the correct part of speech in order to form a grammatically correct sentence.

1. You should not feel **depress** due to failure but view it as a step toward success.

    Incorrect part of speech: ____verb____ → Change to ___adjective___ (__depressed__)

2. A psychologist should be **worth** of the trust that patients give.

    Incorrect part of speech: ____noun____ → Change to ___adjective___ (__worthy__)

3. The foundation of behaviourism lives on in an **update** theory: neobehaviourism.

    Incorrect part of speech: ____verb____ → Change to ___adjective___ (__updated__)

4. Carl Jung rejected Freud's **dogmatic**.

    Incorrect part of speech: ____adj____ → Change to ____noun____ (__dogma__)

5. You must have certain qualities to succeed in electronics: **patient**, caution, and precision.

    Incorrect part of speech: ____noun____ → Change to ____noun____ (__patience__)

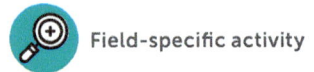
Exercise 4

Create a list of 10 words related to your field of study that have word families (a group of words with a common root to which different affixes are added). For each word, indicate the part of speech and write a definition. Then write a sentence for each word family using at least one of the words from the family.

EXAMPLE

pharmacy (n) place where drugs are prepared and sold

pharmacist (n) a person who prepares and sells prescribed drugs

pharmaceutical (n, adj) a drug or medicine; of or relating to the making and selling of drugs and medicine

I would like to become a **pharmacist** in a big **pharmacy** selling **pharmaceuticals**.

Communicative Activity

People sometimes use English roots and affixes to make up their own words. Take, for example, *Google-ization*, used in the article "Top 10 Weird Job Interview Questions" (Unit 1, page 11). *Google* is the root (noun, referring to the company name). The suffix *-ize* turns it into a verb (meaning "to act like the company Google"). The suffix *-ation* changes it back into a noun (meaning "the action or process of acting like the company Google"). Because of readers' knowledge of the root word and affixes, they are able to determine the meaning of *Google-ization* in context even though it isn't a real word.

With a partner, answer the following questions.

1. Use your knowledge of roots and affixes to guess the meaning of the following made-up words.

   a) I have been to over 50 countries. I am a **circumgeoizer**!

   Word parts: circum = around; geo = earth; ize = verb (action); er = someone who

   Definition: someone who goes/travels around the world a lot

   b) One never knows what you are thinking because you have an **imdicting** personality.

   Word parts: im = not; dict = say/speak (related to words); ing = having the quality of

   Definition: a personality (type) that doesn't speak a lot

You can organize a class contest of the best made-up words!

2. Use your knowledge of roots and affixes to create two of your own made-up words. Use each word in a sentence. Read your sentences out loud and have your classmates guess the meanings of your invented words.

   a) Sentence: _____

   Word parts: _____

   Definition: _____

   b) Sentence: _____

   Word parts: _____

   Definition: _____

Common Vocabulary and Spelling Errors

This unit offers practice with common vocabulary and spelling errors that even advanced learners make. Some of these errors are due to false cognates. Most of the words are academic or work-related.

Review these vocabulary lists provided on the Explore Online website before completing the exercises below:

- Commonly Confused Vocabulary
- Work-Related Vocabulary
- Commonly Misspelled Words

False cognates are words that look the same but have different meanings in two languages. Examples of English/French false cognates are *assist/assister* and *sensible/sensible*).

 S For more information on false cognates, see Vocabulary Strategies, page 149.

  Go to Explore Online to download the vocabulary lists.

Exercise 1

Complete each sentence with the correct word from the word pairs given. Use the plural form of the noun where necessary.

1. **actual / current**

   a) The estimated cost of the equipment was much less than the _____actual_____ cost.

   b) Professors must keep abreast of _____current_____ research in their respective fields.

2. **affect / effect**

   a) Working too many hours can _____affect_____ your grades.

   b) Working too many hours can have an _____effect_____ on your grades.

3. **ancient / former**

   a) In the archaeology course, students get to visit some _____ancient_____ ruins.

   b) I saw many of my _____former_____ teachers at my high school reunion.

4. **bookstore / library**

   a) I paid a $1.40 fine because I returned my books to the _____library_____ two weeks late.

   b) I saw two books that I want to buy from the _____bookstore_____ near my house.

5. **conference / lecture**

   a) That professor always gives interesting _____lectures_____.

   b) The _____conference_____ included workshops given by experts in the field.

CHAPTER 14 | Common Vocabulary and Spelling Errors   217

6. **deceived / disappointed**

   a) I will be very _____disappointed_____ if I do not get accepted into the program.

   b) He _____deceived_____ his teacher by cheating on the test.

7. **experience / experiment**

   a) Doing my master's degree in a foreign country was a great _____experience_____.

   b) We had to do several _____experiments_____ in our final science course.

8. **important / noticeable**

   a) My stress level has become more _____noticeable_____ with exams approaching.

   b) The boss will make some _____important_____ announcements at the next meeting.

9. **journal / newspaper**

   a) Parts of my doctoral research are going to be published in an academic _____journal_____.

   b) The headline on the front page of today's _____newspaper_____ is misleading.

10. **learn / teach**

    a) I want to _____learn_____ some Spanish before I go to Spain.

    b) My friend is going to _____teach_____ me some Japanese expressions.

11. **mark / note**

    a) I got the highest _____mark_____ in the class on the math exam.

    b) The _____note_____ on her door says she will be back soon.

12. **research / study**

    a) The second _____study_____ yielded different findings than the first.

    b) The _____research_____ will involve interviewing experts from many different fields.

13. **say / tell**

    a) You have to _____tell_____ the employees about the upcoming layoffs.

    b) My boss didn't _____say_____ why he was upset.

14. **scientific / scientist**

    a) The study involved _____scientists_____ from around the globe.

    b) _____Scientific_____ cooperation between countries is essential.

15. **sensible / sensitive**

    a) Be _____sensible_____ and do not go to the party the night before your exam.

    b) He is so _____sensitive_____ that he cries even while watching comedies.

Exercise 2

Find the work-related vocabulary error in each sentence below. Underline the error and write the correct word.

1. Each year I do volunteer work for a different organism. _____organization_____

2. If you need to discuss this matter further, you may join me at 438-395-2275.
    _____reach_____

3. As part of the academic program, students must do three months of stage.
    _____on-the-job training_____

4. Be ready to talk about your formation when you go to your job interview.
    _____training_____

5. The syndicate fees that workers at our company must pay are very high.
    _____union_____

6. The direction has decided to change some of its policies. _____administration/ management/director_____

7. On the application form, they asked about my disponibility. _____availability_____

8. The company must engage five new employees. _____hire_____

9. I will take a course in gestion to upgrade my skills. _____management_____

10. She is going to be the responsible of marketing for the entire company.
    _____person in charge of / head_____

11. Along with her new position, she is also going to get a big augmentation.
    _____raise_____

12. When two or more companies join to form one company, it is called a fusion.
    _____merger_____

Exercise 3

Complete each sentence with the correct work-related vocabulary. Use the correct form of verbs and plural nouns where necessary.

1. He got _____fired_____. Now he has to look for a new job.

2. The midnight _____shift_____ is from 12:00 AM to 8:00 AM.

3. Last summer I worked as a _____volunteer_____, so I didn't get paid.

4. My father turns 60 this year, and he is planning to take early _____retirement_____.

5. The company offers the standard _____employee benefits_____, such as vacation pay.

6. Employees also receive some special _____perks_____, such as a big Christmas bonus.

7. How much money do you _____earn/make_____ per year as your salary?

You could have a class spelling bee with these words.

Exercise 4

Correct the spelling errors in the following words.

1. adress _____ address
2. alot _____ a lot
3. buisness _____ business
4. compagny _____ company
5. cours _____ course
6. costomer _____ customer
7. departement _____ department
8. employe _____ employee
9. english _____ English
10. exemple _____ example
11. futur _____ future
12. gouvernment _____ government
13. informations _____ information
14. ponctual _____ punctual
15. realy _____ really
16. recieve _____ receive
17. responsability _____ responsibility
18. shure _____ sure
19. sincerly _____ sincerely
20. sujet _____ subject
21. technicien _____ technician
22. technologie _____ technology
23. usefull _____ useful
24. whit _____ with
25. wich _____ which

Students that spell *with* as *whit* usually pronounce this word incorrectly as well.

 Field-specific activity

Communicative Activity

Choose 15 words from the vocabulary lists of commonly confused words and work-related vocabulary from Explore Online (the ones you find most useful) and create a quiz to test your classmates' knowledge of those words. Your sentences must include information and vocabulary related to your field of study or future career. When you are finished, give your quiz to your classmate(s) to do.

Use the exercises in this unit as a model for the types of questions you may ask, or include other question types such as multiple choice or matching words with definitions.

APPENDIX 1

Overview of English Verb Tenses

	Usage	Past	Present	Future Type 1 – *will*	Future Type 2 – *be going to*
Simple	to describe facts, habits, general truths; can be used to narrate a story	verb + -ed* I/You/He/She/It/They/We **worked**.	verb (+ -s for third-person singular) I/You/They/We **work**. He/She/It/ **works**.	*will* + verb I/You/He/She/It/They/We **will work**.	*be* (present tense) + *going to* + verb I **am going to work**. You/They/We **are going to work**. He/She/It **is going to work.**
Perfect (auxiliary *have*)	to describe actions that have already been completed (which have a connection to a later time)	*had* + past participle* I **had worked** for two hours when my colleague arrived.	*have/has* + past participle I **have worked** here since 2017. He **has worked** here for two years.	*will have* + past participle She **will have worked** here for 30 years when she retires.	*be* (present tense) + *going to have* + past participle I **am going to have worked** 12 hours straight by 8 AM. You **are going to have worked** . . . He **is going to have worked** . . .
Progressive (auxiliary *be*)	to describe actions that are in progress or ongoing	*be* (past tense) + verb + -ing I **was working**. You **were working**.	*be* (present tense) + verb + -ing I **am working**. You **are working**. She **is working**.	*will* + *be* + verb + -ing You **will be working**.	*be* (present tense) + *going to be* + verb + -ing I **am going to be working**. We **are going to be working**. He **is going to be working**.
Perfect progressive	to describe the end of actions that are ongoing or progressive (in relation to a later time)	*had been* + verb + -ing I **had been working** for two hours when my colleague arrived.	*have* (present tense) + *been* + verb + -ing You **have been working** for many hours. It **has been working** for many hours.	*will have been* + verb + -ing She **will have been working** 10 hours in a row.	*be* (present tense) *going to* + *have been* + verb + -ing I **am going to have been working** for 10 hours. You **are going to have been working** for 10 hours. She **is going to have been working** for 10 hours.

NOTE For the past tense and past participles of irregular verbs, refer to Appendix 2, page 223.

Negative verb forms

	Past	Present	Future Type 1 – *will*	Future Type 2 – *be going to*
Simple	I **did not** work.	I **do not** work. He **does not** work.	I will **not** work.	I am **not** going to work. You are **not** going to work. She is **not** going to work.
Perfect (auxiliary *have*)	I had **not** worked.	I have **not** worked. He has **not** worked.	I will **not** have worked . . .	I am **not** going to have worked . . . You are **not** going to have worked . . . He is **not** going to have worked . . .
Progressive (auxiliary *be*)	I was **not** working. You were **not** working.	I am **not** working. You are **not** working. He is **not** working.	I will **not** be working.	I am **not** going to be working. You are **not** going to be working. He is **not** going to be working.
Perfect progressive	I had **not** been working.	I have **not** been working. He has **not** been working.	I will **not** have been working . . .	I am **not** going to have been working . . . You are **not** going to have been working . . . He is **not** going to have been working . . .

Key words

The following table lists certain key words that are used with each verb tense. Note that a key word is not always used in a sentence.

	Past	Present	Future
Simple	yesterday ago last week/month/year	every day/week/year always, usually, sometimes, occasionally, seldom, rarely, never (frequency adverbs)	tomorrow the day after tomorrow next week/month/year soon
Perfect	before by the time	ever/never for/since up to now/so far already	by the end of the day/week/month/year by + specific time, date, or year (e.g., 2050) in + duration of time (e.g., two years)
Progressive	while/as when at + specific time (e.g., 5 PM yesterday)	now currently presently at the moment	at/by + specific time while/as when
Perfect progressive	before when for + duration of time since + specific time	for + duration of time (e.g., many hours) since + specific time all day/week/year	for by the time

APPENDIX 2

Irregular Verbs

Here are some of the most common irregular verbs in English.

Base form	Simple past	Past participle
awake	awoke	awoken
be (is/are)	was/were	been
beat	beat	beaten
become	became	become
begin	began	begun
bend	bent	bent
break	broke	broken
bring	brought	brought
build	built	built
burn	burned/burnt	burned/burnt
buy	bought	bought
catch	caught	caught
choose	chose	chosen
come	came	come
cost	cost	cost
cut	cut	cut
dig	dug	dug
do	did	done
draw	drew	drawn
dream	dreamed/dreamt	dreamed/dreamt
drink	drank	drunk
drive	drove	driven
eat	ate	eaten
fall	fell	fallen
feel	felt	felt
fight	fought	fought
find	found	found
fly	flew	flown
forget	forgot	forgotten
freeze	froze	frozen
get	got	got/gotten
give	gave	given
go	went	gone
grow	grew	grown
have	had	had
hear	heard	heard
hide	hid	hidden
hit	hit	hit
hold	held	held
keep	kept	kept
know	knew	known
lay	laid	laid
lead	led	led
learn	learned/learnt	learned/learnt
leave	left	left

Base form	Simple past	Past participle
lend	lent	lent
let	let	let
lie	lay	lain
light	lit/lighted	lit/lighted
lose	lost	lost
make	made	made
mean	meant	meant
meet	met	met
mistake	mistook	mistaken
pay	paid	paid
put	put	put
read	read	read
ride	rode	ridden
ring	rang	rung
rise	rose	risen
run	ran	run
say	said	said
see	saw	seen
sell	sold	sold
send	sent	sent
set	set	set
shake	shook	shaken
shine	shone	shone
show	showed	shown
sing	sang	sung
sit	sat	sat
sleep	slept	slept
speak	spoke	spoken
speed	sped	sped
spend	spent	spent
stand	stood	stood
steal	stole	stolen
strike	struck	struck/stricken
swim	swam	swum
take	took	taken
teach	taught	taught
tear	tore	torn
tell	told	told
think	thought	thought
throw	threw	thrown
understand	understood	understood
wear	wore	worn
win	won	won
withdraw	withdrew	withdrawn
write	wrote	written

Question Formation

Auxiliaries are added to the main verb to express tense, aspect, modality, voice, or emphasis. Auxiliaries are also used to form negatives and questions.

EXAMPLES

I **have** been to Israel.

Kim **is** talking.

You **can** come.

The dog **was** fed.

I **did** do it!

Richard **does** not smoke.

Does Richard smoke?

There are two main rules for forming grammatically correct questions.

Rule 1: The words in a question follow this order (QASV):

Question word(s)* + **A**uxiliary** + **S**ubject + **V**erb + rest of the sentence

*Yes/No questions do not contain a question word but follow the ASV order.

**If a verb phrase has more than one auxiliary, only the first auxiliary comes between the question word(s) and the subject.

> **EXAMPLE**   You **have been** waiting for the bus for 15 minutes. →
>
>   question words   subject
>   How long **have** you **been** waiting for the bus?

Rule 2: Every question must have an auxiliary. With simple present or simple past tense verbs, add *do* or *does* (present) *or did* (past) as an auxiliary (with one-word verbs) when forming a question If the verb contains a modal, then the modal is the auxiliary.

Example questions

Question word(s)	Auxiliary	Subject	Verb	Rest of the sentence
Where	did	you	work	last summer?
Which day	does	your boss	want	to meet?
Where	should	we	hold	the office party?
When	are	we	going to receive	the report?
How often	have	you	travelled	abroad?
How much	will	the team	have finished	by Friday?
X	Are	you	enjoying	college?
X	Have	you	been working	there for a long time?

The last two questions in this chart are *Yes/No* questions—they do not start with a question word.

There are two exceptions to rule 2 on page 224. In these cases, do not add *do, does,* or *did* as an auxiliary to form the question.

EXCEPTIONS

1. Do not add an auxiliary when *be* is the main verb in the sentence. Simply move the verb *be* before the subject.

Question word(s)	Auxiliary	Verb	Subject	Rest of the sentence
Why	X	is	Manny	here?
Where	X	are	the bosses	today?

2. Do not add an auxiliary when the question word *who* or *what* is the subject of the verb.

Question word(s)	Auxiliary	Subject	Verb	Rest of the sentence
Who	X	X	went	to the conference?
What	X	X	happened	at the meeting?

How to Join Ideas with Proper Punctuation

Compound Sentences (Two Independent Clauses)

For more information about dependent and independent clauses, see Grammar Guide, page 152.

Nor, which is used for negative statements and questions, requires a special construction: *nor* + auxiliary + subject + verb

EXAMPLE

I don't have a job, nor does he (have a job).

There are three ways to join independent clauses to create a compound sentence.

1. Use a coordinating conjunction.

    Independent clause +
    {
    , and
    , but
    , so
    , or
    , nor*
    , for
    , yet
    }
    + independent clause

2. Use a semicolon.

    Two independent clauses may be joined by a semicolon when the second idea completes or closely relates to the first. However, do not overuse semicolons.

    Independent clause +   {   ;   }   + independent clause

    Remember: Do not join two independent clauses with a comma (,).

3. Use a conjunctive adverb.

    Independent clause +
    {
    ; consequently,
    ; furthermore,
    ; however,
    ; indeed,
    ; in fact,
    ; moreover,
    ; nevertheless,
    ; then,
    ; therefore,
    ; thus,
    }
    + independent clause

    When using a conjunctive adverb, you may replace the semicolon with a period and create two separate sentences.

Complex Sentences (One Independent Clause and One Dependent Clause)

When creating complex sentences, you may put either the independent clause or the dependent clause first. The punctuation of the sentence differs depending on which clause comes first.

1. When the independent clause comes first, there is no punctuation between the clauses.

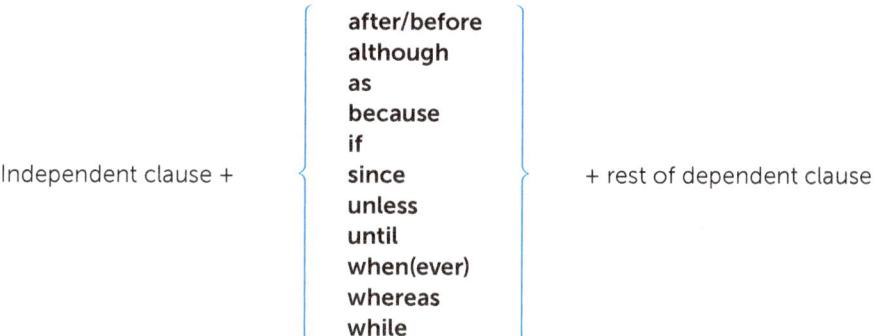

Independent clause +

| after/before |
| although |
| as |
| because |
| if |
| since |
| unless |
| until |
| when(ever) |
| whereas |
| while |

+ rest of dependent clause

2. When the dependent clause comes first, add a comma after the dependent clause.

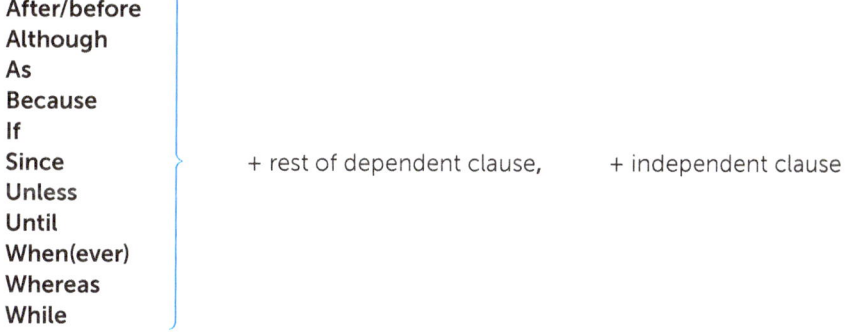

After/before
Although
As
Because
If
Since
Unless
Until
When(ever)
Whereas
While

+ rest of dependent clause,   + independent clause

Capitalization

The basic rule of capitalization is to capitalize **the first word of a sentence** and all **proper nouns** (i.e., the official names of people, places, and things). There are additional capitalization rules for academic and professional writing.

1. Capitalize the days of the week and months of the year.

    EXAMPLE   The meeting will be on Wednesday, September 1.

2. Capitalize geographical names (cities, countries, continents), languages, nationalities, and religions (and derivatives of these words).

    EXAMPLE   He married a Jewish woman from Israel who speaks Hebrew.

3. Capitalize specific geographical regions and people belonging to a specific region, but not generic directions.

    EXAMPLE   It is generally cheaper to travel in Eastern Europe than Western Europe.

    My hometown is located east of Toronto.

4. Capitalize the names of planets.

    EXAMPLE   Elon Musk's company, SpaceX, is developing a rocket to send people to Mars.

5. Do not capitalize seasons.

    EXAMPLE   My favourite season is summer.

6. Capitalize words like *company*, *association*, and *university* only when they are part of an official name.

    EXAMPLE   I will attend Simon Fraser University.

    BUT   I want to go to university.

7. Some organizations require that employees capitalize the names of departments or committees within the organization, but generic references to such departments or committees are not capitalized.

    EXAMPLE   Be sure to send a copy of your email to the Human Resources Department.

    BUT   She works in the human resources department of a big company.

8. Capitalize job titles only when they are used just before the person's name (as an official title).

    EXAMPLE   The employees will meet President Daniels next month.

    BUT   Bob Daniels is the president of the company.

    Bob Daniels, the president of the company, will attend the meeting.

EXCEPTION Capitalize titles of high-ranking officials when that title is referring to a particular person and not just the position in general.

> **EXAMPLE** Satya Nadella became the third Chief Executive Officer of Microsoft in 2014. (refers to a specific person)
>
> BUT *A chief executive officer is the executive of highest rank in a company.* (general position)

9. Capitalize the name of an academic degree only when the full name of the degree is used, not for general references. Capitalize the abbreviated forms of degrees (e.g., BA, MSc, PhD).

> **EXAMPLES** She received a Bachelor of Science degree from McGill University.
>
> She received a bachelor's degree three years ago.
>
> She obtained a BSc from McGill University.

10. Do not capitalize the name of an academic subject or course unless it is the official title of a course.

> **EXAMPLE** I must take a philosophy course. The course is Philosophy 101.

Articles (*a*, *an*, and *the*)

This list of rules is based on the most common errors that students make with articles.

Articles are words that introduce a noun and indicate whether it is specific or general. The definite article *the* indicates a specific item. The indefinite articles *a* and *an* or the lack of any article indicates a general item.

Rules for using articles

1. Use *an* before a word that starts with a vowel sound.

   EXAMPLES   *an* answer, *an* owl, *an* honest guy (silent /h/), BUT *a* university (/u/ is pronounced like a /y/)

2. Use *a* or *an* when the item is unknown to the listener/reader; use *the* when the item is understood from previous knowledge or information given within the context.

   EXAMPLE   The cafeteria will have *a* new menu soon. *The* menu will offer more choices.

3. Use no article before general concepts (e.g., love, peace, war, silence, etc.).

   EXAMPLES   Love can be a powerful motivator.

   Silence is required in the library.

   However, use *the* when referring to such a concept if it is specifically defined by the context of the sentence.

   EXAMPLES   *The* love between my parents is strong.

   The silence during dinner was uncomfortable.

4. Use no article before the name of a disease, food item, or sport.

   EXAMPLES   Dr. Leech specializes in the treatment of cancer.

   My favourite meal is lasagna.

   The most popular sport in Japan is baseball.

   However, use *the* when the disease or food item is specifically defined within the context of the sentence.

   EXAMPLE   I really like *the* lasagna at Emo's Pizza House.

5. Use no article before the name of a city, country, or continent.

   EXAMPLE   In a United Nations 2019 report, Finland was named the world's happiest country.

   There are some exceptions, such as *the* United States, *the* United Arab Emirates, and *the* Netherlands.

Credits

Unit 1

Photo Credits

1, iii   iStock.com/Anchiy
2   O.PASH/Shutterstock.com
3   © Lostafichuk; iStock.com/Mikolette
7   rawpixel/© 123RF.com
9   Andrea De Martin/© 123RF.com
10   KatarzynaBialasiewicz/iStock.com
12   © Fizkes
13   Dean Drobot/© 123RF.com
15   LightField Studios/Shutterstock.com
16   © Guruxox
18   Adapted from www.ClassesAnd Careers.com21
21   © Pressmaster

Literary Credits

7   Reprinted with permission of Eric Siu.
11   Reprinted with permission of CBS News.

Audio/Video Credits

3   Courtesy Seph Fontaine Pennock and Positive Psychology Program
10   With kind permission of Michael Kerr.

Unit 2

Photo Credits

23, iii   © Guruxox
24   Aleksandr Fedorov/© 123RF.com; Adapted from REUTERS INSTITUTE DIGITAL NEWS REPORT 2015
26   © Robert Kneschke
27   iStock.com/fstop123
29   © Piled Higher and Deeper Publishing
31   Wavebreak Media Ltd//© 123RF.com; MNBB Studio/Shutterstock.com
34   diego vito cervo/© 123RF.com
37   © Daniel Draghici
41   © Jevtic

Literary Credits

26   © Telegraph Media Group Limited 2018
27   CBC Licensing
34   Reprinted with permission of T.J. Anderson and Content Customs.

Audio/Video Credits

31   CBC Licensing
37   CBC Licensing

Unit 3

Photo Credits

43, iv   iStock.com/Georgijevic
44 ©   Fromac; Courtesy of Doggles, Inc.; Shutterstock.com; Kenishirotie/Shutterstock.com
45   Courtesy of Skipping Rocks Lab
46   Courtesy Sam Van Aken Studio
49   © Michael Johansson/Studio Michael Johansson; © Michael Johansson/Studio Michael Johansson
50   © Murdock2013
52   dennizn/© 123RF.com
53   Photo by Devin Edwards on Unsplash
55   Photo by Scott Webb on Unsplash
56   fizkes/Shutterstock.com
57   RPBaiao/Shutterstock.com
59   Photo by Carles Rabada on Unsplash
60   Adapted from "What Really Fosters Innovation" developed by MindJet and Spigit
62   Sarawut Aiemsinsuk/© 123RF.com

Literary Credits

45   © 2015 The Atlantic Media Co., as first published in The Atlantic Magazine. All rights reserved. Distributed by Tribune Content Agency, LLC.
46   From CNN.com. © 2015 Turner Broadcast Systems. All rights reserved. Used under license; Excerpt from "The Preschool Inside a Nursing Home" by Tiffany R. Jansen, The Atlantic, January 20, 2016. Reprinted with permission from The Atlantic Monthly Group. All rights reserved. Permission conveyed through Copyright Clearance Center, Inc.
53   Reprinted with permission of HubSpot, Inc.

Audio/Video Credits

50   Courtesy New York Public Radio
58   From Reason.com. Used with permission. https://reason.com/reasontv/2016/01/22/the-geography-of-genius

Unit 4

Photo Credits

65, iv   iStock.com/nico_blue
66   © Stefan Malloch; Photo by Vlad Tchompalov on Unsplash
68   © William Attard Mccarthy

70   stocksolutions/© 123RF.com
72   Slavek Ruta/Shutterstock.com
75   Graham Oliver/© 123RF.com
80   TY Lim/Shutterstock.com
83   Sirisak_baokaew/Shutterstock.com
84   © Viacheslav Iacobchuk

Literary Credits

65   Excerpt from THE SHORT REIGN OF PIPPIN IV by John Steinbeck, copyright © 1957 by John Steinbeck; copyright renewed © 1985 by Elaine Steinbeck, John Steinbeck IV and Thom Steinbeck. Used by permission of Viking Books, an imprink of Penguin Publishing Group, a division of Penguin Random House LLC. All rights reserved.
68   Reprinted with permission of Project Syndicate.
75   Copyright Guardian News & Media Ltd 2018

Audio/Video Credits

72   CBC Licensing
80   Courtesy of WNET/Thirteen Productions, LLC.

Unit 5

Photo Credits

87, iv   rawpixel/© 123RF.com
88   iStock.com/NoSystem images
89   rawpixel/© 123RF.com
90   EtiAmmos/Shutterstock.com
92   Gustavo Frazao/Shutterstock.com
93   iStock.com/Rawpixel
94   Dariusz Jarzabek/View/Shutterstock.com
95   Image courtesy of Canam Buiildings, a Canam Group Business. All rights reserved.
96   © Leszek Wrona
97   tabthipwatthana/© 123RF.com
103   anatoliygleb/© 123RF.com
104   Adapted from the Zombie Survival Guide with permission of Haynes Publishing
106   razihusin/© 123RF.com

Literary Credits

89   Copyright © 2014 Coaching Positive Performance. Reprinted here with permission of Carthage Buckley.
96   Copyright Guardian News & Media Ltd 2018

Audio/Video Credits

93   Courtesy of London Business School. With permission of Tom Hulme.

100   Courtesy New Hampshire Public Radio

Projects

Photo Credit

109   luchschen/© 123RF.com

Learning Strategies

Photo Credit

115   Viktoriya/Shutterstock.com

Literary Credit

125   Olympians look for an edge with brain stimulation. MIT Technology Review, Mike Orcutt, July 26, 2016.

Grammar Guide

Photo Credits

151   Giorgio Bizzotto/© 123RF.com
156   Photo by Ross Sneddon on Unsplash
159   rawpixel/© 123RF.com
161   Spiroview Inc/Shutterstock.com; Photo by Dex on Unsplash
167   Photo by Reinhart Julian on Unsplash

171   Photo by Thandy Yung on Unsplash
172   © Hongqi Zhang (aka Michael Zhang)
175   Photo by Jehu Christan on Unsplash
176   © Tharathip Onsri; © Fizkes
177   © Photographerlondon
183   Photo by Emma Paillex on Unsplash
194   only4denn/© 123RF.com
195   Photo by rawpixel on Unsplash
200   Photo by Micheile Henderson on Unsplash
204   Photo by Ricardo Gomez Angel on Unsplash
209   Photo on Visual Hunt
213   Photo by Yuki Dog on Unsplash

Index

About the Authors

Becky McKnight has a BA in English Literature, a TESL Certificate from Carleton University, and an MA in Applied Linguistics from Concordia University. She has taught English in secondary schools in Japan, university-level ESL at Concordia, intensive English in the Explore program at Bishop's University, and business English at O'Sullivan College. She currently teaches ESL at Cégep Saint-Jean-sur-Richelieu.

Patrick Peachey has a BA in English Literature and a BEd TESL from Concordia University. He also has a graduate certificate in Education from the Université de Sherbrooke. For the past 23 years, he has worked at Cégep André-Laurendeau as a teacher and department coordinator.